Liberalism and Islam

Liberalism and Islam

Practical Reconciliation between the Liberal State and Shiite Muslims

Hamid Hadji Haidar

First published in 2008 by
PALGRAVE MACMILLAN™
175 Fifth Avenue, New York, N.Y. 10010 and
Houndmills, Basingstoke, Hampshire, England RG21 6XS.
Companies and representatives throughout the world.

PALGRAVE MACMILLAN is the global academic imprint of the Palgrave Macmillan division of St. Martin's Press, LLC and of Palgrave Macmillan Ltd. Macmillan® is a registered trademark in the United States, United Kingdom and other countries. Palgrave is a registered trademark in the European Union and other countries.

ISBN-13: 978-0-230-60525-1
ISBN-10: 0-230-60525-7

Library of Congress Cataloging-in-Publication Data

Haidar, Hamid Hadji.
Liberalism and Islam: practical reconciliation between the liberal state and Shiite Muslims / Hamid Hadji Haidar.
    p. cm.
  Includes bibliographical references and index.
  ISBN 0-230-60525-7
  1. Liberalism. 2. Shi'ah. 3. Islam and politics. 4. Islam and state. I. Title.

JC574.H35 2007
320.5'57—dc22

                                                                          2007030419

A catalogue record for this book is available from the British Library.

Design by Macmillan India Ltd.

First edition: February 2008

10 9 8 7 6 5 4 3 2 1

Printed in the United States of America.

To my wife for her patience

Contents

Introduction

This book examines the relationship between Islamic thought and liberal theory, as well as the relationship between a liberal state and its Muslim citizens. Put another way, this book intends to explore the extent to which contemporary political liberalism has more successfully accommodated religious people through softening the secularity of liberalism than traditional comprehensive liberalism. This task is undertaken by critically examining two key theories of liberalism: that of John Stuart Mill (1806–1873) as one of the clearest representative of traditional comprehensive liberalism, which belongs to the "Enlightenment Project," and that of John Rawls (1921–2002) as a powerful representative of contemporary political liberalism, which belongs to the "Reformation Project." To illuminate the degree to which the secularity of liberalism has been softened, Shiite Islam is adopted as a test case.

What distinguishes Mill's liberal theory for this study lies in the general viewpoint, as John Gray suggests, that "if anyone is a liberal, it is surely John Stuart Mill."[1] Furthermore, Mill occupies a unique place in the history of philosophy by writing about many branches of knowledge such as logic, philosophy of science, ethics, epistemology, metaphysics, economics, psychology, religion, education, literature, history, political theory, social philosophy, and on current public affairs. However, as J. B. Schneewind and Bertrand Russell suggest, Mill was not noticeably as original a theorist as Descartes or Hume, despite his undeniable influences on all fields mentioned above.[2]

What is significant with Rawls's liberal theory is his unequivocal influence on political philosophy in the twentieth century.[3] Even those who disagree with Rawls's theory admit that the discipline of political philosophy has been promoted by his work.[4] Not only is the international influence of Rawls's work even on European intellectual thought undeniable,[5] but also his theory marks a "turning point for political philosophy."[6] He left legacies of inquiry and debate not only in political philosophy, but also in other branches of social sciences, such as law, economics, education, and political science.[7] In the clearest appreciation of Rawls's influence on political philosophy, Brian Barry labeled the current period a "post-Rawlsian world."[8]

Nozick points to the remarkable position that both Mill and Rawls have occupied in political philosophy, and argues that Rawls's theory is "a powerful, deep, subtle, wide-ranging, systematic work in political and moral philosophy which has not seen its like since the writings of John Stuart Mill." He contends that Rawls's work is so central that all political philosophers "must either work within Rawls's theory or explain why not."[9] In addition, the comparison between Mill's and Rawls's liberalism lies in Rawls's reiteration that, contrary to the comprehensive liberalism of Kant and Mill, his political liberalism is a freestanding view that is compatible with various reasonable comprehensive doctrines. More explicitly, taking it for granted that comprehensive liberalism is incompatible with religion, Rawls's major purpose of theorizing about liberalism is to answer affirmatively the "torturing question in the contemporary world, namely: Can democracy and comprehensive doctrines, religious or nonreligious, be compatible?"[10]

The adoption of Islam lies in the general acknowledgment that in the late twentieth century, Islam has "experienced an international resurgence and a renewed vitality."[11] Although in the past 20 years, the study of liberal democracy and democratization has been central to the comparative study of politics,[12] a particular attention has been given to the debate on the relationship between Islam and liberal democracy.[13] There is a serious and general concern in the West with the examination of probably an inherent hostility between Western liberal democratic values and Islamic values.[14] What persuades us to adopt Shiite Islam as a test case lies in its possession of certain elements that make reconciliation between liberal democracy and religion more likely. In addition, in contemporary world order, Shiite Islamic political theory manifested in the Islamic Republic of Iran has caused considerable concern for the degree to which this religious regime can and should be accommodated in the world order.

This book examines Rawls's achievement at two levels. First, at the theoretical level, I will examine Mill's liberal philosophy to show its unjustifiability from the Shiite Islamic perspective. This leads to an investigation into Rawls's theoretical achievement in softening the secularity of liberal philosophy. Second, at the practical level, I will examine the Millian liberal state to show its acceptability to Shiite Muslim citizens of liberal democratic societies. Then, I shall explore Rawls's practical achievement in broadening the scope of tolerance of the liberal state. My concern is not with specific liberal states at a given time. This would be an empirical examination that needs undertaking a survey of some specific liberal societies. Rather, since this book is a philosophical research, I am concerned with what

Millian and Rawlsian ideal liberal states are expected to provide for their citizens. The precise questions this book poses are the following:

> Is Rawls's liberal theory less secular than Mill's liberal theory, and hence can it become partially compatible with Shiite Islam? Is the Rawlsian liberal state less secularist than Mill's liberal state, and hence can it be more tolerant of, and more acceptable to, Shiite Muslim minorities?

As opposed to a general liberal ambition, this book argues that neither Mill's comprehensive liberalism nor Rawls's political liberalism is justifiable in the view of Shiite Islam, and hence liberalism cannot lead Muslims at home. Furthermore, in agreement with Rawls, this book argues that liberalism and religion can partially become compatible by confining the demand of liberalism and Shiite Islam to distinct societies that are mutually disengaged from each other. Moreover, as opposed to a general worry, this book demonstrates that since the Millian and Rawlsian ideal liberal states show sufficient tolerance toward Shiite Muslim citizens, the latter should reciprocally accept the basic structure of the former. In brief, Rawls's achievement is confined to the theoretical domain, whereas Mill's ideal liberal state is as tolerant of, and acceptable to, Shiite Muslim citizens as that of Rawls. Hence, my answer to the first question is "yes" and to the second is "no."

Shiite Islam, Its Ideas, and Values

The Arabic term *din*, which is used in the same notion as religion, has different meanings, such as punishment, judgment, and obedience.[15] When one says that Islam is a *din*, it means that Islam is one lifestyle through which one can obey God. Hence, *din* refers only to theist religion, meaning a way of life God has introduced to mankind[16] to lead them to eternal happiness. The terms *islam, istislam,* and *taslim* have the same meaning as *din*, that is, to obey and to submit to someone.[17] The Qur'an interprets the term "religion" as equal to the term *islam:* "Religion in the sight of God is *islam*,"[18] where *islam* means submission. Hence, religion, according to Tabatabai's interpretation of this verse means to submit oneself to God and His will.[19] In the course of time, however, Islam has become a particular name for the religion introduced by Prophet Muhammad. A Muslim, therefore, is a person who has submitted to God and obeys the Islamic laws, which have been delivered by Prophet Muhammad. The Qur'an affirms that all Divine religions derived from the same source and the major developments of the Divine religion occurred in five religions:[20] the religions of Noah, Abraham, Moses, Jesus, and Muhammad.[21]

Every Divine religion is composed of two major parts: a particular worldview and a particular moral system. With regard to the worldview, all Divine religions have in common the faith in God, in Judgment Day, and in God's Messengers who have conveyed His messages to people, though there is disagreement about the details of these basic doctrines. In addition, every divine religion has introduced a particular moral system by following which religious people are expected to move toward eternal happiness.[22] The moral system of a religion can be interpreted as demanding a particular direction in politics, as was the case with Christianity in the Middle Ages. Alternatively, a religion can be interpreted as restricting its demands to nonpublic domain, as has been the case with Christianity in modern times. Leaving aside the interpretation of other sects of Islam, this chapter now moves on to discuss the demands of Shiite Islam.

Literally, the term *shia* derives from the term *mushayaa* meaning a group of people who follow someone. In the course of time, Shia has become a particular name for a group of Muslims who adore and follow Imam Ali and his progeny.[23] In fact, it was Prophet Muhammad himself who for the first time called the followers of Imam Ali as shia.[24] Hence, Shia as a particular sect of Islam appeared at the time when Prophet Muhammad was still living among his followers. However, after the demise of Prophet Muhammad, two major sects with many subgroups have developed in the Islamic world: Sunni Muslims as the majority, and Shiite Muslims as the minority. The mainstream subgroup of Shiite Islam is Twelver Shiite Muslims who believe that twelve infallible Imams have succeeded Prophet Muhammad. The Twelver Shiite Muslims are the majority of the minority of Muslims. Two other Shiite Muslim subgroups are *Zeydi* and *Ismaili*.[25] Throughout Islamic history the Twelver Shiite Muslims have been residing in many parts of the Islamic world, such as Egypt, Saudi Arabia, Lebanon, Iraq, Iran, and Yemen.[26] Since the sixteenth century, however, Iran has been the main Shiite country with a vast majority of Shiite population;[27] the majority of population in Oman, Bahrain, Azerbaijan, and Iraq is also Twelver Shiite Muslims.[28] It is estimated that Twelver Shiite Muslims constitute between 10 and 25 per cent of the whole Muslim population in the world.[29]

The most important principle that divided Muslims into Sunni and Shia, and Shia into its subgroups, is the issue of leadership or Imamate. While Sunni Muslims hold that the Prophet has entrusted the leadership of Muslims to them, Shiite Muslims affirm that he appointed his successors.[30] The Twelver Shiite further believe that Prophet Muhammad has named twelve infallible Imams to lead the Muslim people consecutively. It is a particular Twelver Shiite conviction that the last infallible Imam, al-Mahdi, was born in 869 and is believed to be miraculously alive since then.[31] According to Shia, the last Imam disappeared from view in 939 and he is believed to reappear at the end of history to make justice rule on earth.[32]

Shiite Muslims unanimously believe that Prophet Muhammad and his twelve successors were all infallible and they possessed Godly-inspired superior knowledge.[33] Explaining Shiite basic doctrines, Muzaffar, a contemporary Shiite scholar, says: "We believe that God's Messengers, as well as Imams, are all infallible and pure from any sin, mistake or ignorance."[34] Similarly, Imam Khomeini argues that "Messengers of God and their successors [Imams] possess an eminent position in spirituality called *rouh al-qudus* [sacred spirit], with the help of which they have access to the perfect and comprehensive superior knowledge." He further argues that one consequence of that superior knowledge is their infallibility with regard to understanding, interpreting, and implementing divine laws.[35]

As for the way of discovering such infallible figures with divine knowledge, Twelver Shiite Muslims generally maintain that only God has the ability to recognize them. Furthermore, to distinguish the authentic Messenger and Imam from any person who might deceitfully assume this highly position, Shiite Muslims argue that the Messengerhood and Imamate can be only proved by a miracle. Alternatively, a Messenger, whose Messengerhood has already been proved by a miracle, can confirm the Messengerhood or the Imamate of another person.[36] Explaining the general doctrines of Shiite Muslims, Muzaffar argues that "we believe that when God the Almighty appoints a Messenger for people He should introduce him to people by showing a sign to his Messengerhood." He goes on to argue that "this sign is what is called the miracle."[37] Likewise, with regard to a successor of a Messenger, Muzaffar explains that "the Imamate of a person is only acknowledged by a Messenger's or a previous Imam's report about his appointment by God."[38] All Shiite scholars as well as ordinary Shiite Muslims unanimously have faith in this principle.[39] Overall, the belief in Imamate distinguishes Twelver Shiite sect from all other Islamic sects.

What distinguishes the Shiite moral system lies in its affirmation that the particular set of Islamic moral values consists of two major collections: individual and social.[40] The first and the most significant collection concerns those individual practices that lead to self-development and individual progress. Individual progress is obtained through performing some practical duties, such as daily prayer, annual fasting during Ramadan, and a pilgrimage to Mecca at least once in a lifetime. In addition, through commitment to some practical codes, individuals can develop some positive traits in their souls, such as gratitude, patience and tolerance, goodness, a sense of duty, sympathy, kindness, loyalty, cheerfulness, fairness, benevolence, politeness, and contribution to charity.[41] The second collection of Islamic moral values includes those social norms that are intended to establish an Islamic social order, covering familial values, principles of distributive and criminal justice, foreign policy of Islamic society, and the like.[42] As will be explained in chapter 8, this book prefers to call the first collection as "Islamic ethical theory" and the second collection as "Islamic political theory."

As will be argued in chapter 8, Islamic ethical theory is universal, and hence should be followed by Muslims everywhere and all the time, irrespective of the religiosity of the political system or the society in which they reside. Obviously, however, the society in which they are allowed to reside should provide them with a minimum freedom of religion in order for them to overtly pursue their personal religious duties. It is the assumption of this book that Muslims are religiously allowed to reside in Millian and Rawlsian liberal societies where a set of individual freedoms is guaranteed for each citizen. By contrast, Islamic political theory is particular to those societies that have already submitted to Islam and constitute the majority of the population of the society involved. These societies are religiously obliged to establish Islamic states with the aim of pursuing Islamic social values through the state apparatus.

It should be noted that by Shiite Islam this book refers to the theory that justifies the Islamic Republic of Iran in its ideal form. There are, however, many basic principles and values that are characteristic to all Twelver Shiite Muslims throughout the world. Yet, in controversial and sensitive cases, this book constructs its arguments largely on views and ideas developed by Imam Khomeini (1902–1989), the political theorist and founding leader of the Islamic Republic of Iran, established in 1979. In addition, in many cases a reference will be made to the views and ideas developed by Muhammad Hussein Tabatabai (1903–1981), the most prominent philosopher and the greatest interpreter of the Qur'an in the contemporary Shiite world.[43] Finally, where necessary, I also resort to views and ideas developed by the students of Imam Khomeini and Tabatabai who have supported and developed the political theory of the Islamic Republic of Iran.[44] Therefore, what is introduced in this book as Shiite Islam can be definitely regarded as the political theory of the Islamic Republic of Iran, as interpreted and developed by the author.

Liberalism, Its Ideas, and Values

The English term "liberal" is derived from the old French word *liberal,* from the modern French term *libéral,* and from the Latin term *liberalis.* These terms, formed from the root *liber* meaning free, denote pertaining to a free man.[45] More than being a moral philosophy, liberalism was originally a "fighting doctrine," a "theory of government" whose major goal was personal liberty. Its aim was to oppose political absolutism and arbitrariness by setting limits to the exercise of political power.[46] While at the beginning liberalism was a revolutionary movement against the absolutism of religious orthodoxy, it has further become a moral and political philosophy.[47] The fundamental value of liberal philosophy is the respect for "autonomy."[48] It possesses a cluster of specific features that distinguish it from other intellectual traditions, even though there is no single consensual definition. What distinguishes liberalism from all other political doctrines and philosophies is the priority it gives to "individual liberty" over all other human goods.[49] Among all other human values, such as equality, social justice, democracy, stability, and order, none can compete with freedom in liberal thought.[50]

According to Bellamy, the priority of liberty as the minimum value shared by all theories of liberalism will be subject to deep controversies when it comes to determining the precise conception of liberty and different categories of human freedoms. Similarly, there is no consensus with regard to the reasonable way to order different liberties when conflict among them arises.[51] One famous controversy concerning the very meaning of liberty is noticed by Constant's dichotomy between the "liberty of moderns" in the sense of a space of individual independence and the "liberty of ancients" in the sense of entitlement in participation in public decision making.[52] A similar disagreement concerns defining liberty negatively in terms of "freedom from chains, from imprisonment, from enslavement by others,"[53] or defining it positively in the sense of "self-control," "self-direction," "self-mastery," and "self-realisation."[54] A deeper disagreement here concerns determining a set of basic rights that should be protected.[55] While Rawls, as will be discussed in chapter 6, suggests an extensive list of basic liberties, Kukathas proposes only two rights as fundamental: the right to join and leave a community, and the right against inhumane, cruel, and degrading behavior.[56] Here, some writers argue that there is a core of norms that are widely accepted among liberals regarding what rights we have. These rights include "freedom of expression or belief, fair arrest and trial, or humane conditions of detention."[57] Beyond this core, there is no uniformity in defining rights or determining the cases of rights among liberals.[58]

A further source of controversy concerns the boundaries of each kind of civil right and freedom, as is the case, for instance, with regard to freedom of speech. While in the United Kingdom individuals are not free to reproduce classified information, or to slander each other, in the United States the limitation of freedom of speech is put on "maliciously shouting 'fire' in a crowded room or incitement to racial hatred." One more source of disagreement amongst theorists of liberalism is in ranking the importance of different types of freedom such as freedom of speech, freedom of association, and the like when they clash in some cases. A clear case of competition between two irreconcilable civil freedoms concerns liberals' view about freedom of speech including insulting religious sacred figures that conflicts with religious believers' notion of a right not to be offended by insulting their sacred figures.[59]

Disagreement about liberalism does not remain confined to the ultimate value it supports. One more controversy derives from its philosophical outlook about man and society. In his *Liberalism,* John Gray proposes that all variants of liberal thoughts share some basic ideas, though these ideas have been refined and redefined in the course of history: individualism, equality, uniformity of human beings, and improvability of social institutions and political arrangements.[60] In a similar manner, Bellamy characterizes liberalism with the "commitment to the concepts of equality, liberty, individuality and rationality."[61] Yet, in his later work, *Post-Liberalism,* Gray withdraws this view and suggests, instead, that none of mentioned four fundamental ideas "can withstand the force of strong indeterminacy and radical incommensurability among values."[62] Likewise, Bellamy firmly rejects the agreement amongst even liberals themselves about the affinity between the mentioned core conceptions. Nor is there any compromise among them with regard to the political consequences of these four principles.[63]

Two Forms of Liberalism

Given the ultimate purpose of liberalism, it is suggested that theories of liberalism can be classified into two kinds: (1) traditional, substantive, comprehensive, or ethical, (2) and contemporary, neutral, or political.[64] The first type of liberalism, regarded as a moral philosophy, intends to introduce the best form of life for all humankind in the sense of freedom, autonomy, or happiness. By contrast, the second kind is aimed just at guaranteeing a just and peaceful situation for different conceptions of the good life to coexist. Put another way, while the norms of comprehensive liberalism apply to all collective and individual aspects of human life, political liberalism is merely a scheme for political domain of human life.

Traditional Comprehensive Liberalism

Comprehensive liberalism, like that of Mill, is an alternative not only to any form of absolutist political arrangement, but also to all transcendental philosophy and religions.[65] It is for this feature that all theories of liberalism of this form are "comprehensive" in the sense that they challenge all previous transcendental philosophies and religions and suggest that the specific liberal way of life is distinctively the best pattern of life. Comprehensive liberalism suggests not only that all individuals should adopt and follow the liberal way of life, but also that the state should promote it using its coercive apparatus. Autonomy, self-determination, privacy, liberty, and the like are *universal values;* not only can the state impose them on citizens, but the legitimacy of government is also based upon pursuing them.[66] Larmore argues that the ideal of freedom as self-determination and individuality, in Berlin's term, "positive liberty," is the ultimate goal of traditional liberalism, which liberals would prefer as the best conception of the good life.[67]

Connecting comprehensive liberalism with a historical background, Galston maintains that this type of liberalism is related to the "Enlightenment Project." According to this project, (1) reason is the major source of authority, (2) a life based on experience is considered as privileged in comparison to confidence in religion, and finally (3) self-determination is superior to external determination.[68] Rawls, on the other hand, seems to disagree with Galston on the origin of liberalism. In *Political Liberalism,* Rawls states that "the historical origin of political liberalism (and of liberalism more generally) is the Reformation and its aftermath, with the long controversies over religious toleration in the sixteenth and seventeenth centuries." Likewise, he would seem to cast doubt on Enlightenment Project by arguing that "whether there is or ever was such an Enlightenment project we need not consider; for in any case political liberalism . . . has no such ambitions."[69]

In a more detailed exploration about the history of liberalism, Rawls suggests that the task of moral philosophy has always been to find the best answer to the following questions: (1) Does every human being have access to the knowledge of how to act directly, or is this awareness restricted to a few persons, such as clerics? (2) Do the moral values related to human actions originate from human nature and the requirements of social life, or are they derived from God's intellect? (3) Are human beings constituted in such a way that there are naturally adequate elements to motivate them to act as they have to, or do they need a type of external motivation to act in accordance with moral values, such as divine reward and punishment or state threats and encouragements?[70] Characterizing comprehensive liberalism as a moral philosophy, Rawls describes both Hume and Kant—and certainly Mill—as asserting the first option in all three above questions with regard to *all* aspects of human life, the fact that leads Rawls to label their account of liberalism as "comprehensive."[71]

However, it would seem credible to assume, following Galston's view about the origin of liberalism, that an intrinsic feature of this form of liberalism is the dismissal of the transcendental doctrines and ideas by liberal philosophy as untrue, or at least skepticism toward them. Evidence of this dismissal or skepticism can be found in the debates surrounding the concept of "toleration."

The term "tolerant" employed to describe a person, a group, an institution, or a government implies disagreement and disapproval.[72] Fotion and Elfstrom convincingly observe that "[i]n order to be able to say that we tolerate something . . . [w]e must have a certain negative attitude toward it." This negative attitude can be "one of dislike or disapproval, or it must cause us discomfort or inconvenience in some way that we may assume will cause us to have a negative attitude toward it."[73] According to Warnock, if the situation or action with which one puts up is merely "distasteful" there is a "weak" sense of toleration, whereas in the cases where the situation or action with which one puts up is held to be "immoral" there is a "strong" sense of toleration.[74] In a more explicit explanation of the term "toleration," Preston King distinguishes a strong notion of toleration from indifference or neutrality. By incorporating the notion of "unequivocal objection" as well as "voluntarily endure" in the concept of toleration, he defines it as "a function of initial and continuing objection to an item, action against which is at least suspended, because cut across by incompatible action that is accorded a higher priority."[75]

Contemporary Political Liberalism

As the major representatives of "political liberalism," one can point to Bruce Ackerman, Ronald Dworkin, Charles Larmore, and John Rawls, who have employed the concept of "neutrality" to justify political liberalism.[76] To these thinkers the central concern of liberalism lies in developing a political arrangement in order to reconcile various ideas about the good life. Two decisive notions are purposefully invoked by contemporary theorists of liberalism, particularly by John Rawls, that shed light on this distinction: the idea of neutrality and the notion of politicality of liberalism.

The attention of political liberalism has shifted from tolerance to the idea of "neutrality" in the sense of "silence" about and "non-interference" with competing ideas about the good life. Thus, it is not any longer the chief purpose of liberalism to discuss what the best life is for humankind. Rather, based on a deeper commitment to "equality" among citizens and their values, liberalism has focused on suggesting a neutral political arrangement to deal with the diversity of ideas about the good life.[77] Nevertheless, irrespective of the possibility of neutrality and more substantial equality it embodies, the replacement of the concept of tolerance by the concept of neutrality could be taken as a definite indication to the alteration from denial of otherworldly values to prioritizing this-worldly values without taking sides in disputes about the former.

The other key notion that characterizes contemporary liberalism concerns the proposition that liberalism is a "political philosophy," rather than a "moral philosophy." Hence, in contrast with comprehensive liberalism, Rawls's political liberalism avoids taking sides in the three questions mentioned above in *all* aspects of life. Rather, his political liberalism affirmatively answers the above-mentioned questions only "with respect to a political conception of justice for a constitutional democratic regime." Therefore, political liberalism does not address the question: What is the worthy life for all human beings? the answer to which *requires* a specific political arrangement. Rather, it is aimed directly at addressing the question: How should we establish a just and stable society among those who affirm various reasonable conceptions about the good life?[78]

With regard to historical ground, as opposed to traditional liberalism, political liberalism originated from the Reformation Project. According to this project, given the plurality of religions, the political domain should be designed such that the followers of different religions or sects of a religion respect each other. Justification for this mutual respect, according to Galston, concerns (1) the impossibility of endless division of a given state into homogeneous subunits, (2) the failure of the attempt to return the homogeneity by imposing one religion, and finally (3) the failure of efforts to establish a single religion of reason.[79]

Secularism and Political Theory

The term "secular" is derived from the old French term *seculer,* from the modern French term *seculier,* and from the Latin term *secularis,* and formed on the term *saecul-um,* which meant "the world," especially as opposed to the church, in Christian Latin in the past. Secular means civil, temporal, nonecclesiastical, nonreligious, or nonsacred; something that belongs to the world and its affairs; something that originates from, or belongs to, the present and visible world.[80] Secularism can be generally defined as the idea of the "detachment of a state or other body from religious foundations."[81] However, there are various sources as well as forms of secularization and secularism in the West.[82] As Bhargava suggests, rather than implementing a program required by the values embedded in secularism, each Western country exercises a particular political compromise. Disagreement on secularism pertains both to the meaning and the degrees of separation of religions and state, and to the justification for this detachment.[83]

Thus, according to Bader, all types of Western compromise on religion-state relationship can be categorized into five groups.

1. "Strong establishment" marks the establishment of one monopolistic church in constitution, monism in administration and politics, as approximately found in recent Greece and Serbia.
2. "Weak establishment" establishes one church in constitution and administration, yet recognizes freedom of religion and plurality of religious affiliation, as recently approximated by England, Scotland, and the Scandinavian states.
3. "Constitutional pluralism" or "plural establishment" requires the constitutional recognition as well as pluralization of administration and politics of more than one organized religion, as found in Finland.
4. "Nonconstitutional pluralism" combines two elements of a power-sharing system: first, the plurality of religions should not only be recognized, but it should also be incorporated and integrated into the processes of decision making, such as problem defining, deliberating, proposing alternatives, and finally voting. Second, a fair amount of independence in specific issues should be guaranteed for each organized religion. This model can be found in Australia, the Netherlands, Belgium, India, and Germany.
5. "Nonestablishment and private pluralism" requires strict separation of religion and state at all levels ranging from constitution, through administration, to politics. Hence, religious pluralism is permissible only in a "civil society" and not in social and political arenas, as ideally sought in the United States.[84]

However, before secular and related terms were used in philosophical discussions in twentieth century, the term was used to promote a certain program or policy. Originally, the term *seculariser* was used by the Frenchman Longueville in the negotiation that led to the Peace of Westphalia in 1648, in the sense of nonecclesiastical. In 1846, Holyoake used the term "secularism" to free public education from religion in England. In twentieth-century United States, secularism pointed to the independence of this-worldly issues from religious considerations, irrespective of whether or not God exists. However, secularism unambiguously opposes the sacred and implies "a cultural emancipation from religion."[85] Steve Bruce points to the centrality of nonreligiosity to secularism when he argues that the less a society is influenced by religious beliefs, the more secular it is.[86] Similarly, Holyoake defines secularism as "a code of duty pertaining to this life, founded on considerations purely human, and intended mainly for those who find theology indefinite or inadequate, unreliable or unbelievable."[87] Likewise, contrasting "secular" and "religious" or "sacred," Meland defines secularization as a movement away from a traditional lifestyle in which religious sanctions directed human conduct and shaped his life.[88]

With regard to secularism the distinction between "political secularism" and "ideological secularism" is worthy of attention.[89] For instance, Munby quotes an extract from a worldwide conference on secularism held in 1959 that emphasized the importance of distinguishing between a "secularist State" and a "secular State." While the former is based upon "secularist assumptions" or aimed to promote "secularism" and atheism, the latter is merely neutral toward different religions present in it.[90] One extremist view about secular society supported in the nineteenth century attempts to eliminate religion from human life and maintains that a secularized society is an atheist society. Building its principles on the belief of nonexistence of God and aiming to provide a reasoned basis for freedom, this view is hostile to God and religion as the source of authority.[91] A softer view, usually associated with liberalism, rather than engaging in controversial discussion about the truth of God and religion, merely "disclaims any religious intention or capability." Distinguishing between religious and political purposes, the "separation view of secularism" suggests that there should be some political institutions pursuing political purposes, as well as religious institutions distinctively pursuing religious purposes.[92]

In line with the latter view, Munby best characterizes a secular society "ideally" as having the following features: (1) the widest possible private sphere where individuals can entertain independent decision making, (2) the narrowest possible public sphere where common purposes should be inevitably served, (3) tolerance of diversity and heterogeneity, (4) encouragement of diversity by providing opportunity for presentation of plural doctrines and convictions amongst citizens, (5) plural doctrines that are expected to counter "official image" and "ideal pattern of life" for all citizens, and (6) the government considers its citizens as bearers of certain rights irrespective of their religious beliefs and behavior.[93] The demand of a secular state is less than the demand of a secular society, or a secularist state. Defining a theocratic state as one "which formally and openly incorporates religious dictates and directives in the exercise of government," Meland quotes Donald Smith as defining secular states as meeting the following conditions: (1) freedom of religion, (2) recognition of citizens' rights irrespective of their religion, and finally (3) the separation of church and state institutionally.[94]

As an opponent of Rawls's political liberalism, Wolterstorff argues that the liberal view about the public space assumes that "citizens (and officials) *are not* to base their decisions and/or debates concerning political issues on their religious convictions." Rather, they should build the principles of political and public affairs on "some sources *independent of* any and all of the religious perspectives to be found in society" in the pursuit of justice as the ultimate value of liberalism. As a proponent of Rawls's political liberalism, Audi suggests that a perfect concept of secularism has two complementary sides. First, not only is the state obliged morally to prevent the prioritizing of one religion over others, but the state should also refrain from favoring or disfavoring any religion as such. The ground for this separation, according to Audi, lies in freedom supposed by principles of liberal democracy. The other side of secularism requires mature, rational, religious citizens as individuals living in contemporary liberal societies to ground their public debates in secular principles. Hence, they should avoid resorting to pure religious principles that are not in reflective equilibrium with relevant secular principles. What justifies this abstinence on the part of committed religious citizens, according to Audi, lies in their ability to pursue their religious obligations within the limit set by the secular state along with the requirements of civility. The separation of religion and state, further, requires that religious institutions such as churches refrain from political activities and keep themselves officially neutral with regard to policies and to candidates competing for political offices. What accounts for this abstinence, suggests Audi, lies in the preservation of purity of the very religion, and refraining from harming the freedom of religious citizens in their political activities.[95]

Overall, as far as the relation between religion and political theory is concerned, this book prefers to distinguish between "theism" and "humanism" on the one hand, and "religiosity" and "secularity" on the other. The neutrality of a political theory is basically inconceivable. Hence, the following definitions are proposed to precisely examine Rawls's achievement in softening the secularity of liberalism.

1. Theism: A political philosophy can be theist in its worldview if the starting point and the highest idea is the existence of God as the original source of existence in the world. Admittedly, a theist political philosophy takes into account the moral principles God has revealed to human beings in its overall system of morality. Furthermore, the dignity of man and his possession of certain rights in theist political philosophy derives from his relationship with God, rather than from being intrinsic. The dependence of man upon his

creator will, further, result in his authority being secondary to God's original authority.

2. Humanism: A political philosophy can be humanist in its worldview if central attention is paid to man as intrinsically possessing certain rights not based on any consideration about his relationship with God. In humanist political philosophy, the reverence for God derives from the intrinsic worth of man who might believe in God. God is respected as *something* man believes in, rather than as *someone* who has created man.

3. Religiosity:[96] The concept of religiosity points to the idea that draws its moral principles on both human intellect and godly revelation. Constructing its starting point on human intellect, a religious political theory attempts to develop a system of morality by combining the principles of human reason with those of revelation. While recognizing the right of man and his entitlement to this-worldly enjoyments, a religious political theory prioritizes the otherworldly perpetual happiness over this-worldly temporal pleasures. This recognition, admittedly, might vary from one religion to another. However, religious political theories might range from those that forcefully denounce every secular theory as untrue, to those theories that attend to human fallibility.

4. Secularity: The concept of secularity connotes the opposite of what religiosity points to. A secular political theory in its moral system seeks the domination of nonreligious values in human society on the assumption that modern human societies no longer need religious values. The replacement of God's revelation with human reason and dismissing the sacrifice of this-worldly pleasure for the attainment of heavenly enjoyments are intrinsic components of a secular political philosophy. Admittedly, secular political philosophies range in the degree to which they respect religion, from aggression by denouncing it as untrue, through keeping silent about any judgment about the truth, to accepting its usefulness for meeting some requirements of human society.

The distinction between theism and religiosity on the one hand, and humanism and secularity on the other, far from being a mere technical conceptualization, encompasses considerable advantages. Confronted with the dominant humanist language of political philosophy, theist political theorists can justify their religious concerns in the manner of humanist theorists who defend the rights of religious people. What is more, it is through this dichotomy that Rawls's achievement can be more precisely captured.

It is worth noticing, however, that while there is controversy about the possibility of a neutral/secular state, it seems inconceivable to construct a political philosophy that is neutral between theism and humanism, as well as religiosity and secularity. For the acceptance of the concept of God as the original source in the chain of causes and effects, as well as the idea of the superiority of perpetual life over temporal life, along with invocation to god-revealed morality, make a political philosophy theist and religious, whereas the absence of these concepts in philosophical arguments makes a political theory humanist and secular. Hence, according "the law of the excluded middle," a third option is inconceivable.

It is obvious that Mill happily constructs his liberal philosophy upon secular principles and values with no claim about its neutrality. Likewise, Rawls explicitly dismisses the possibility that liberal philosophy can be procedurally neutral. He contends that "a procedure that can be legitimated, or justified, without appealing to any moral values at all," be they religious or nonreligious, "seems impossible, since showing something justified appears to involve an appeal to some values." Therefore, he unequivocally admits that his political morality is not procedurally neutral. For, "clearly its principles of justice are substantive and express far more than procedural values, and so do its political conceptions of society and person, which are represented in the original position."[97] Overall, Mill's liberal philosophy and Rawls's liberal theory are both secular.

As far as the relation between religious citizens and the state is concerned, this book prefers to categorize states into three types: religionist states, secularist states, and neutral states.

1. Religionism: The concept of religionism points to the purpose of a religious state in seeking to promote certain religious values through the state apparatus, whether coercively or peacefully. A religionist state receives its moral justification from a religious political theory aimed at determining the good life for humankind. A religious political theory proposes its values as unequivocally true principles, which have been revealed by God. Hence, the major concern in all variants of religionist states is to find a secure ground for toleration of those who are committed to religions other than the official religion or to no religion at all. Historically speaking, despair about finding a secure ground in religionist states for toleration moved liberals toward the idea of the separation of state and religion. Therefore, both Mill and Rawls as liberal theorists are committed to the separation of state and religion. However, while the intolerance of religionist states of the Middle Ages in Europe between Protestants and Catholics, not

to mention against agnostics and atheists, is indisputable, intolerance should not be thought to be an intrinsic feature of religion in general. Conceivably, there are varieties of the religionist state that are committed to the toleration of others.

The famous variant of the religionist state is the "intolerant monist religionist state," in which the unique dominant religion suppresses all who believe in other religions, as well as agnostics and atheists. The intolerant religionist states of the Middle Ages in Europe should be categorized under this variant.[98] The religious intolerance derives, first, from the assumption that there is one true way of life. Second, this unique, true way of life is a particular religion, or a particular sect of a certain religion. Third, there is an exclusive means to unmistakably comprehend the creeds of that religion or sect. Fourth, the value of salvation, which can exclusively be obtained through following the unambiguous collection of religious creeds, is so supreme that all means to achieve it, even torture, are justifiable. Therefore, those who claim to possess the unambiguous truth have the right, even the duty, to impose the truth on others. Another conceivable variant of the religionist state is the "tolerant monist religionist state," where the dominant religion combines the pursuit of its values, through peaceful governmental means, with toleration of others on fallibility grounds and the like. Conceivably, the dismissal of any of the four premises necessary for religious intolerance mentioned above can lead to toleration of others. The only genuine religious ground for toleration of those who do not believe in the allegedly true religion, as Preston King suggests, is the insufficiency of force for achieving religious ends. In other words, a religion can maintain its exclusive access to the truth, while tolerating others by recognizing human fallibility.[99]

Alternatively, the tolerant monist religionist state can be a reasonable combination of the value of the truth followed by an absolute majority of citizens with the value of the protection of a minimal set of human rights for all human beings. In differing degrees of toleration of others, this variant of the religionist state can be found in contemporary Britain, Indonesia, Pakistan, the Scandinavian states, and the like, where the weakly or strongly established religion is not the only legitimate religion in society; that is, the followers of other religions possess certain civil rights, though not necessarily with an equal weight to the followers of the official religion.

A third variant of the religionist state can be shaped in the form of a "corporative religionist state," as is the case in Finland, where all major religions supported by citizens are incorporated into the power body.

A power-sharing strategy adopted by a religionist state brings this variant of the state in practice very close to a supposedly neutral rule, where no religion is privileged by the state. For just as the removal of bias and suppression of diversity is conceivable by a strategy of disengagement of the state from controversial conceptions of the good life, it is achievable, too, through a strategy of compromise between rival religions, provided that aggression can be removed from participating religions.

2. Secularism: As opposed to the religionist state, the concept of a secularist state implies a situation where the state seeks deliberately to promote nonreligious values in society on the basis of the idea that the necessary requirements of modern social life no longer depend upon religious values. Alternatively, secularism can be established on the basis of commitment to the rationalization of the intellect by assuming that the intellect is the exclusive means to the truth. Hence, religion and its principles are valid insofar as they can receive the assent of the intellect. This form of governance derives from the Enlightenment Project with its inclination toward scientific discovery and modernization of human life. The first variant of the secularist state is the "tolerant secularist state," which promotes this-worldly interests through allocating all, or nearly all, governmental resources in advancing nonreligious values. Yet, it abstains from the suppression of religion by granting the freedom of religion to all citizens. Both the contemporary United States of America and France are examples of this variant of the secularist states. For example, France shows less tolerance toward religion than the United States by prohibiting the appearance of Muslim girls in public schools, clothed as the Islamic dress code requires. Alternatively, the "intolerant secularist state," in line with intolerant religionist states, shows its bias against religion by depriving religious citizens from overtly and securely pursuing their values.[100] An ideal Marxist secularist state is the best example of this variant, in which the allegedly corrupted commitment to religion should be suppressed in order to arrive at a just social order. Mill's liberal state is an obvious case of a tolerant secularist state.

3. Neutrality: The term "neutrality" of the state has been employed to manifest the idea that a liberal state can abstain from secularism and religionism by setting its ultimate task as a freestanding agency that does not take sides on controversial doctrinal issues. A neutral state is supposed to play the role of an impartial arbiter whose task is to set a general framework for impartially settling disputes over conceptions of the good. This idea is based on the assumption that the statesmen

have no personal interests. Hence, they can be expected to pursue only the minimum values shared by followers of conflicting doctrines of the good life. The tolerance offered by the neutral state to various religions is grounded in the disengagement of the state, which possesses exclusive access to coercive power, from controversial issues. Put another way, the competition between the followers of competing doctrines will be handled peacefully if their dangerous coercive power is disarmed. In addition, the state, which has exclusive access to coercive power, refrains from involvement with such disputes. Hence, ideally, no suppression and intolerance is exercised by the state and competing groups.

Since the major intolerance in the history of Western liberal societies has been manifested by the religionist states of the Middle Ages, the idea of neutrality is connected with the idea of the secularity of the state. According to the Reformation Project, since the possession of coercive power by a religion or one sect of a religion has led to suppression of other religions or atheism in its extremist fashion, the only solution to persistent bloody conflicts among competing religions is the secularization of the state and the separation of church and state. A neutral state is not supposed to adopt any religion as official in order to provide the most favorable situation for the promotion of various moral, philosophical, and religious doctrines of the good life. The major task the neutral state is expected to fulfill is restricted to impartial arbitration, as well as to promoting the minimum values shared by all rival doctrines and religions. As will be discussed in the following chapters, although Rawls's liberal state is alleged to be neutral in a sense with regard to competing doctrines of the good, it should be categorized as a tolerant secularist state.[101]

As far as the stages of the relationship between politics and religion are concerned, William Safran distinguishes among three phases: "unification," "separation," and "independence." (1) He argues that in ancient times religion and politics were inseparable and they were thought to derive from God. (2) In the Middle Ages, although the spiritual power was distinguished from the territorial power, in European countries religion had an unchallenged supremacy over secular states. (3) Finally, modern times can be marked not by a mere separation of religion and politics, but rather by the doing away with of the supremacy of religion over the state.[102] Modernity, thus, can be characterized by the independence of politics and public square from religious concerns.

Modernism, as European cultural heritage, occurred between the fifteenth and eighteenth centuries, from the late Renaissance to the Age of Enlightenment. Modernism has brought with it three phases of secularization. (1) "Rationalism," as the first phase, has secularized the intellect and rejected a fundamental religious conviction that there is such revealed absolute truth. (2) "Reformation" has secularized political theory by proposing the availability of several truths, even over religious doctrine. Hence, the state should be separated from various religious doctrines, each of which might carry a degree of truth with it. (3) Finally, the "Industrial Revolution" and market economy with its emphasis on the trade of land, labor, and capital has secularized economics as another sphere of collective life.[103] Hence, "modernity has come, in most parts of the world, in a package with secularisation,"[104] and the separation of religion and politics is an essential principle and value of modernism.[105]

Historically, the independence of the state from religion derived initially from a political struggle between two sects of Christianity to achieve freedom in eighteenth-century England. In a further stage, secularism was furnished with a theoretical foundation provided by scientific movement.[106] And finally, industrialization of the nineteenth century in England and elsewhere pushed secularism toward more expansion. Consequently, while initially secularism merely meant "nonreligious," by the end of the nineteenth century it meant "scientific naturalism that expressed full allegiance to the truth of the sciences and the demands of industry, and commitment to those procedures in education and other institutions of society which could implement these scientific findings and serve these technical demands." Since a secular state allocates its major resources for the physical well-being of its citizens, secularism not only competes against traditional religious lifestyles, but it also strengthens the indifference of people to religious principles.[107]

Consequently, between the late seventeenth century and the late twentieth century, in most Western societies there has been a move from affiliation to Christianity to a situation in which a "significant proportion of the population professes no religious belief." Starting from England, the Netherlands, and some British colonies in North America in the late seventeenth century and spreading to other parts of Western Europe in the eighteenth century, the gradual development of religious toleration was an essential precondition for this situation. What has followed from religious toleration is the legal permission of unorthodox religion, irreligion, and religious nonpractice as alternatives to orthodox religion.[108] However, although social theorists of the nineteenth century, such as August Comte, Herbert Spencer, Emile Durkheim, Max Weber, Karl Marx, and Sigmund Freud, predicted that religion would gradually fade away from social life,[109] recent surveys show that the majority of people still consider themselves to be religious.[110]

Liberalism, Secularity, and Secularism

Analytically, liberalism that is concerned with tolerance, individual liberty, and rights is a distinct concept from secularism that is aimed at separating life or politics from religious concerns. Hence, conceivably there can be "theological liberalisms," as some Muslims seem to suggest a theory of Islamic liberalism,[111] as well as "non-liberal secularism," such as communism. Nevertheless, not only does liberalism historically derive from secular considerations, but it also analytically receives its strength from some secular assumptions. Nowadays, most theorists of liberalism, republicanism, feminism, and socialism share the commitment to complete "separation" between state and church in all aspects of social and political issues, such as constitution, administration, legislation, policymaking, and culture. Dworkin, Ackerman, Galston, Rawls, Macedo, and Audi, among other American political philosophers, believe that the secularization of politics and privatization of religion are both to the benefit of religious practice and pluralistic democracy.[112]

"Liberal political philosophy, we are told, starts with the assumption that men are born free, no matter what historical chains might suggest the contrary." Giving top priority to human liberty rejects the contrary foundation that suggests "seriously a god who says different things to different men at different times" that "seems to compromise the intentions of liberal political philosophy from the very start." In addition, the liberal intention to guarantee the primacy of self-preservation dismisses the establishment of the state on some contradictory assumption, such as divine right, that might subordinate self-preservation to some more significant values determined by God. Furthermore, there are three ideas located at the center of liberalism—natural rights, individual interest, and the efficacy of reason—all of which distance liberal political philosophy from any dependency on religion.[113]

At any rate, both Rawls's liberalism and Mill's liberalism are secular in essence, though different in degree. Mill's liberalism is one example of comprehensive liberalism that is *deeply* secular. By contrast, Rawls's liberalism is one example of political liberalism that is *mildly* secular. Mill's and Rawls's ideal liberal states, however, are tolerant of religious citizens. This research intends chiefly to show that the incompatibility between liberalism and religion, as far as Shiite Islam is concerned, is theoretical and not practical. Moreover, this theoretical incompatibility has been decreased to a large degree by Rawls's political liberalism in three considerable ways.

First, Rawls keeps silent with regard to the truth of religion by introducing the notion of reasonableness for assessment of doctrines. Hence, the reasonableness of Rawls's liberal theory is compatible with the truth of religion. Second, Rawls's particularist theory of justice as fairness, which disengages from Shiite Muslim societies, does not provide any ground for incompatibility between his political morality and Shiite particularist political theory. In addition, his theory of decency, which engages with Shiite Muslim societies, provides a ground for partial-compatibility between his political theory and Shiite political theory of religious democracy. Third, what Rawls expects of Shiite Muslim residents in liberal democratic societies is restricted to the concept of "reasonable citizens," which is compatible with the concept of "the self-restrained Muslim" that Shiite political theory expects of them.

Yet, Rawls's particularist theory of justice as fairness is not justifiable to Shiite Muslims, and hence cannot be adopted by them in constructing the basic structure of their societies. Nor is his final argument for the liberty principle compatible with Shiite Islamic views. For the last two qualifications, this book suggests the notion of partial-compatibility.

At the practical level, as opposed to a general expectation, there is a wide scope for reconciliation between liberal states and Shiite Muslim minorities. This reconcilability is chiefly due to the distinction made by Shiite Islam between ethical theory and political theory. While the latter applies only to majorities of Shiite Muslims at home, the former is the leading idea for Shiite Muslims, irrespective of the place of their residence. It will be argued that the ethical duties and obligations Shiite Islam sets for its followers can be fulfilled in Millian and Rawlsian liberal societies.

Briefly, this research investigates three propositions, which initially seem incompatible, regarding the secularity of liberalism:

(TP/1a) *Theoretical Incompatibility Proposition:* Mill's liberal theory is *deeply* secular, and hence is incompatible with Shiite Islam.

(TP/1b) *Theoretical Partial-Compatibility Proposition:* Rawls's liberal theory is *mildly* secular, and hence is partially compatible with Shiite Islam.

(TP/2) *Practical Reconcilability Proposition:* The Millian and the Rawlsian liberal states should tolerate, and should be reciprocally acceptable to, Shiite Muslim minorities.

Two practical recommendations, which are highly significant, will reasonably result from this research:

(PR/1) Shiite Muslim majorities at home should refrain from constructing the basic structure of their societies in accordance with liberal theory. Yet, it does not follow that Shiite political theory might be illiberal. Rather, it proposes "religious democracy," which guarantees human rights, for an Islamic society that possesses a majority of Shiite Muslims.

(PR/2) Since liberal societies tolerate Shiite Muslim citizens, the latter should reciprocally accept the basic structure of the former. Shiite ethical theory demands a Shiite Muslim resident in liberal societies to be a "self-restrained Muslim," which is compatible with Mill's concept of a harmless person and Rawls's concept of a reasonable citizen.

The Organization of the Research

This research is organized in three parts. Part One is devoted to examining the Theoretical Incompatibility Proposition regarding comprehensive liberalism and Shiite Islam. It explores Mill's deeply secular liberalism by focusing on his methodology, utilitarian moral theory, and principle of liberty. Part Two is a parallel examination of the Theoretical Partial-Compatibility Proposition with respect to political liberalism and Shiite Islam. It explores Rawls's mildly secular liberalism by focusing on his methodology, egalitarian moral theory, and principle of liberty. Part Three examines the Practical Reconcilability Proposition with respect to the Millian and Rawlsian liberal states and Shiite Muslim citizens. It explores, first, how the Millian and Rawlsian liberal states tolerate Shiite Muslim citizens, and, second, how these liberal states are acceptable to Shiite Muslim citizens. This part examines some cases, such as public education and headscarf (*hijab*), to support practical reconciliation between the liberal state and Shiite Muslim minorities. The conclusion will, then, review all chapters and summarize the result of their examinations.

PART ONE

Mill's Deeply Secular Liberalism

CHAPTER 1

Mill's Methodology

This chapter examines the theoretical incompatibility between Mill's liberalism and Shiite Islam by looking at Mill's methodology. It will, first, discuss Mill's preferred method in theoretical sciences. It will explore the school of "deductive intuitionism," which is supported by Whewell and Hamilton among others, as the main rival to Mill's method. Second, Mill's alternative positivist method of reasoning, which this book calls "inductive experimentalism," will be critically examined. Furthermore, Mill's scientific methodology in ethics, again as a rival to intuitionism, will be discussed.

As this chapter will show, Mill defines the external world in terms of possible, permanent, perceivable things, distinct from our perception. He holds that our immediate knowledge about those permanent possibilities derives from experience, rather than mere self-examination. The expansion of our knowledge is due to induction from immediate awareness or further experiences, and not a deductive method of inference. In ethics, Mill suggests the following two major principles. First, there should be one ultimate moral value that receives its validity from some scientific consideration, rather than from scientific proof. What this ultimate evaluative judgment expresses is merely a specific relation between the components of the judgment in human feeling or mind, rather than reporting a causal relation between two facts in the external world to which the report can be compared. Second, apart from the ultimate moral value, there are many other moral codes, the validity of which lies in their serving as means to the single ultimate value and their consistency with each other. Therefore, the assessment of all moral values, other than the highest one, should be made on the basis of two criteria: their causal relations to the ultimate end as discovered through inductive experimentalism and their consistency with one another.

The major incompatibility between Mill's methodology and Shiite Islamic methodology lies in Mill's assertion that inductive experimentalism is the unique method for scientific explanation and investigation about the truth. For Shiite Islam, however, proof can be provided by revelation and intellectual demonstration, as by experiment.

The Logic of Theoretical Sciences

What has made Mill a renowned philosopher is his *A System of Logic,* published in 1843, which enjoyed a paramount position compared to other logic books for about half a century. However, the rise of logical positivism and the philosophy of logic have gone far beyond the point that Mill reached.[1] Generally speaking Mill is "the most distinguished philosopher of British positivism."[2] As far as Mill's terminology implies, he can be called a supporter of what I call "inductive experimentalism." First, in contrast to Hamilton who maintains that there is a persistent world out there that can be perceived by our faculty of intuition, externality for Mill amounts to the idea of being the "permanent possibility of sensations."[3] Therefore, to the question: What is the external world? Mill's answer is "that there is concerned in our perceptions something which exists when we are not thinking of it; which existed before we had ever thought of it, and would exist if we were annihilated; and further, that there exist things . . . which have never been perceived by man."[4] To clarify, Mill firstly accepts the existence of the perceived as something different from our perceptions. Furthermore, he distinguishes between the "actual sensations" that are present so long as we have them, and the "possible sensations" that we did not have in the past, nor do we have at present, but we may experience in the future. The latter cases are permanent. In addition to the permanence of the perceived as one character of externality, publicity is its other characteristic feature. While the actual sensation is only perceivable by particular individuals, possibilities are capable of being perceived by different individuals.[5] "The belief in such permanent possibilities," says Mill, "seems to me to include all that is essential or characteristic in the belief in substance."[6]

As for the discovery of these permanent possibilities, Anschutz argues that Mill always declares himself an "experientialist" in opposition to intuitionists, yet avoids seeing himself as an adherent of "empiricism." According to Mill, while experience provides us with necessary materials of knowledge, further valid knowledge can be obtained only when the scientific method of generalization is employed. For Mill, the scientific method of inductive experimentalism he advocates can be compared with the job of a bee, which firstly collects materials from the garden and then with its power analyzes and transforms them. Empiricism can be compared with the job of an ant, which merely gathers materials and uses them. Intuitionism can be compared with the job of a spider, which uses its power to spin its web out of itself. Hence, distinguishing among empiricism, intuitionism, and experimentalism, Mill associates empiricism with Burke, Mackintosh, and Macaulay; intuitionism with Coleridge, Carlyle, and Whewell; and experimentalism with himself.[7] Therefore, Mill should be counted as an adherent of the school of "inductive experimentalism," as opposed to the school of deductive intuitionism.

The School of Deductive Intuitionism

In his attack on intuitionism, Mill's major target is Sir William Hamilton.[8] Intuitionists in the first place suggest that there are truths out there we have access to by "immediate intuition." In this belief, Mill associates Spencer with metaphysicians such as Reid and Stewart, as well as with philosophers of the intuitive school, such as Descartes, Whewell, Sir William Hamilton, and Cousin.[9] "That there exists a material world," says Mill, and "that this is the very world which we directly and immediately perceive, and not merely the hidden cause of our perceptions; that Space, Time, Force, Extension, Figure, are . . . objective realities; are regarded by Mr. Spencer" in agreement with others mentioned above, as truths we know by intuition.[10] Intuition, as Coleridge states, is "the direct Beholding, the immediate Knowledge, which is the substance and true significance of all."[11] Not only are there such necessary truths that, argues Whewell, we can arrive at,[12] but they are also so obvious that "we see that they could not be otherwise." In other words, Whewell suggests that the rejection of such necessary truths "is not only false, but impossible," so that one cannot "even by an effort of imagination, or in a supposition, conceive the reverse of that which is asserted."[13]

The test of the correctness of all beliefs, according to intuitionists, is "inconceivableness" of the negative of those beliefs. Hence, according to intuitionism, if all persons believe in a proposition at all times so that its contradictory belief becomes inconceivable, the proposition is an infallible primitive truth that constitutes the premise of our further knowledge.[14] These necessary truths, which can be found in every philosophical issue, are the subject of "simple self-examination." In the process of this self-examination, Mill quotes Cousin as suggesting, we can find with certainty some primary truths that are the sources of all our knowledge. Our consciousness, as the only evidence, approves the correctness of our immediate knowledge.[15]

In addition to our immediate knowledge about necessary truths, what constitutes our understanding about reality lies in our secondary affirmations inferred from immediate knowledge by deduction, as deductive intuitionists propose. It is worth noticing that there is no agreement among deductivists about the logic of scientific reasoning, as is the case with inductivists.[16] However, according to Mill, deductivists believe that while the validity of our immediate knowledge about some subjects depends upon the "inconceivability of their negation," the reliability of the knowledge we obtain indirectly through reasoning depends upon the inconceivability of inferences through which we conclude our secondary knowledge. According to deductivism, "inconceivability is thus the ultimate ground of all assured beliefs."[17] Hence, by mixing our different forms of direct knowledge with one another, through the method of deduction, deductivists affirm that we arrive at secondary beliefs with the same assurance and certainty.

This method of deduction employed to produce the secondary convictions states that any scientific inference consists of two sets of premises: the first set should comprise one or more universal laws, whereas the second set should consist of some singular statements or "the initial conditions." The first part in its turn should be deduced from some more general statements.[18] According to Ryan's formulation of the deductive tradition, the deductive account of explanation is the view that "a science aims at explaining as wide a range of phenomena as possible from as few initial assumptions as possible; these assumptions feature as axioms from which all more specific laws are to be deduced."[19]

The method of deductive intuitionism was employed by Mill's contemporaries to justify basic religious convictions and values, at the top of which is the knowledge of God. For God is assumed to be something to which the hands of experimental experience have no access. Therefore, while rejecting the possibility of proving the existence of God by experience, Coleridge did not infer the impossibility of the knowledge of God. Rather, he maintained that there are many truths we know a priori, such as "the fundamental doctrines of religion and morals."[20] By contrast, Mill intends to reject these religious consequences by his method of inductive experimentalism as the only reliable method of scientific investigation.

However, as for the development of Mill's view, he seems to affirm two views about scientific explanation. In 1828, when reviewing Archbishop Whately's views on logic, although rejecting intuitionists' claims about immediate knowledge, Mill suggests that "reasoning" is made by deduction. Mill took it for granted that "the process of philosophising consisted of two parts, the ascertainment of premises, and the deduction of conclusions." While the original premises can be obtained only through experience, which is called "induction," syllogism concerns only the process of reasoning and helps prevent drawing wrong conclusions on true premises.[21]

Here Mill seems to reject the possibility that there might be any system of inductive reasoning. He approves Whately's view in rejecting the assumption "that mathematical reasoning, and theological, and metaphysical, and political, and moral, are so many different *kinds of reasoning*." Rather, Mill suggests, "what in reality is different in these cases is not the *mode* of reasoning, but the nature of the premises, or propositions *from* which we reason."[22] Initially, then, Mill subscribed to the deductive method in political and moral philosophy, in the sense it is used in mathematics, geometry, and the like, although he was certainly an experimentalist in that the original source of knowledge to him is experience and not intuition.[23]

The School of Inductive Experimentalism

As was indicated above, initially Mill's view was similar to his father's and Bentham's. Hence, Mill believed that "the principles of political philosophy and the practical rules of political action were to be deduced from a few simple laws of human nature, i.e., psychological axioms." Macaulay criticized this view on the basis that in political philosophy the observed events of human history should be added to our conception of human nature.[24] Therefore, Mill shifted from his early view to the view that experience is the ultimate source of human knowledge even in those cases in which reason is employed.[25] According to Mill, "axioms" are "simply our earliest inductions from experience," rather than being deductions from immediate knowledge.[26] Our intuitive knowledge derives from "science," rather than being "a matter of simple self-examination."[27] By this, Mill opposed intuitionists who suggested, instead, that the original source of our knowledge is the self-evident knowledge we have access to through self-examination.

Thus, in 1833 Mill had expanded his primary idea about deduction.[28] In *A System of Logic,* he undoubtedly departed from his previous view and proposed instead that induction is another kind of reasoning in contrast with deduction.[29] Logic, Mill argued, as the "science and art of reasoning" is "the science of Proof, or Evidence,"[30] rather than being merely a science of formal inference. Proof, or evidence, in its turn should be considered as singular statements about particular facts that provide explanation and prediction, rather than being general statements constituting the major part of syllogisms.[31] Developing his view further in *Hamilton's Philosophy,* Mill rejects the idea that the only logic is formal logic, namely syllogism, and suggests that "what the Logic of mere consistency cannot do, the Logic of ascertainment of truth, the Philosophy of Evidence in its larger acceptation, can. It can explain the function of the Ratiocinative process as an instrument of the human intellect in the discovery of truth."[32] Yet, it is worth considering that Mill does not reject the usefulness of syllogism as an empiricist such as Locke affirms. Nor does he conceive the syllogism as an indispensable method for reasoning as deductivists firmly assert.[33] Against these two standard views, Mill suggests that syllogistic reasoning is useful, although it is not unavoidable.[34]

In his new logic, Mill defines "induction"[35] as "the operation of discovering and proving general propositions," or as "the process of establishing the general proposition."[36] In his expanded view about scientific reasoning, Mill argues against syllogism, by which we conclude a particular from general statements, concluding that in every syllogism there is a petitio principii. Mill's criticism of syllogism states that only when the conclusion is already known in general statements used as premises can one infer that particular.[37] Assuming that one intends to conclude that John is mortal, a syllogistic reasoning should be organized as follows:

> Premise 1: John is a man.
> Premise 2: Every man is mortal
> Conclusion: John is mortal

According to Mill, when we affirm in accordance with premise 2 that "Every man is mortal" either we already knew that "John is mortal," or we did not. If we knew that fact already, the conclusion will add nothing to our knowledge. On the other hand, if we did not know already the fact of John's mortality, premise 2 is incorrect. In both cases, this syllogistic reason is useless.[38] What Archbishop Whately resorts to as the solution to this problem, that is, this reasoning will "expand and unfold the assertions wrapt up" in the premises, Mill finds unconvincing. He casts doubt on the possibility that "a science, like geometry, can be all 'wrapt up' in a few definitions and axioms."[39]

Having dismissed the view that mere syllogistic reasoning can give us new knowledge, Mill proposes his alternative to syllogism, that is, the inductive method by which we infer particulars from particulars. "All inference," Mill explicitly states, "is from particulars to particulars."[40] The ground for this affirmation, according to Mill, lies in the fact that in the world where we live, every fact is particular; hence the only knowledge initially available to us is particular. However, the aggregation, made of several pieces of evidence, each of which reveals a picture about a particular fact, will further enable us to make a generalization.[41] A "general truth is but an aggregate of particular truths; a comprehensive expression, by which an indefinite number of individual facts are affirmed,"[42] rather than being a deductive inference from a more general law. Mill explicitly proposes that our understanding about general laws derives from the process of aggregation in which we combine different particular facts to infer generalities. Similarly, when the issue at stake is a particular, the evidence and proof can only be a set of information about relevant particulars. Hence, all inference occurs through a process from particulars to particulars, be the unknown fact a general law, or a particular. It is because of this strong inductive view about inference that Mill dismisses the "logical" need for general statements in the process of inference.[43] "Since the individual cases," says Mill, "are all the evidence we can possess . . . and since that evidence is either sufficient in itself, or, if insufficient for the one purpose, cannot be sufficient for the other; I am unable to see why we should be forbidden to take the shortest cut from these sufficient premises to the conclusion."[44]

Nevertheless, the intermediate general statements in logical inference are so advantageous that in "practice" they are indispensable. The advantages of general statements lie in the simplification of the process of inference, along with compensation for human forgetfulness, and a check of our inference from particulars to particulars.[45] "Those facts, and the particular instances which supplied them, may have been forgotten, but a record remains," Mill concludes. "Generalisation," Mill further suggests, is "a process of inference," that is, inference from a given set of particulars to a given particular at stake along with inference to one general law. This general law is "the whole of what our evidence must prove if it proves anything."[46] Thus, the unnecessary intermediation of general laws deduced from particular facts known by experimental experiences cannot compel Mill to accept the validity of anything except experiment.

However, Mill admits that there are some laws we know a priori. These immediate cases of knowledge are not attainable by inductive experimentalism. Our knowledge of them rests on the inconceivability of their negation. Among these are three "Fundamental Laws of Thought," upon which all other laws are based. The first is the "Law of Principle of Identity," which expresses that "a thing is the same as itself." The second is the "Law of Contradiction," according to which "contradictory propositions cannot both be true." And the third is the "Law of Excluded Middle," which indicates that "contradictory propositions cannot both be false." Not only does Mill accept the independence of these laws from experiment, but he also admits that any assertion which "conflicts with one of these laws . . . is to us unbelievable."[47]

There are, however, other immediate laws, although not as the bases for every conviction, we firmly hold, with no derivation from experiment. These are all laws that express the "impossibility" of an event, such as the "Law of Contrariety," which indicates that one subject cannot possess two or more contrary qualities at a given time. This law rejects, for instance, the possibility of a given piece of paper being white and black at the same time. Another impossibility law is the "Law of Causation,"[48] which not only requires the dependence of every phenomenon on a cause, a fact that brings it under the control of experimental experiences, but also sees it as "impossible" that any phenomenon can exist with no cause, a fact that excludes it from being accessed through experience.[49] The subject of experience is what we can reach by sense, which requires in the first place that it be possible. Hence, all impossibilities are out of the reach of experiment.

More importantly, consider the very fundamental statement of experimentalism that says "the experimental experience is the only method for achieving the truth." If you consider this basic law as a priori it contradicts itself and will require rejecting experimentalism's denial of any a priori; and if you ground its validity on the very experimental experience it leads to petitio principii about the validity of experimentalism.[50] Hence, for experimentalism to start from somewhere it is necessary to admit in advance some a priori on the basis of which we can build our experimental discoveries. What is necessarily required by acknowledgment of an a priori is the task of more contemplation for other possible a priori in human knowledge.

However, Mill's opposition to his contemporary religious thinkers, such as Coleridge, shows that his method of inductive experimentalism, as the only reliable method of scientific discovery, is expected to reject even the *possibility* of accessing transcendental facts. Hence, since Mill's contemporary religious thinkers rely upon nonscientific method with regard to their basic religious convictions, by refuting their methodology Mill seems to intend to guarantee the secularity of his moral and political philosophy.

As far as the sources of moral and political values of Shiite Islam are concerned, the Qur'an is the key source. The Qur'an consists of 6,666 verses that explain many issues, such as doctrines, history of previous peoples and their Messengers, and moral values. The second source is prophetic traditions, in which the Prophet interprets the Qur'an and expands its teachings. At the same level of validity is traditions reported from the twelve infallible Imams who have consecutively succeeded the Prophet in his mission. Yet, the very validity of the Qur'an and Islamic traditions derives basically from some intellectual demonstration and reasoned reflections that direct man to accept the truth of revelation.[51] In addition, Shiite Muslims receive intellectual demonstration as another source for Islamic doctrines and moral values.[52] Overall, intellectual demonstration and revelation are two sources of moral and political values that

Shiite Islam introduces. Hence, the exclusiveness of the validity of inductive experimentalism opposes the teachings of Shiite Islam and its holy book.[53] This is a strong case for the Theoretical Incompatibility Proposition.[54]

The Logic of Ethics

Like his view about the theoretical sciences, Mill's rationalist position in ethics should be envisaged as an attack on intuitionism. The focal point of intuitionist morality, according to Mill, consists of two claims about moral judgments: first intuitionism is the idea that "the principles of morals are evident *a priori*, requiring nothing to command assent, except that the meaning of the term be understood." Intuitionists, further, affirm that there are many self-evident moral judgments, and not only one. The plurality of moral judgments can neither be reduced to a single value, nor is there any self-evident umpire standard by which we can settle the conflicts among those moral judgments.[55] What Mill suggests against intuitionism is utilitarian morality starting from a single ethical value with the ability to explain all other evaluative judgments at the lower levels. The highest value—in Mill's morality, the utility principle—which is not susceptible to scientific proof, gives validity to other codes of actions, along with playing the role of the ultimate judge for settling any conflict among lower standards when disagreement arises.

Distinguishing fundamentally between "factual statements" common in theoretical sciences and "evaluative judgments" employed in ethics, Mill rejects the possibility of supporting the ultimate ethical judgment by proof.[56] "Questions of ultimate ends," argues Mill, "are not amenable to direct proof. Whatever can be proved to be good, must be so by being shown to be a means to something admitted to be good without proof." By the latter statement, Mill points to the utility principle as the ultimate ethical value.[57]

The following chapter shows that Mill resorts to the very method of inductive experimentalism in justifying his utility principle. What completes Mill's methodology lies in his distinction between "scientific proof" and "rational consideration."[58] While the former explores a cause-effect relation through inductive experimentalism, the latter explores an ethical principle through inductive experimentalism without there being any *cause-effect* relation. Therefore, as will be discussed in the following chapter, Mill's advocacy of the utility principle is based upon his inductive experimentalism, by collecting evidence from the feelings of individuals. Furthermore, he argues that his experimental findings indicate that each individual desires only "happiness." Moreover, as for the types of happiness, Mill again attempts to collect evidence from the most experienced members of society. Hence, his argument for the Greatest Happiness Principle rests upon purely observed experiences. Yet, his argument here differs from the cause-effect relation explored in theoretical sciences, as well as all ethical values other than the ultimate one. In both categories, however, there is a type of experiential argumentation, rather than any intuition or a priori principle. Put another way, Mill maintains his commitment to a posteriori knowledge in ethics, to which he is ontologically committed.

The distinction between factual statements and ethical judgments, according to Mill, lies in the difference between science and arts. The former is a set of truths supposedly corresponding to the external world aimed at describing facts as they are, whereas the latter consists of a collection of rules and codes of actions aimed at directing human actions as they have to be. Mill explains the different nature of ethical judgments by suggesting that a proposition of which the predicate is expressed by the words 'ought' or 'should be', is generically different from one which is expressed by 'is' or will be'. He further goes on to suggest that "even these propositions assert something as a matter of fact. The fact affirmed in them is that the conduct recommended excites in the speaker's mind the feeling of approbation."[59] To Mill, moral judgments are indisputable real "moral feelings."[60] Speaking about moral judgments made by people, Mill argues that "the practical principle which guides them to their opinions on the regulation of human conduct, is the feeling in each person's mind," although "no one, indeed, acknowledges to himself that his standard of judgment is his own liking." What is more, "if reasons, when given, are a mere appeal to a similar preference felt by other people, it is still only many people's liking instead of one."[61] Therefore, all moral judgments are merely the expression of our individual preferences with no independent order of moral values in reality. By this, Mill subscribes to the positivistic principle of "naturalism"[62] that suggests "goodness and right are *natural properties*—they are ultimately properties of things that can be located in the natural world."[63]

Therefore, the reason why ethical judgments about ultimate values are not amenable to any scientific proof lies in the fact that in essence they are not "statements" that can bear truth or falsity, even when they are uttered in the form of ostensible statements of facts. For instance the statement "Happiness is the supreme good" is in essence an expression of a judgment, such as "Happiness ought to be sought as the primary goal," and hence is not amenable either to truth or falsity. The criterion for assessment of these types of judgments can be desirability, acceptance, approbation, or, conversely, undesirability, rejection, and disapprobation, rather than truth or falsity.[64] Further illumination in distinguishing the essence of factual statements from that of evaluative judgments seems useful here.

Any "genuine" factual statement either affirms or denies the "co-existence" of two concepts in the external world. For instance, the statement: "Fire is burning" suggests the coexistence of the concept of "fire" and the concept of "burning" in the external world, rather than assuming that they are congruent in my mind; for obviously the kind of fire I can imagine or remember in my mind lacks the capability of burning, otherwise whenever I remember a fire my mind should be burned. "When I say that fire causes heat," says Mill in this regard, "I mean that the natural phenomenon fire causes the natural phenomenon of heat," as opposed to asserting anything about ideas in the mind.[65]

The essence of an evaluative judgment is fundamentally different from factual statements in that the former in whatever form it is uttered does not suggest the coexistence of two independent concepts in the external world. Consider the judgment: "Keeping one's own promise is necessary." While the concept of "keeping," as well as "the person" and "promise," are all external phenomena, the concept "necessary" does not point to anything in the external world that can be perceived, experienced, or seen. There is obviously disagreement as to what the "source" of our evaluative judgments is. Our personal desires, God's knowledge, and the requirement of human nature, or *telos*, are well-known views in this regard. Likewise, our incentives for uttering evaluative judgments varies from teaching the interlocutor about one human value, through reminding one who knew the value before, to encouraging him toward action, to examining his potential for obedience. However, it is apparent that the judgment itself does not assert any concrete entity in the external world. The mere meaning of "necessary" is that the person who is addressed by this utterance "is asked to keep his promise." Owing to the lack of any report about coexistence of two distinct concepts the assessment of evaluative judgments as true/false is impossible. In brief, factual statements should be assessed as "true/false," and the criterion for this assessment should be "compatibility" or "incompatibility" of our statements with the external state of affairs.

Since in the case of evaluative judgments the assessment of a value as true/false is irrelevant, a question arises over how to assess them. To this question, Mill's answer distinguishes between the ultimate moral value and all other values, and suggests that it is the ultimate moral value that is essentially different from factual statements, for all other ethical judgments can be converted to causal statements describing the causal relation between means and ends, even when they are uttered ostensibly in the form of evaluative judgments.[66] Hence, in line with Mill's morality, when one advises another to not tell a lie, or to "tell the truth," one is describing the dependence of the ultimate value of general utility on the general commitment to truth telling of the members of society. In this way, the interaction between science and art can be envisaged. "The Art," argues Mill, "proposes to itself an end to be attained, defines the end, and hands it over to the science. The science receives it, considers it as a phenomenon or effect to be studied, and having investigated its causes and conditions, sends it back to Art with a theorem of the combination of circumstances by which it could be produced. . . . Art concludes that the performance of these actions is desirable, and finding it also practicable, converts the theorem into a rule or precept."[67]

For Mill, justification of evaluative judgments would be due to their causality for the higher values, along with consistency with other rules of conduct.[68] Consistency and efficacy with regard to the highest value, Mill affirms, are the criteria for assessing ethical judgments. In addition to these criteria, the whole system of morality has the potentiality for being explained by a single rule, which is not susceptible to any proof, namely, the principle of utility.[69] Put another way, the whole system of morality,[70] in Mill's account, should encompass several evaluative judgments that are consistent with each other serving one ultimate value. Being located at the top of evaluative judgments, the ultimate evaluative judgment does not need any proof.[71] Rather, it is supported by "some considerations."[72] Still, as will be explored in the following chapter, Mill is committed to experiment and induction in supporting his utility principle, though not in cause-effect fashion.

As far as the Theoretical Incompatibility Proposition is concerned, Shiite Islam agrees with Mill that evaluative judgments are different from factual statements in that the former do not report any causal relationship between two facts, and hence cannot be assessed as true/false.[73] Yet, the particular Islamic conception of the common human constitution determines a particular end for life. According to this view, human nature is constituted so as to determine some specific values and virtues to promote and crystallize man's natural tendencies and potentialities.[74] Here, Shiite Islam agrees with MacIntyre who suggests that once we conceive of the human nature as having a telos, the linkage between "is" and "ought" can be grasped, since the human telos should be assumed as the effect and the "ought" judgments including the very ultimate moral value as causes to that end. Hence, what leads to that end should be judged as good and what prevents man from moving toward that end as bad.[75] In this sense, even the ultimate moral value should be conceived of as being a factual statement that shows the cause to achieving human happiness.

Conclusion

This chapter examined the Theoretical Incompatibility Proposition regarding Mill's liberalism and Shiite Islam by looking at Mill's methodology. The depth of the secularity of Mill's methodology, which confirms this incompatibility, can be chiefly noticed in the following points.

(1/a) Mill asserts that inductive experimentalism is the unique method for scientific explanation and investigation about the truth. To Mill, knowledge of God, Messengerhood, and the basic doctrines of Islam, which altogether rest heavily on intellectual demonstration and revelation, are not possible.

(1/b) By contrast, according to Shiite Islam, although Mill's inductive experimentalism is a reliable method for providing proof in sciences, it is not a unique reliable method. In addition to experiment, proof can be provided by revelation and intellectual demonstration. Even those Shiite Muslim philosophers who attempt to prove only the basic doctrines of Islam by following inductive experimentalism do not agree with Mill that the experiment is the unique method for providing proof.

(2/a) Mill maintains that the ultimate moral standard is subjective and does not report any causal relationship between two facts in the external world, and hence cannot be assessed as true/false, whereas it can be confirmed by a "scientific consideration."

(2/b) By contrast, according to Shiite Islamic philosophy, it is true that evaluative judgments in essence are different from factual statements. Yet, since the common human constitution determines a particular spiritual path toward human progress, all evaluative judgments should be assumed as causes to that end. In this sense, even the ultimate moral standard should be conceived of as being a factual statement that shows the cause to achieving that particular human progress.

CHAPTER 2

Mill's Utilitarian Moral Theory

This chapter examines the theoretical incompatibility between Mill's liberalism and Shiite Islam by looking at Mill's utilitarian moral theory. First, the major rival to utilitarianism, namely moral intuitionism will be explored. Whewell and Kant are the major rivals with whom Mill competes. Then, Mill's utilitarianism, which develops both his father's and Bentham's utilitarianism, will be analyzed.

As will be demonstrated in this chapter, recent interpretations of Mill's account of morality claim that he is proposing a kind of rule-utilitarianism. This recent interpretation not only adds some strength to his moral theory, but also allows his utility principle to be reconciled with his "veto principle" of justice, which derives from the very principle of utility. Overall, Mill's moral system amounts to suggesting that the this-worldly happy life, which is full of different kinds of utility at different levels, is the unique criterion for moral judgments. At the top of different kinds of utilities stands security, requiring the establishment of just laws with the veto power to define the boundaries of all other moral values.

Having established his secular method, Mill expounds a deeply secular system of morality in all the steps of his conceptualization and argumentation. Not only does Mill allow no recourse to religion, but he also establishes his alternative notion of the Religion of Humanity. The secularity of his moral theory can be seen, first, in his "humanism," rejecting its rival theist systems of morality by focusing its attention on human beings. Second, not only does Mill refrain from any recourse to religious principles in his moral theory, but he also ignores the feelings and desires of religious citizens when referring in his argument to what man desires. In this respect, he only looks at nonreligious persons in society and their desires in determining what is desirable. Hence, he restricts the concept of utility to "this-worldly" happiness, whereas religious people expand the notion of happiness and apply it at a higher level to "otherworldly" happiness.

More explicitly, he proposes that his utilitarian morality can play the role of a religion with some privileges over all supernatural religions. All these features of Mill's moral theory confirm the theoretical incompatibility between Mill's secular morality and Shiite Islamic morality.

Moral Intuitionism

Mill contrasts moral intuitionism with his moral theory of utilitarianism. As "Whewell was probably the most influential of the academic opponents of utilitarianism in the early nineteenth century,"[1] when Mill criticized intuitionism he had in mind views such as Whewell's in *Elements of Morality*.[2] To capture what precisely Mill opposes, a brief examination of the intuitionism of Whewell and Ross is required.

Comparing the "Laws of Human Action" with the "Laws of Nature" in that both are general principles about their subjects, Whewell characterizes the latter as bearing "imperative" rules or "commands" aiming to "direct the Will" as opposed to the descriptive nature of the former. The purposiveness of human actions, according to Whewell, requires that every action be taken in order to produce an intended consequence. Whewell argues that in a chain of actions each inferior action aims to produce the superior action as an end or a good. The "imperative force" of those rules, which allow a given action, derives from the value of the consequence it produces. Thus, the superior rule justifies the inferior rule. Since the chain of means and ends should logically terminate somewhere as "the highest end" that "had a value of its own . . . there is a Supreme Rule of Human Action" from which all other rules of actions derive. That ultimate rule "is called *right*" as opposed to "*wrong*." Since the supreme rule of right and wrong is ultimate, there can be no reason to obey it except that it is evidently our duty to do the right and avoid the wrong. "Why must I do what is right?" argues Whewell. "Because it *is* right." Whewell seems to mean by the Supreme Rule of Human Action the *ultimate term* by which we make our moral judgments, rather than providing an *ultimate standard* by which we can evaluate all inferior actions as good or bad. Put another way, he merely defines a "Duty" as something that should be done, as appears from his further discussion about right and wrong: "That which is right we *approve;* that which is wrong we *disapprove.*"[3]

Therefore, with regard to the ultimate standard of human actions Whewell argues that what determines right and wrong actions are "*Moral Rules.*" There are many moral rules that determine right and wrong actions, and not only one. Here we arrive at the core element to which Mill points when he describes intuitionism as affirming several self-evident moral standards. Since each moral rule derives from a human "Right," such as the right to one's property, and since there are five "primary and universal Rights of men," there are five primary moral rules as the ultimate standard for human actions. Those five primary rights, argues Whewell, include "*the Right of Personal Security; the Right of Property; the Right of Contract; Family Rights; and the Rights of Government.*" Suggesting that every man's right corresponds to others' obligation to respect that right, Whewell arrives at the core point in his "duty-based" theory of morality, that is, "the Doctrine of Duties, which is *Morality,* presupposes a Doctrine of Rights and Obligations."[4]

To justify those rights that are the source of our obligations, Whewell regularly resorts to the concept of necessity, requirements, and the like. Thus, he seems to assume that these rights are self-evident in the sense that they are the necessary requirements of the special constitution of human nature and human society. According to Whewell, not only do moral rules "exist necessarily," but they are also the "necessary truths" derived from "the moral nature of man." Therefore, they are "universal and unchangeable" as all necessary truths must be.[5]

Like Whewell, Ross's intuitionism assumes that there are prima facie duties known self-evidently with no umpire rule to settle cases of conflict between them. As his list of those prima facie duties, Ross mentions the following cases "without claiming completeness or finality for it."

(1/a) The duty of "fidelity," such as keeping implicit promises we make not to tell a lie when entering into a conversation.

(1/b) The duty of "reparation" derived from a "previous wrongful act."

(2) The duty of "gratitude" in responding to a service we receive from others.

(3) The duty of "justice" derived from the "possibility of distribution of pleasure of happiness."

(4) The duty of "beneficence" derived from the mere fact that by being virtuous we can improve others' condition.

(5) The duty of "self-improvement" derived from the fact that through virtue and intelligence we have the ability to make our situation better.

(6) The duty of "not injuring others."[6]

At the beginning of *Utilitarianism,* Mill also mentions Kant's constructivist moral system as another failed rival to his utility principle, alongside intuitionism. Kant's morality, again duty-based, affirms that there is only one universal first principle from which all moral duties derive.[7] Assuming that by self-examination we clearly are aware that everyone ought to fulfill his duty unselfishly and completely,[8] Kant provides us with two "ought" propositions regulating all our actions. The single ultimate law of prudence expressed in "ought" form states that "whoever wills an end ought to will the means." He calls this single prudential first principle a "hypothetical imperative" in the sense that its command toward an action is *conditional* upon willing the relevant end producible by that action. The second "ought" proposition that regulates all our moral actions states: "Act only according to that maxim through which you can at the same time will that it should become a universal law," where "maxim" means one's plan of action. Kant calls this ultimate moral principle the "categorical imperative" in the sense that it commands an *unconditional* action with no reference to the relevant end.[9]

What accounts for the validity of the categorical imperative is the necessary requirement of being committed to three suppositions: (1) everyone is morally worthwhile, (2) we should do the right actions, and (3) we should pursue a good state of affairs. All these suppositions can only be achieved, maintains Kant, by starting from the rationality or the goodness of the agent. Hence, the binding force of the categorical imperative as the ultimate moral law derives from the centrality of the concept of a good agent "whose will is wholly determined *a priori*" in morality. Hence, moral law is the pattern of the will of the good agent. What follows from this assumption is the priority of the notion of the right action over the concept of the good end. Rather than defining the rightness of an action on the basis of the goodness of the result it produces, the goodness of an end should be defined on the basis of the rightness of the action that leads to the end. By disconnecting the notion of moral law from the consequences of actions, then, Kant proposes that the only criterion for judging an action as moral is to see if the good agent would do that action.[10] On the whole, Kant is concerned with what the right action is irrespective of its consequences.

Overall, what is located as the center of any duty-based moral theory is the "individual." Here, the moral rule demands that the individual take a specific action because the action corresponds to some standard known either "self-evidently" or "deductively," irrespective of its consequences.[11] However, Mill rejects all types of duty-based moral theories with recourse to the scientific method of inductive experimentalism and instead suggests a "goal-based" utilitarian moral theory, to use Dworkin's term.

Mill and the General Theory of Utilitarianism

Mill was the greatest utilitarian theorist who explained vigorously "the strengths and the weaknesses of the utilitarian philosophy" in comparison with his predecessors.[12] Recent reinterpretations and explorations of Mill's philosophy by writers such as Alan Ryan, David Lyons, Don Brown, John Gray, Henry West, and Fred Berger have been attempts to redress former unsympathetic interpretations and to present Mill more accurately.[13]

As was just demonstrated, Mill's utilitarian moral philosophy should be conceived of as opposing Whewell's intuitionism and Kant's rationalism. Crusius's religious morality, which derives all moral laws from one duty, namely the "necessity" of complying with "God's Will," seems to be the view to which Mill most objects. Overall, intuitionist morality generally disregards the consequences of human conduct in shaping the moral rules, a fact that to which Mill fundamentally objects.[14]

Mill asserts that a system of morality should and can be organized in a coherent order with some principles deriving from the others up to the point that the chain or chains arrive at one ultimate value.[15] He further suggests that all moral values, except the ultimate value, receive their validity from their causality to the ultimate moral value. He emphasizes that the ultimate moral value receives its validity from a "scientific consideration" that is independent of all other moral values. Speaking about the ultimate moral standard, he emphatically suggests that "whatever that standard is, there can be but one: for if there were several ultimate principles of conduct, the same conduct might be approved by one of those principles and condemned by another; and there would be needed some more general principle, as umpire between them."[16] Having established the necessity of coherence in morality, Mill suggests that the ultimate moral rule is "utility" or "the happiness of mankind, or rather of all sentient beings." It is this ultimate standard of utility "with which all other rules of conduct were required to be consistent, and from which by ultimate consequence they could all be deduced."[17] In this way, Mill registers his name as an advocate of utilitarianism in moral and political philosophy.[18]

Furthermore, Mill's utilitarianism should be understood as being in line with Hume and Bentham with regard to English political and ethical theory. Hume suggested utilitarianism as the alternative to the dominant view of natural law and social contract in Europe. While Hume introduced the principle of utility as a descriptive principle, which explains the "received morality," Benthamite utilitarianism offered a moral standard by which human actions *should* be judged.[19] "Nature has placed mankind under the governance of two sovereign masters, pain and pleasure," says Bentham in his famous passage. "It is for them alone," he continues, "to point out what we ought to do, as well as to determine what we shall do."[20]

Combining utilitarianism with radicalism, James Mill argued that given the untutored nature of humankind, people tend to exploit one another to their own benefit, unless restrained. Therefore, in order for government to pursue general happiness it is essential that the representative system of democracy guarantee the identification of governmental decisions with that of the community. In this way, democracy would be an essential instrument to the realization of utilitarian purposes. What will further strengthen the pursuit of general happiness, in addition to the governmental apparatus, is education in reformed society.[21] Inheriting some notions of utilitarianism from Bentham and his father, Mill has enriched utilitarianism in some aspects and has proposed it as both a moral theory and a political theory.[22]

Mill's Particular Theory of Utilitarianism

According to Mill, while the utility principle supplies a compelling ground for all individual and collective actions, his notion of justice draws the inevitable boundaries for those actions that belong to the collective domain. Nevertheless, the fact that the validity of justice derives from utility resolves any potential contradiction between them. The point is that utility as the general term consists of different types of pleasures in various degrees in quantity and quality. The most valuable type of utility is "security." Thus no other utility can resist its demand, no matter how great the latter and how small the former. Justice, in this reading, is a term for respecting those rights that should be respected for achieving the utility of security. On this reading of Mill's moral theory, the rightness and wrongness of actions are accounted for by general utility, whereas justice as the most vital utility counteracts all other utility when conflict arises. Hence, utility is the unique criterion for rightness and wrongness without the possibility of any unsolvable contradiction between utility and justice.

To clarify: in morality, where we make a "judgment" about the rightness/ wrongness of a conduct, what is needed is a "satisfactory justification" for that judgment. A satisfactory justification consists of two complementary components: "the requisite" and "the absence of nullifier." The requisite either is a "pre-act ground" or a "post-act ground," as I call them. The former points to something existing before the action and ranges from human nature and society, as Whewell suggests, through autonomy of man as Kant proposes, to God's commands, as Crusius affirms. On the other hand, a post-act ground points to something expected to result from the action, which ranges from the narrowest, namely "this-worldly hedonistic happiness," as Benthamite utilitarianism suggests, through Mill's middle view of "this-worldly multilevel happiness," to the religious view of "this-worldly and otherworldly happiness." No moral rule can rationally be justified without reference to one of these requisites to judge something as right or wrong.

Yet, the effectiveness of a requisite rests on the absence of any nullifier. Hence, since justice in Mill's understanding can only play a veto role in human conduct, no morality can be built on a mere conception of justice. Justice can enter in the realm of morality as a complementary component to the requisite. Justice tells us what not to do, and prohibits the violation of others' rights. After respecting others' rights in our social interactions, when it comes to choosing among different alternatives, none of which will do harm to others' rights, justice is silent. What we can justifiably choose to do while different alternatives are available is entrusted to a requisite, be it a pre-act or a post-act ground. Assume that a man intends to have intercourse with a woman. In the case where that woman does not consent to the man's desire, the principle of justice prohibits this intercourse as a violation of that woman's right. Yet, in other cases the principle of justice is silent. What may permit or prohibit the intercourse in cases where the woman consents to the intercourse is a requisite, such as the Benthamite post-act ground of hedonism that permits the intercourse absolutely on the basis that it produces pleasure.

Nevertheless, the binding force of the very principle of justice derives from the ultimate standard, namely the utility principle, that is, neither is the validity of justice intrinsic nor does it derive from any other source except the very general utility. Answering the question of what the binding force of justice is, Mill resorts to "general utility." To the question of what type of utility justice produces, Mill's answer is this: "The interest involved is that of security, to every one's feelings the most vital of all interests. Nearly all other earth[l]y benefits are needed by one person, not needed by another; . . . but security no human being can possibly do without; on it we depend . . . for the whole value of all and every good."[23] Overall, justice as a veto principle, which overrides all other human values in social life, derives its force as a rule from the ultimate standard of all moral rules, that is, general utility.

What follows from the above clarification, first, is that the concept of justice as the highest value with its veto function nullifies the function of all requisites when they are contradictory. Mill points to this position of justice in morality when he says: "Justice is a name for certain moral requirements, which, regarded collectively, stand higher in the scale of social utility, and are therefore of more paramount obligation, than any others."[24]

Second, when two interpretations of justice are applicable in a given case, the umpire principle, which prefers one of them to the other, is the utility principle. Pointing to this function of the utility principle, Mill says: "Not only have different nations and individuals different notions of justice, but in the mind of one and the same individual, justice is not some one rule, principle, or maxim, but many, which do not always coincide in their dictates, and . . . any choice between them, on grounds of justice, must be perfectly arbitrary. Social utility alone can decide the preference."[25]

Third, in all self-regarding conducts where there is no ground for justice to enter, the only element of the satisfactory justification is a requisite. Mill refers to the exclusive requiring function of utility when he suggests that "the creed which accepts as the foundation of morals, Utility, or the Greatest Happiness Principle, holds that actions are right in proportion as they tend to promote happiness, wrong as they tend to produce the reverse of happiness." He is explicit that "pleasure, and freedom from pain, are the only things desirable as ends; and that all desirable things . . . are desirable either for the pleasure inherent in themselves, or as means to the promotion of pleasure and the prevention of pain."[26] The following part of this chapter will expand the above interpretation of Mill's moral theory.

The Principle of the General Greatest Happiness

The briefest and the most thorough passage in which Mill expresses his theory of utilitarianism is the following: "According to the Greatest Happiness Principle, . . . the ultimate end, with reference to and for the sake of which all other things are desirable (whether we are considering our own good or that of other people) is an existence exempt as far as possible from pain, and as rich as possible in enjoyments, both in point of quantity and quality; the test of quality, and the rule for measuring it against quantity, being the preference felt by those who in their opportunities of experience, to which must be added their habits of self-consciousness and self-observation, are best furnished with the means of comparison. This, being according to the utilitarian opinion, the end of human action, is necessarily also the standard of morality; which may accordingly be defined, the rules and precepts for human conduct, by the observance of which an existence such as has been described might be, to the greatest extent possible, secured to all mankind; and not to them only, but, so far as the nature of things admits, to the whole sentient creation."[27]

In the above passage, Mill explains his psychological theory as a premise to arrive at his moral theory, namely the Greatest Happiness Principle. His whole argument in support of the utility principle consists of the following premises:

1. The only "desired" end of human beings, which ultimately motivates all human conduct, is attainment of a life with the most possible

amount and the best kinds of happiness and the prevention of the most likely and the worst kinds of pains. Expanding the notion of happiness to incorporate mental happiness, too, Mill suggests that as there are different degrees of happiness there are various qualities in different kinds of happiness. This is a descriptive statement about human psychology that explains why human beings do what they do.

2. The only "desirable" end is to secure a life with the most possible amount and the best kind of happiness and prevention from the most possible and the worst kind of pain, not only for all human beings, but also for all sentient creation. As there are differences in the quality of happiness, the more valuable kind of happiness should take precedence over the inferior kinds of happiness. The criterion for measuring the quality of happiness and pain is the view of the "experienced wise" group. What the experienced wise group prefers is the happiness human beings really desire and what they ought to desire. This principle is an evaluative judgment about the ultimate moral standard that shows why we should take a specific action.

The Happy Life as the Only Desired End

Mill's first premise indicates that happiness is the only desired end. "The utilitarian doctrine," argues Mill, "is, that happiness is desirable, and the only thing desirable, as an end; all other things being only desirable as means to that end." The second assumption expands the subject of happiness to a "happy life" as the ultimate goal of every individual. Therefore, it is not Mill's argument that each individual in each action pursues his own momentary happiness. Nor does he prescribe this as the ultimate moral standard. Thus, the subject of happiness is the whole life, rather than every single action. Furthermore, a happy life is not that which is full of happy moments, free from all pains. What "the philosophers who have taught that happiness is the end of life" have in mind is "not a life of rapture; but moments of such, in an existence made up of few and transitory pains, many and various pleasures, with a decided predominance of the active over the passive." It is this type of life that is "worthy of the name of happiness."[28]

A further assumption Mill invokes is that every individual seeks his own happy life. Combining the previous premises with a further assumption that "each person's happiness is a good to that person," we arrive at the conclusion that every individual seeks a happy life for himself as the ultimate end in his life. What is more, this common inclination toward one's own happy life is a requirement of human nature. Mill's explicit conviction in this regard is that "human nature is so constituted as to desire nothing which is not either a part of happiness or means of happiness."[29]

As for the meaning of "happiness," expanding the Benthamite notion of pleasure, Mill suggests that happiness has different "qualities" just as there are different degrees in the quantity of every kind of happiness. Hence, what motivates human beings is a combination of the quality as well as the quantity of happiness that different types of conduct might produce. "Human beings have faculties more elevated than the animal appetites," says Mill. Regarding the importance of the quality of happiness, Mill argues that "utilitarian writers in general have placed the superiority of mental over bodily pleasures chiefly in the greater permanency, safety, uncostliness, etc., of the former." This innovation about the degrees of worth of different kinds of pleasure, according to Mill, "is quite compatible with the principle of utility."[30] Mill, therefore, has revised Bentham's hedonistic utilitarianism in two related aspects. While to Bentham good is restricted to the sensation of pleasure or happiness, Mill expands the notion of the good by residing it in "complex mental experiences" rather than a mere sensation of pleasure. Furthermore, he appraises the good on the basis of the quality of pleasures in addition to their quantity.[31]

Mill rejects the interpretation that the quality of a pleasurable experience means its overall value in an agent's ranking of pleasures. Rather, he affirms that the overall value of an action that places it in a specific degree when ranked by an agent should be measured on the basis of the following features. While the quantity of a pleasure in the sense of its intensity and duration is one dimension of measurement, the complementary dimension is the quality of that pleasure.[32] Rosen argues that Mill can be regarded as a leading modern Epicurean for his distinction between quantity and quality of pleasures. By emphasizing the worth of mental pleasures, an Epicurean doctrine suggests that no wise man may be unhappy while all foolish persons are destined to unhappiness. This is because a wise person fears neither death nor God owing to the fact that he knows he is destined to death. Furthermore, a wise person enjoys remembering the past pleasures, which make him happy and grateful in the present. Also, the wise person obtains happiness by comparing his life with that of a foolish person. Finally, the wise person, by resorting to reason, can overcome the obstacles created by fortune in his path.[33]

On the whole, Mill's complex notion of happiness incorporates, first, those inferior pleasures man shares with animals. Second, there are such superior pleasures that are particular to man as "'the love of liberty," "personal independence," and "a sense of dignity." It is the superiority of human pleasures that leads to the idea that "it is better to be [a] human being dissatisfied than a pig satisfied; better to be Socrates dissatisfied than a fool satisfied." Third, Mill introduces a kind of "pleasurable means" that receives its pleasurability from its instrumentality to any kind of the pleasurable end. What is significant about pleasurable means is that in the course of time they become a secondary type of end desired even when being considered per se. To clarify: Mill resorts to the desirability of money originally as the means to obtaining what pleases us that finally becomes pleasant per se so strongly that one may love money even more than the happiness to which money was considered originally as an instrument. To Mill, the desirability of virtues per se derives from this consideration. Hence, "utilitarian moralists," argues Mill, "not only place virtue at the very head of the things which are good as means to the ultimate end, but they also recognise as a psychological fact the possibility of its being, to the individual, a good in itself, without looking to any end beyond it; . . . They are desired and desirable in and for themselves; besides being means, they are a part of the end."[34]

Therefore, contrary to psychological hedonism, Mill does not maintain that all our actions are motivated by anticipation of pleasure and pain.[35] As Mill explains, in many cases our actions are motivated by our firm character or habits. He says: "It is at least certain that we gradually, through the influence of association, come to desire the means without thinking of the end: the action itself becomes an object of desire, and is performed without reference to any motive beyond itself. . . . As we proceed in the formation of habits, and become accustomed to will a particular act or a particular course of conduct because it is pleasurable, we at least continue to will it without any reference to its being pleasurable. . . . It is only when our purposes have become independent of the feelings of pain or pleasure from which they originally took their rise, that we are said to have a confirmed character." Assured that the "original source" of all actions is intrinsic happiness, Mill's utilitarianism definitely approves the possibility of other desirable means and secondary ends deriving from intrinsic happiness.[36] What proof does Mill provide to support this assumption about the end of human actions?

As was discussed in the previous chapter, the only method of investigation about facts that Mill approves is the scientific method of inductive experimentalism. The very desirability of pleasure can be discovered by experiment about the preference of mankind through collecting evidence about every individual's desires.[37] Since this is a factual statement about human conduct in the real world, the only way to prove it like all similar questions, is to resort to evidence. "It can only be determined by practised self-consciousness and self-observation, assisted by observation of others." What we find by self-examination is that we desire something that pleases us, as Mill argues. For "desiring a thing and finding it pleasant . . . are phenomena entirely inseparable, or . . . two different modes of naming the same psychological fact . . . and that to desire anything, except in proportion as the idea of it is pleasant, is a physical and metaphysical impossibility. So obvious does this appear to me," Mill continues, "that I expect it will hardly be disputed."[38] By equating desirable with pleasant in connotation, Mill's experimental method of investigation leads to an obvious proposition: we all find ourselves as well as others desiring everything that pleases us and makes us feel happy. Therefore, the proposition "Every pleasure is desirable to us"—while the term desirable here means merely "desired" or "wanted," rather than meaning "worthy of being desired"—is a mere observation of two sides of one fact about human conduct obviously known to every individual.

As for the criterion of measurement of the quality of happiness, Mill's suggestion is to entrust this measurement to a wise person who has experienced all types of pleasures.[39] The procedure of measuring the overall value of a pleasurable experience to Mill starts from the measurement of the intensity and duration of a given pleasurable experience and ends in the measurement of its quality in the sense of receiving higher preference by a competent agent who has experienced all kinds of pleasures. Implicit in the notion of an experienced wise person is the idea of a self-developed moral agent whose preference is the criterion for evaluation of the quality of pleasurable experiences.[40] Mill's scientific method of inductive experimentalism should also be used to approve of the ranking of pleasures and pains. Hence, the ranking of different kinds of pleasures should be entrusted to wise people who have experienced all possible pleasures. To wise people, human dignity, pride, love of liberty, and personal independence are preferable to other types of pleasures. The induction would lead us to the fact that all wise persons who have experienced different kinds of pleasures would rank them in a scale of value.[41] To the objection that some people choose lower pleasures while they have access to higher kinds, Mill's answer suggests that those individuals have lost the desire for the higher due to the education they have received from their society.[42]

It is worth noticing that the broad scope of the meaning of happiness and its types in Mill's moral theory would prevent the objection that apart from happiness, there are unquestionably some individuals, such as "the hero or the martyr," who sacrifice themselves for some valuable purposes other than happiness, which is meaningless in their case. For Mill considers human virtues as a means to general happiness, or as a part of an individual's happiness. "The utilitarian morality," argues Mill, "does recognise in human beings the power of sacrificing their own greatest good for the good of others. It only refuses to admit that the sacrifice is itself a good. A sacrifice which does not increase or tend to increase, the sum total of happiness, it considers as wasted."[43] To capture Mill's precise view about sacrifice two qualifications are worth attention. First, the sacrifice of an *individual's life* is only to be approved if it serves the general happiness and is made voluntarily. Second, the sacrifice of an *individual's happiness,* less than his life, is justifiable if it serves the total sum of happiness.

The Desirability of the Happy Life
The above discussion of Mill's psychology about human desire constitutes one premise of his Greatest Happiness Principle. It is worth noticing that Mill is not an act-utilitarian, as are Sidgwick, Moore, Rashdall, Laird, and Smart. Act-utilitarians affirm that "an action is morally right if and only if it will—or probably will—do as much good in the total circumstances as any other act the agent could perform instead."[44] Appreciating Urmson's new interpretation of Mill's theory as a type of rule-utilitarianism, Mabbott "doubt[s] whether Mill himself realised the fundamental differences between the two views."[45]

Comparing utilitarianism with consequentialism, Frey dismisses the necessary connection between consequentialism and all accounts of utilitarianism. He argues that for egoistic consequentialists the only criterion of the rightness and wrongness of an act is its capability to produce a given person's interests. By contrast, rule-utilitarianism does not evaluate rightness and wrongness of an act on the basis of its consequences.[46] As Urmson convincingly explains Mill's rule-utilitarianism, the criterion of rightness of an action is its agreement with some moral rule. Hence, an action that disagrees with a relevant moral rule is wrong. The role of utility concerns the evaluation of moral rules: a correct moral rule is one that promotes the general welfare. Furthermore, it is the task of moral rules to evaluate actions as right and wrong. Therefore, when no moral rule is applicable, another way of assessment of an action should be invoked. Terminologically speaking, Urmson uses moral rule in the sense Mill uses "moral law" and "secondary principle," such as "Keep promises," "Do not murder," and "Tell no lies."[47] Also Mill speaks of them as "ethical standards," "codes of ethics," and the "rules of morality."[48]

This interpretation, first, can be supported by the way in which I reconcile Mill's utility principle with his justice principle. For it is only by interpreting Mill as a rule-utilitarian that his principle of utility can be reconciled with his veto principle of justice. The general objection to unconstrained utilitarianism concerns its negligence of the vital interests of persons. This objection can be answered by the idea of rule-utilitarianism developed in the 1960s and 1970s, whereas the other solution is the rights-based theory of moral philosophy.[49] Furthermore, Mill's employment of the term "intermediate generalisations" as well as "corollaries from the principle of utility" in pointing to moral rules can be taken as evidence for proposing that he is a rule-utilitarian rather than an act-utilitarian.[50] Because, if he were an act-utilitarian there would be no need for any other rule except that an action produces utility without the mediation of any other rule.[51] One striking passage through which Mill states his view of rule-utilitarianism,[52] is: "In the case of abstinences indeed—of things which people forbear to do from moral considerations, though the consequences in the particular case might be beneficial—it would be unworthy of an intelligent agent not to be consciously aware that *the action is of a kind which, if practised generally, would be generally injurious, and that this is the ground of the obligation to abstain from it.*"[53]

Therefore, Mill's rule-utilitarianism suggests that our interactions with each other are directed by some moral rules the ultimate source of which is happiness in its various types. In other words, morality requires us to follow some rules the binding force of which is that general compliance with them will promote the general happiness. What consideration can Mill provide to compel us to accept this ultimate moral rule that demands us to pursue the general happiness?

Mill's argument is what he mentions in chapter 4 of *Utilitarianism* under the title "Of what sort of Proof the Principle of Utility is Susceptible." "The only proof," says Mill, "capable of being given that an object is visible, is that people actually see it. The only proof that a sound is audible, is that people hear it. . . . the sole evidence it is possible to produce that anything is desirable, is that people do actually desire it. . . . No reason can be given why the general happiness is desirable, except that each person, so far as he believes it to be attainable, desires his own happiness. This, however, being a fact, we have not only all the proof which the case admits of, but all which it is possible to require, that happiness is a good: that each person's happiness is a good to that person, and the general happiness, therefore, a good to the aggregate of all persons."[54]

The problem with the quoted passage is that while it is true by definition that "visible" means "capable of being seen," "desirable" has a different meaning from "capable of being desired"; it means "worthy of being desired," as its location in morality obviously requires.[55] For in morality we are concerned with prescribing actions rather than describing them. Hence, Mill needs to bridge desirable in the sense of desired and desirable in the sense of worthy of being desired.

One persuasive argument aimed at filling this gap is provided by Mandelbaum. He contends that Mill's argument should be understood as being based upon the following complementary premises. As an obvious *necessary* condition of the desirability of an action, though not as a sufficient condition, a given action should be capable of being desired. With regard to human goals, it necessarily follows that the desirability of a goal is dependent upon the capability of human beings of desiring that goal. A further assumption Mill explicitly affirms indicates that happiness is the *only* goal that human beings are capable of desiring. Therefore, since there is no other end we can desire except happiness, the necessary condition turns out to be the sufficient condition of desirability.[56]

In this way, *we bridge the desirability of a happy life for every individual and its moral goodness for every individual*. However, this is not what utilitarianism proposes. Mill is explicit that "good" to utilitarians is general good. The "happiness which forms the utilitarian standard of what is right in conduct," suggests Mill, "is not the agent's own happiness, but that of all concerned."[57] Yet, Mill should fill another gap between the individual happiness and the general happiness with recourse to the ultimate moral value, that is, maximization of happiness.

One proposition to fill this gap is Britton's elitist interpretation of Mill's utilitarianism. He suggests that since wise persons desire the general happiness for its own sake and their preference is the criterion of good, general happiness is good.[58] "What is there to decide," Mill asks, "whether a particular pleasure is worth purchasing at the cost of a particular pain, except the feelings and judgment of the experienced?"[59] This is a successful Millian attempt to fill the gap between the desirability of individual happiness and the desirability of the general happiness.

Another connection is made through resorting to one other moral value, impartiality. "As between his own happiness and that of others," argues Mill, "utilitarianism requires him to be as strictly impartial as a disinterested and benevolent spectator. In the golden rule of Jesus of Nazareth, we read the complete spirit of the ethics of utility. To do as you would be done by, and to love your neighbour as yourself, constitute the ideal perfection of utilitarian morality."[60] Why should we appreciate impartiality, if self-interestedness benefits us more?

To arrive at an appreciation of the general good through impartiality, Ryan resorts to the Hobbesian mode of argument in Mill's utilitarianism as the central point in Mill's system of morality.[61] In this interpretation, suggests Ryan, we resort to Mill's proposition that men are self-interested and happiness is the only desirable end each pursues. Furthermore, the "social state," proposes Mill, "is at once so natural, so necessary and so habitual to man, that, except in some unusual circumstances, or by an effort of voluntary abstraction, he never conceives of himself otherwise than as a member of a body." Hence, men are naturally inclined to pursue their individual happiness in a society of self-interested persons. What each of these self-interested members of society should admit is that all are equal. "Society between human beings, except in the relation of master and slave," Mill goes on to suggest, "is manifestly impossible, except on the footing that the interests of all are to be consulted." Not only should the interests of all members of society be should be taken into account in the determination of collective purposes, but also the interests of each one should be *counted equally.* "Society between equals," affirms Mill, "can only exist on the understanding that the interests of all are to be regarded equally."[62] In this way, Ryan seems to be constructing Mill's concept of the general happiness on the desirability of individual happiness through the mediation of a presupposition of the "equality" of all members of society that requires impartiality in the pursuit of happiness.[63]

However, if Mill intends to suggest that the existence of human society on the assumption of the inequality of its members is *logically* inconceivable and practically impossible, this suggestion contradicts the experimental evidence we possess about the history of human society. If he is proposing that equality is *morally* desirable independently of utility, his conviction about the monopoly of happiness as the ultimate end will be questioned.

As for the feasibility of the pursuit of the general happiness when it conflicts with individual happiness, Mill proposes two solutions. First, laws and social institutions should be arranged so as to harmonize the two as much as possible. Second, society through education should convince each member firmly to see his individual happiness in the promotion of the general good.[64] Therefore, an impartial government that is *democratically* organized should aim to increase the general good, rather than sectarian interests.

However, the secularity of Mill's utilitarian moral theory can be noticed both in his conceptualization and argument.[65] As for his conceptualization, he confines the notion of happiness in the domain of this-worldly pleasures, rather than incorporating otherworldly happiness. When he argues that all human conduct is motivated ultimately by the desire for a happy life he means nothing except life in the earthly world, whereas religious people act for a happy eternal life as they act for a happy present life. Shiite Islam disagrees with Mill's restricted conceptualization of life. Rather, it expands the concept of life by proposing two realms for life: one before death and the other after death, which is eternal. While it is true that the ultimate end for human conduct is happiness,[66] life is not restricted to a this-worldly temporary life. Rather, it consists of the temporary life before death and an eternal life after death.[67]

As for the secularity of Mill's argument, when he intends to collect evidence about what man really desires, which is the first premise of his argument, he concludes that the only thing human beings desire is happiness in this temporary life. Likewise, when Mill intends to rank different pleasurable experiences in quantity and quality, he refers to the wise, experienced man who is definitely secular. As for the second premise of Mill's argument, there are other secular assumptions in his theory. The first bridge between what is desired and what is worthy of being desired is built on a secular assumption. He suggests that the *only* thing man desires is happiness, where happiness means an earthly happy life. Hence, Mill articulates the second premise of his Greatest Happiness Principle in ignorance of the obvious desires of religious people who pursue, also, an otherworldly happy life. To Mill, the notion of desirability of individual happiness is secular and points to the pleasures of the earthly world. The second bridge he builds between the desirability of an individual happy life and the general happiness is made secularly. The first interpretation that fills the gap between individual happiness and the general happiness by resorting to the experienced wise persons, selects only secular men. Since they have not experienced religious life, the result of their contemplation approves only the desirability of general happiness in its earthly sense.

In contrast to the above views, the Qur'an declares: "The life of the present world is only amusement and pastime and the real life is in The Last Home if the people could understand it."[68] Hence, according to Shiite Islam, the worth of the eternal life is superior to the present life, when happiness of the temporary life clashes with happiness of the eternal life. Describing Paradise, the Qur'an states: "Now enter the Paradise you and your wives happily. They will be served food and drink in golden plates and cups, and there will be all that man desires and enjoys looking at; and you will stay there forever."[69]

More explicitly, Mill declares that God has no right to set moral rules for human beings, a fact that contradicts a basic Shiite Islamic principle. He says: "That the received code of ethics is by no means of divine right . . . I admit, or rather, earnestly maintain." Even if God intends to reveal something about morality, he should follow Mill's idea of utilitarianism in its earthly sense: "[w]hatever God has thought fit to reveal on the subject of morals, must fulfil the requirements of utility in a supreme degree."[70]

Mill's expectation of God runs counter to the teachings of Shiite Islam. As for determining or discovering the principles of morality, the Qur'an indicates that knowledge of good and evil is incorporated in human nature and is discoverable by practical reason.[71] Yet, religion and Godly revelation act as a complementary source for morality. This completion is realized in expansion of the natural knowledge of good and evil, as well as completing the motive to human progress, along with activating the natural endowments by reminding humankind of his common constitution facilitated with the knowledge of good and evil.[72] Hence, God completes human knowledge of good and evil by sending his revelation.

As for the Shiite Islamic view about the appropriate moral system, first, the Qur'an locates justice at the top of human values, and hence asks Muslims to stand for justice even toward their enemies, because justice is required by righteousness.[73] Moreover, the Qur'an explicitly contrasts between human utility in the present life and justice and asks Muslims to follow the requirements of justice even at the cost of losing their temporary utility.[74] In fact, the eternal happy life for human beings is connected with justice in the temporary life. In this way, the value of justice and the general concept of utility are unified.

More directly and in opposition to supernatural religions, Mill introduces himself as an atheist who is detached from conventional religion and the church, as his contemporaries also acknowledge.[75] Mill supports, instead, Comte's notion of Religion of Humanity, which serves secular purposes without God.[76] He suggests that his utilitarian morality deserves the name of the Religion of Humanity. Initially, in his essay "Nature," Mill casts doubt on the consistency between believing in God as all benevolent and omnipotent and the cruelty of the universe he is believed to have created. Furthermore, in "Theism," he dismisses epistemologically the possibility of proving the truth or the falsity of religion by evidence.[77] Moreover, he argues that man's conviction in supernatural religions and gods in the past was based on shortage of his knowledge about the world, along with the hope to achieve those goods "he has failed to find on earth." Yet, he acknowledges the usefulness of any religion for understanding right and wrong behavior, as well as motivating man toward right actions.[78]

The above-mentioned utility of religion added to the indefensibility of supernatural religious doctrines, along with the possibility of achieving the benefits of religion more thoroughly by the Religion of Humanity leads Mill to support the latter as necessary and sufficient.[79] The value of the Religion of Humanity, to Mill, lies in its role in individual satisfaction and elevated feelings, and its superiority over all supernatural religions for two reasons. First, the Religion of Humanity is disinterested because its followers do not expect to be rewarded in the Hereafter for their compliance with its moral rules. Second, it is free from some intellectual inconsistencies such as belief in a perfect God as the creator of the imperfect world. In addition, the Religion of Humanity has a social value in that it educates individuals to value the happiness of others as much as they value their own happiness. As the corollary of the feeling of unity with others, the achievement of the greatest happiness of the greatest number of society will become more likely.[80]

Mill admits only one privilege for supernatural religions over his Religion of Humanity. He says: "One advantage, such as it is, the supernatural religion must always possess over the Religion of Humanity; the prospect they hold out to the individual of a life after death. . . . I cannot but think that as the condition of mankind becomes improved, as they grow happiness in their lives, and more capable of deriving happiness from unselfish sources, they will care less for this flattering expectations." He continues that "if the Religion of Humanity were as sedulously cultivated as the supernatural religions are . . . all who had received the customary amount of moral cultivation would up to the hour of death live ideally in the life of those who are to follow them. . . . Nor can I perceive that the sceptic loses by his scepticism any real and valuable consolation except one; the hope of reunion with those dear to him who have ended their earth[l]y life before him. That loss, indeed, is neither to be denied nor extenuated."[81]

All the above-mentioned statements by Mill confirm the theoretical incompatibility between his utilitarian morality and Shiite Islamic thought.

The Veto Principle of Justice

Apart from Mill, all other utilitarians neglect the consideration of the concept of justice and its problems in their idea of the utility principle. What accounts for this negligence is their major obsession with such values as pleasure and pain, happiness, and welfare. Mill's discussion of the principle of justice and its relation with the utility principle, argues Lyons, is so "complex" and "often confusing" that it gives rise to the general objection that "he is inconsistent or unreasonable."[82] Mill's discussion of the principle of justice and the language he uses here have recently given rise to an interpretation of Mill's moral theory that ascribes to him a type of an "indirect utilitarianism," as Lyons and Gray have proposed.[83] According to Lyons, "'Mill's moral theory is . . . a theoretical alternative to both act *and* rule utilitarianism" in the sense that the principle of utility does not determine directly what is right or wrong. For Mill, the criterion for right and wrong, as Lyons asserts, is the "punishability" of an action deserved by the breach of a right that an individual person can claim as his moral right.[84] Similarly, Gray ascribes to Mill the idea of indirect utilitarianism for two reasons. First, Mill connects between the wrongness of an action and its punishability. Second, the direct appeal to utility for settlement of moral questions is self-defeating due to human fallibility.[85]

As opposed to the aforementioned interpretation of Mill's principle of justice, he is explicit that the criteria for the wrongness and rightness of actions are pleasure and pain.[86] In addition, through interpreting Mill as an advocate of a type of rule-utilitarianism, his principle of utility can be successfully reconciled with his principle of justice. What is more, as will be shown in the next chapter, Mill directly resorts to the principle of utility to justify his liberty principle. What this chapter would prefer to ascribe to Mill is a type of rule-utilitarianism as implied above and developed below.

What Is Justice?

Mill starts his principle of justice with the primitive proposition that justice means "conformity to law" and injustice means the breach of law. Yet, since human laws might be made wrongly, the respect of those laws that "ought" to be made is justice, and the breach of those laws is injustice. Therefore, "the sentiment of injustice came to be attached," infers Mill, "not to all violations of law, but only to violations of such laws as *ought* to exist."[87] By this second assumption, Mill promotes his view of justice in comparison with a mere correspondence of an action to the positive law.[88]

As to the criterion for just law, Mill's answer suggests that any law, the breach of which justifies the punishment of those who have broken it, is a law that ought to be. In this way, Mill arrives at the point that punishment for injustice is both justifiable and pleasant to us. The sense of justice, thus, derives from the general pleasure we instinctually and intellectually deem in punishing persons who have done harm to society.[89]

Up to this point, Mill has suggested that justice is the respect of those laws the breach of which justifies punishment of those who break them. A further assumption Mill affirms here concerns the criterion for the justifiability of punishment: "There is involved . . . the conception of some definite person who suffers by the infringement; whose rights . . . are violated by it." Hence, what justifies punishment lies in the existence of a violated right for an individual. Connecting the concept of right with legitimate "claim" on others, Mill argues that a "moral right" is something "which it is not only right to do, and wrong not to do, but which some individual person can claim from us." Distinguishing between "duties of perfect obligation" and "duties of imperfect obligation," Mill connects the existence of a right with a perfect obligation for others to respect that right. He contends that "duties of perfect obligation are those duties in virtue of which a correlative *right* resides in some person or persons; duties of imperfect obligation are those moral obligations which do not give birth to any right . . . as in the case of charity or beneficence, which we are indeed bound to practise, but not towards any definite person, nor at any prescribed time."[90]

Through the above discussions, Mill arrives at his definition of justice: justice concerns those obligations of morality that deal with rights, as opposed to other moral obligations. Thus, "justice," infers Mill, "appears generally to involve the idea of personal right—a claim on the part of one or more individuals."[91] This emphasis on individual persons is the most significant feature of Mill's conception of justice and a moral right.[92] Still, the question arises as to what are those rights the respect of which is the obligation of others? The right to security and the right to freedom are the most basic rights to Mill.[93] He contends that security from harm by others, and freedom from intervention by others in one's private life "are more vital to human well-being than any other maxims . . . the punishment of those who violate them . . . [are] the dictates of justice."[94] These two basic rights, as they appear, derive from the value of well-being, rather than being intrinsic to or based on any contract. Rights, to Mill, are utility based.[95]

Overall, Mill's notion of justice indicates two *negative* demands. First, justice requires us not to infringe others' rights in the sense of noninterference in others' life and actions, along with not doing them harm. Second, justice is connected with impartiality and formal equality in the sense of equal treatment of every individual with regard to his rights.[96] As for the subject of justice, it is other-regarding actions where the two sides of right and obligation are specifically determinate. Hence, all self-regarding actions, as well as those social obligations that are not to benefit some determinate individuals, along with the domain of permissible actions, become the subject of other moral rules.

How Is Justice Reconcilable with the General Utility?

For Mill, justice and utility, far from being contradictory, are closely connected so that the well-being of individuals account for a collection of rights.[97] The way Mill draws the principle of justice on the Greatest Happiness Principle will prevent any unsolvable contradiction between the two principles. First, Mill divides the ultimate standard of morality into two distinctive kinds: the first interest, which is the highest, the most vital, and the only general one absolutely all human beings benefit from, is "security." The ground for the supremacy of security, one might suggest, lies in the fact that a "happy life" should be in the first place "a life." Hence, all threats and harm to life itself are the worst pain. What can confirm this interpretation is Mill's firm conviction that "to save a life, it may not only be allowable, but a duty, to steal, or take by force, the necessary food or medicine."[98]

The task of preservation of life is so absolutely crucial that in this case, not only should any account of justice give way to the preservation of life but the very meaning of justice here is also changed in support of saving life.

Second, all other interests should be placed at a level lower to security. Thus, in all cases of conflict between security and all other kinds of pleasures, the latter should give way to security, no matter how great the other interests, for the value of security is so intense in quality that no other interest can resist its demands. The most immediate demand of security is that of the rule of law. Predictability, which can be guaranteed by the rule of general laws, is the most vital requirement of security. "Rules are necessary," says Mill, "because mankind would have no security for any of the things which they value, for anything which gives them pleasure and shields them from pain, unless they could rely on one another for doing, and in particular for abstaining from, certain acts."[99] While different kinds of general pleasures require the establishment of several different values, security singularly restricts the demands of those general pleasures in two ways. First, those values should be established in the form of general laws. Second, the law directly demanding security, justice, is superior to all other interests when conflict arises.[100] In brief, Mill's moral theory attaches the greatest importance to this-worldly happy life and restricts utility seeking by the requirements of justice and respecting others' rights.[101]

Conclusion

This chapter examined the Theoretical Incompatibility Proposition regarding Mill's liberalism and Shiite Islam by looking at Mill's utilitarian moral theory. The depth of the secularity of Mill's utilitarian moral theory, which confirms this incompatibility, can be noticed chiefly in the following points.

(1/a) Mill explicitly declares that God has no right to set moral rules for human beings. He says: "That the received code of ethics is by no means of divine right . . . I admit, or rather, earnestly maintain."

(1/b) By contrast, according to Shiite Islam, although the knowledge of good and evil is incorporated in human nature and is discoverable by practical reason, religion and Godly revelation act as a complementary source for morality.

(2/a) Mill maintains that even if God intends to reveal something about morality, he should follow Mill's idea of utilitarianism in its earthly sense: "Whatever God has thought fit to reveal on the subject of morals, must fulfil the requirements of utility in a supreme degree."

(2/b) By contrast, the Qur'an explicitly contrasts human utility in the present life and justice, and asks Muslims to follow the requirements of justice even at the cost of losing their temporary utility. In fact, eternal happy life for human beings is connected with justice in the temporary life.

(3/a) Mill confines the notion of happiness in the domain of earthly life. When he argues that all human conduct is motivated ultimately by the desire for a happy life, when he collects evidence about what man really desires, when he ranks different pleasurable experiences in quantity and quality as the wise, experienced man does, and when he bridges individual happiness and the general happiness, he means only happiness of earthly life.

(3/b) Shiite Islam agrees with Mill that the ultimate end for human conduct is happiness. Yet, it expands the meaning of life, by proposing two realms for life: one before death and the other after death, which is eternal. According to Shiite Islam, the worth of the present, temporary life is inferior to that of the eternal life where there will be all that man desires.

(4/a) Mill introduces his substitute for supernatural religions as the Religion of Humanity, which serves secular purposes without God. The general utility of religion added to the indefensibility of supernatural religious doctrines, along with the possibility of achieving the benefits of religion more thoroughly through the Religion of Humanity leads Mill to support the latter as necessary and sufficient.

(4/b) By contrast, Shiite Islam introduces divine religion as a necessary part of the good life on earth by which man can establish a plausible temporary life and move toward an eternal happy life.

CHAPTER 3

Mill's Liberty Principle

This chapter examines the theoretical incompatibility between Mill's liberalism and Shiite Islamic thought by looking at Mill's principle of liberty. First, his view about free will as the prerequisite for any meaningful discussion of civil liberty will be analyzed. Furthermore, the discussion will examine his distinctive conception of civil liberty, which has successfully combined positive and negative conceptions of liberty. In addition, Mill's particular principle of liberty together with a short list of basic liberties will be discussed. Moreover, his arguments for the liberty principle, which invoke various ideas, such as the utility argument, the fallibility argument, and the individuality argument, will be critically explored.

As will be shown in this chapter, Mill has successfully tackled a problematic philosophical issue by reconciling necessaritarianism, based upon the law of universal causation, and free will in human conduct by distinguishing between fatalism and necessaritarianism. Mill maintains that the resistibility of our motives dismisses the idea of causality of our motives in relation to our actions, that is, fatalism. The conception of moral freedom is a prerequisite for any meaningful discussion of civil liberty. For if man from an ontological perspective lacks the power to make decisions, the discussion of the right to make decisions from a moral perspective is irrelevant.

Furthermore, it will be argued that Mill's conception of civil liberty combines two conceptions of liberty, that is, positive liberty and negative liberty. What protects Mill's idea of positive liberty from the danger of authoritarian consequences is his idea of spontaneity and individuality. Hence, in addition to affirming negative liberty, which protects individuals against suppression by any paternalistic consideration, he enriches his idea of negative liberty with a conception of positive liberty, which is not amenable to any paternalistic consideration. Consequently, one can find in Mill a full-blooded liberalism.

Not only do these two conceptions of liberty agree with his utilitarian morality, but Mill's liberty principle is also the logical consequence of the application of utilitarianism to politics. Although Mill's argument for the liberty principle invokes various ideas, he successfully reconciles his utility principle, his veto principle of justice, and his liberty principle. When the Greatest Happiness Principle is applied to the domain of politics, the result will be a liberal state tasked with guaranteeing absolute freedom of thought, conscience, and expression, as well as freedom of action for individuals in the private sphere. A happy life for all individuals as the ultimate and unique standard of morality requires the establishment of a liberal state, the supreme goal of which is to guarantee liberty for each individual. The only restriction on individual freedom justifiable in utilitarian views is prevention of harm to others. What accounts for this restriction, while liberty is the most crucial component of a happy life, lies in justice, which sets limits on different utilities to guarantee the supreme interest of all individuals—security. Therefore, in contrast to other nonliberal theories of utilitarianism, Mill's just-utilitarianism is the very foundation of liberalism.

However, Mill's liberty principle is deeply secular and is incapable of fully accommodating the beliefs and feelings of those religious citizens who are committed to supernatural religions. To them, the major theoretical failure of Mill's liberty principle concerns his narrow conceptualizations of human progress and harm. Shiite Islam disagrees with Mill's humanist picture of man and conceives of man as being dependent on his source of existence and progress, that is, on God. The path toward progress is one that is determined by human nature so conceived. In addition, Mill's conceptualization of harm rests upon pure secular considerations with less attention to religious values and concerns. One such case is blasphemy, which harms religious individuals and is prohibited in Islam.

The Conception of Moral Freedom

Logically, theoretical philosophy should firstly deliver an unambiguous portrayal that man possesses the capability to act free from transcendental forces, surrounding circumstances, his own fixed character, and unchangeable beliefs, which individually or altogether may be assumed to force him to act in a specific way. Then, moral philosophy should argue for the value of liberty. Hence, before dealing with Mill's arguments about reasons supporting the value of liberty, there should be a reference to the way through which a picture of human free will can be drawn.

In *A System of Logic,* Mill argues that similar to causality in natural sciences, which explains the relation between natural phenomena, the functions of mind should be explained in accordance with the same law of causation. In the latter, the subject of explanation concerns human mind rather than nature. Following Enlightenment naturalism, Mill holds that causal laws that explain man's individual behavior can account for social phenomena. Disagreeing with a further assumption about steadiness of human nature, Mill suggests that history and society can change human nature. To this end, he proposes the science of "ethology," which deals with different forms of human character in different social environments.[1] Here, the question arises as to whether this naturalistic supposition about the law of universal causation in human actions can be compatible with human free will.[2] Put another way, ostensibly the rule of the law of universal causation over human actions and determinacy of any cause in relation to its effect dismisses the possibility of decision making for man about his actions. If man is free no certain determinacy should necessitate a given action; and if determinacy of a given cause necessitates a specific action from man he cannot have any control over his action.

To tackle this dilemma, Mill distinguishes between the principle of necessity in natural events and in human conduct. In natural events, the word "necessity" implies, in addition to "uniformity of sequence," "irresistibleness." In human conduct, necessity merely "means that the given cause will be followed by the effect, subject to all possibilities of counteraction by other causes." Hence, the notion of irresistibility in natural events plays a crucial role, whereas in human conduct irresistibility leads to "fatalism," which should be distinguished from "necessaritarianism." At this point, in line with Hume's view about causation in human actions, Mill maintains that all of us share an internal image that our actions are determined by our character, motives, and convictions. Nevertheless, argues Mill, "we know that we are not compelled . . . to obey any particular motive."[3] Therefore, the resistibility of our motives rejects the idea of causality of our motives in relation to our actions.[4] Through this argument, Mill distinguishes between necessaritarianism and fatalism that seems to constitute the negative part of his argument. He asks us to refer to our conscience about the resistibility of our motives on many occasions. Consciously, we all admit that although sufficient motives sometimes invite us to move in a specific direction, we still possess the ability to resist that motive and act differently. An apparent distinction between a compelled action and a free one can be acknowledged through an ordinary event; the difference between a man whose hands are shaking of old age or cold weather and a young person who shakes his hands when leaving home in the morning. However much might be assumed about the law of universal causation over human actions, the difference between these two types of hand shaking is unquestionable. Hence, the first argument for distinction between fatalism and necessaritarianism in human conduct may be provided through an indirect reason that rejects fatalism with regard to some human conduct by differentiating between obvious cases of fatalism and those actions that we feel free to resist.

As the positive part of his argument for human free will, the notion Mill invokes is "moral freedom." Mill defines moral freedom as the power to control one's desires in accordance with a stable rational purpose, which is the central condition of self-realization as the ideal life. Then, he suggests that man has the capability to weigh, balance, and resist his motives on the basis of reason and reflection. Consequently, although the law of universal causation explains the relation among human actions, motives, and character, the ability to change one's own character, and resist one's motives grants a person free will.[5] Therefore, I should be said to be free as long as I act on the basis of a motive I could have resisted if there had been sufficient reason for me not to follow it. Still, I act from a motive determined by circumstances, which are beyond my control. Yet, I am capable of considering my motives and changing or resisting them when I find rational grounds to do so. A similar analysis applies to our character and convictions. While the law of universal causation still rules the relation between our actions and our characters and convictions, our obvious capability to alter our characters and to amend our beliefs grants us moral freedom.[6]

Hence, Mill's solution to the charge of the law of universal causation about human actions does not invoke an Owenite and Kantian philosophical picture that the will comes from nowhere, and therefore is not determined by circumstances that are out of one's control.[7] Rather, Mill argues that although the will is determined by circumstances and conditions, we feel conscientiously that we are capable of resisting those previously determined motives and wishes. This capability to resist the determined wishes and motives is what Mill calls "moral freedom."[8] With appeal to the notion of moral freedom—the ability to act upon reason—Mill draws a picture of human free will while preserving the universality of the law of causation. This picture of human free actions provides us both with a safe ground for discussion on the value of liberty and with the method and possibility to study scientifically human free actions.

The Conception of Civil Liberty

Having drawn a convincing picture of human free will, Mill arrives at his political principle of "Civil, or Social Liberty," its definition, its boundaries, and its justification.[9] Given the prevailing distinction between negative and positive conceptions of liberty made by Berlin, it is worth examining briefly

Berlin's famous conceptualization. According to Berlin, "The fundamental sense of freedom is freedom from chains, from imprisonment, from enslavement by others." To Berlin, negative freedom means "liberty from; absence of interference" by deliberately imposed restrictions from other human beings. The other kind of liberty, the "positive" conception of liberty is "not freedom from, but freedom to." In this sense, Berlin connects liberty with some notions such as "self-control," "self-direction," "self-mastery," and "self-realisation."[10]

Habibi convincingly interprets Berlin's major worry as the political abuse of positive liberty by authoritarian regimes, whereas Western liberal regimes, which emphasize the importance of negative liberty, have provided their citizens with greater scope for individual choice and opportunities.[11] Yet, Berlin's worry about a positive sense of liberty lies in the "historical" fact of authoritarian rule under the guise of positive liberty, rather than any conceptual deficiency or the implausibility of positive liberty. Thus, he contends that the positive and negative conceptions of freedom in the course of history "came into direct conflict with each other." This conflict derived from opposite notions of "self" held by adherents of negative and positive freedom. The proponents of negative liberty are concerned with "actual" man and his actual desires and wants, whereas the advocates of positive liberty pursue self-realization and self-mastery for a "real," "true," or "ideal" self. Berlin suggests that the positive sense of freedom is historically connected with the idea of division of the self into two: "the transcendent, dominant controller, and the empirical bundle of desires and passions to be disciplined and brought to heel. It is this historical fact that has been influential."[12] Hence, to Berlin, argues Habibi, negative liberty should be taken as superior to positive liberty when conflict between the two arises.[13] However, as Richard Bellamy has convincingly argued, Berlin's dichotomy of negative/positive liberty is inadequate. For "the central liberal value of autonomy" and negative freedom "presupposes a particular moral and social context which fosters individual liberty" by providing them with meaningful choices, hence the mere absence of external obstacles cannot be appreciated as an independent value.[14]

As for Mill, there is serious disagreement as to whether he advocates positive or negative liberty.[15] What Habibi and Vernon affirm about Mill is that he is both an advocate of negative and positive conceptions of liberty, though Mill did not refer to this distinction at all.[16] The ground for this interpretation lies in Mill's argument in the beginning of *On Liberty* about freedom as the lack of interference, and in the chapter entitled "On Individuality" his advancement of the notions of "self-realisation" and "human progress," and the like.[17] Skorupski argues that Mill's conception of negative liberty is a crucial instrument to positive liberty. "The central Millian claims are that developed spontaneity and rational autonomy are 'permanent' and general human interests [per se]; and that positive freedom flourishes only in conditions of civil liberty."[18]

Still, there is room for taking a further step in interpreting Mill's conception of civil liberty, by suggesting that it is a unitary conception that *requires* some external but necessary concepts. He defines freedom persuasively in terms of acting as one wishes. "The only freedom which deserves the name," writes Mill, "is that of pursuing our own good in our own way": a man can be said to be free to the degree that he can act as he wishes. The absence of all external obstacles in the way of acting as one wishes is an external but necessary concept required for liberty, rather than being a constituent of the concept of freedom, or another concept of freedom. As the concept of social liberty presupposes internally some "active desires" in addition to "free will," it requires externally the absence of coercion by others. At the beginning of *On Liberty*, Mill writes: "The subject of this Essay is . . . Civil, or Social Liberty: the nature and limits of the power which can be legitimately exercised by society over the individual."[19] This absence of external coercion, to Mill, is not another conception of freedom, since he defines freedom as the absence of external coercion and the ability of "pursuing our own good in our own way." What distinguishes Mill's definition of freedom lies in combining what Berlin calls negative freedom and positive freedom in one concept with no contradiction. Only when "freedom to" is intended to lead to *a specific* "self-realisation" not determined by each individual does it contradict "freedom from." Thus, with regard to Mill's conceptualization of liberty it seems credible to ascribe to him the idea that liberty is a unitary conception.[20] Liberty means the ability to act as one wishes, which *requires* the following external but necessary concepts: (1) the existence of free will, (2) the existence of some active desires, and finally (3) the absence of external coercion.

The Principle of Liberty

Having established his own conception of liberty, Mill arrives at his significant principle of civil liberty. His first assertion here is that the "very simple" principle of liberty is the supreme principle "entitled to govern absolutely."[21] It seems that what primarily concerns Mill in *On Liberty* is the liberty of individuals as an independent value, which requires different guarantees in different stages of social development. "The struggle between Liberty and Authority" is what Mill intends to deal with. Mill argues that "in old times this contest was between subjects, or some classes of subjects, and the

Government." In representative democratic societies where "the rulers should be identified with the people," the evil against which individuals should be protected is "the tyranny of the majority." In modern times, "Protection, therefore, against the tyranny of the magistrate," concludes Mill, "is not enough: there needs [to be] protection also against the tyranny of the prevailing opinion and feeling; against the tendency of society to impose, by other means than civil penalties, its own ideas and practices as rules of conduct on those who dissent from them."[22]

Having located civil liberty at the top of human values, Mill contends that the right to civil liberty should be guaranteed equally for each individual, that is, our right to freedom holds "so long as we do not attempt to deprive others of theirs, or impede their effects to obtain it." In this way, Mill expresses his commitment to the "equal right to freedom" for all individuals. "Each is the proper guardian of his own health, whether bodily, or mental and spiritual."[23] Since everyone is the best judge of their own mental and bodily interests, each should be free to act as he wishes. This demarcation of individual liberty is different from the harm principle, which sets another limit to individual liberty. Here, Mill suggests that the right to freedom should be accorded equally to each individual over his actions. I have no authority over others' body or mind so as to expand my freedom to interfere with what concerns others.

The Liberty-Limiting Principle of Harm

Having established the superiority of civil liberty over other human interests, along with recognizing the equal right to freedom for all individuals, Mill arrives at the demarcation of this equal right through the harm principle. Mill proposes that "the only purpose for which power can be rightfully exercised over any member of a civilised community, against his will, is to prevent harm to others, that is, for 'self-protection.'" The restriction of civil liberty by the harm principle, as will be discussed later in this chapter, derives from the supremacy of security and justice over all other human interests, including individual liberty. Hence, each individual is equally free to pursue his own good in his own way to the extent that he does not "produce evil to some one else." Nor is he permitted to pursue "such actions as are prejudicial to the interests of others." With regard to making damage to others' interests, "the individual is accountable," accordingly.[24] As for the precise meaning of terms such as "harm," "evil," "injure," "damage," and "hurt," there is no Millian technical terminology. Hence, the ordinary meaning should be relied upon.[25] Contrasting between liberalism and varying degrees of perfectionism, Feinberg argues that "the harm principle" and "the offense principle" are accepted more or less by liberals as valid moral principles. Yet, he suggests that Mill's "extreme liberal position" accepts only the harm principle as a valid "liberty-limiting principle."[26]

The limits to individual liberty, hence, are as follows:

1. Each individual is obliged not to interfere with others' freedom. Therefore, a person must refrain from compelling others to serve his interests, that is, exploitation of people is prohibited because they are free men. This part amounts to the recognition of each individual as a free person in contrast with slaves. Thus, a person has no right to even sell himself.

2. Moreover, no one is permitted to injure others under the guise of individual freedom. For instance, Mill argues that gambling and fornication concern the two sides involved with free consent and hence these would be permissible. In these cases, the actions involved are "injurious only to the agents themselves," and hence "ought not to be legally interdicted." Yet, if they are "done publicly," they should be counted as "offences against others" and "offences against decency," and hence "may rightly by prohibited."

3. Finally, each person should avoid making obstacles for another person in the way of obtaining his personal interests. For instance, the state or society cannot prevent individuals from free transactions of goods and services, such as alcohol, as long as they do no harm to others.[27]

However, the boundaries of the right to freedom and the harm principle has received the most criticism.[28] The ground for this continuous criticism derives from a misunderstanding of Mill's liberty principle by ascribing to him the division of actions into "actions which concern only the agent and actions that concern others besides the agent"; an interpretation that "is impossible to sustain." The problem is that there are mutual influences among different parts of society, as there are mutual influences among different parts of the body of a person. In addition, since "the nature of man is unity . . . his sociality and his individuality cannot belong to two different spheres." Hence, if we accept the analogy made between different members of society and different parts of human body, "whatever he is, and whatever he does, affects others and therefore concerns them." This misunderstanding overlooks the fact that Mill's harm principle denies individual freedom "in cases where the *interests* of others are either threatened or actually affected," not in cases where others are merely affected. The ground for this distinction, Rees convincingly argues, lies in two factors. First, there are some passages in which Mill uses the term "interests" rather than mere effects, as quoted above. Moreover, Mill acknowledges that a self-regarding action can have indirect or minor effects on others, a fact that rejects his affirmation of the private sphere as a realm that has no influence on others.[29]

"I fully admit that the mischief which a person does to himself may seriously affect . . . those nearly connected with him, and in minor degree, society at large," contends Mill. This argument does not distinguish the private sphere from the public sphere. Yet, "whoever fails in the consideration generally due to the interests and feelings of others, not being compelled by some more imperative duty, or justified by allowing self-preference, is a subject of moral disapprobation for that failure, but not for the cause of it, nor for the errors, merely personal to himself, which may have remotely led to it."[30] Therefore, a person who spends a large proportion of his earnings on alcohol resulting in failure in supporting his family should not be condemned for drinking alcohol, whereas he might be rightfully condemned for his failure to support his family, irrespective of the fact that this failure is the result of his spending money on alcohol.

It should be noted, however, that Mill explicitly restricts the scope of application of equal liberty to the "adults of civilised society," rather than all societies across time and space. Liberty is a definite value for adult citizens of civilized societies who can take advantage of it without jeopardizing their own fundamental interests and threatening others' interests. Hence, those "backward states of society in which the race itself may be considered as in its nonage," suggests Mill, "must be protected against their own actions as well as against external injury" much the same as "children" and "young persons below the age" who need to be "taken care of by others."[31] Thus, Mill's view about the right to freedom amounts to the principle of equal liberty for all citizens of already civilized societies.[32]

As was indicated above, there are some external but necessary concepts required by individual freedom. This brings us to the negative concept of liberty, to use Berlin's terminology. If each individual has an equal right to freedom within its boundaries, the state and society have the duty to refrain from passing laws that violate the equal rights of each individual to freedom. Consequently, not only is any legal prosecution in the scope of individual freedom not just, but social condemnation should also be prevented. What would violate the right to freedom is "compulsion and control," suggests Mill, "whether the means used be physical force in the form of legal penalties, or the moral coercion of public opinion." Furthermore, the person who uses his right to freedom "is not accountable to society for his actions." Thus, the recognition of the right to freedom requires the absence of all forms of coercive interference, ranging from the social pressure and legal threat prior to, and legal punishment and social condemnation after, the free act. Here, the *aim* of civil liberty is "to set limits to the power" of the rulers in the way of interference with individual affairs. Since only coercive interference should be considered as a violation of the right to civil liberty, social interference by way of inducement, advice, and encouragement does not contradict the recognition of the right to civil liberty. While an individual "cannot rightfully be compelled to do or forbear because it will be better for him to do so, because it will make him happier, because, in the opinions of others, to do so would be wise, or even right," all these grounds "are good reasons for remonstrating with him, or reasoning with him, or persuading him, or entreating him."[33]

A List of Civil Liberties

Although some interpreters of Mill's liberalism reject the view that he aimed to provide a list of basic liberties and rights, one might categorize the liberties and rights to which Mill strongly adheres into two basic groups that are not of course as comprehensive and detailed as liberal lists of freedoms.[34]

1. In the first group Mill mentions the right to "liberty of conscience in the most comprehensive sense"; the right to "absolute" and unqualified "liberty of thought and feeling"; and the right to absolute liberty of expression. "If all mankind minus one were of one opinion," writes Mill, "and only one person were of the contrary opinion, mankind would be no more justified in silencing that one person, than he, if he had the power, would be justified in silencing mankind."[35] This is the most explicit expression of the absoluteness of the right to liberty of thought and discussion.

2. The second group concerns the right to limited liberty of action and "tastes," as well as the right to limited liberty of association. "No one," admits Mill, "pretends that actions should be as free as opinions."[36] What limits the right to free actions are not considerations concerning spirituality of society, religious sanctities, communal values, and the like. Rather, the limitation comes from the harm principle.[37] In demarcating freedom of action and freedom of discussion, given the probable harm by some free discussion when leading to action, Mill emphasizes that "as long as discussion remains discussion, it ought to be permitted absolute freedom; but once it passes beyond

discussion to action, it ought to be treated as action," and hence restricted by the harm principle.[38]

It is worth noticing that Mill, as John Gray persuasively argues, is not concerned with the maximization of freedom, as is the early Rawls.[39] Rather, Mill invokes the concept of "absolute freedom" in the realm of thought and expression. Hence, none of the objections that are addressed to the inconceivability of maximization of freedom, can be addressed to Mill's conception of absolute freedom. I will now turn to Mill's argument for absolute liberty of thought and discussion, along with his argument for limited liberty of action.

The Argument for Absolute Liberty of Discussion

Regarding the right to the absolute liberty of thought and speech, Mill seems more to be arguing more *against* coercive interference by the majority or government, rather than arguing directly *for* independence of thought and discussion. Put another way, rather than being concerned with providing a straightforward "proof" for free discussion and autonomy of persons in thought and opinion, he seems to be moving between dismissing dialectically an imaginary absolutist disputant and supporting the value of freedom of thought and speech with proof. His argument for absolute liberty of thought and speech incorporates various reasons, which I will now discuss.

Fallibility Argument

Here, Mill connects all justifications for the legitimacy of coercive interference by government or society with claim of the "infallibility" of human beings. "All silencing of discussion," writes Mill, "is an assumption of infallibility," whereas "every one well knows himself to be fallible." Any suppression of opinions implicitly presupposes that the view adopted by the authority or society is the true one, and all opposing views apparently would be false. It does presuppose also that the suppression of false views is legitimate. By questioning the infallibility of government and society, Mill dismisses this authoritarian view, which is based implicitly upon the infallibility of some individuals. By referring to their conscience everyone admits that they make mistakes in exploring the truth. Even if the imposition of the truth through coercive instruments is legitimate, since no one is infallible "the opinion which it is attempted to suppress by authority may possibly be true." Therefore, the imposition of one view as the truth on others who hold different views is illegitimate. The state and society, thus, "have no authority to decide the question" of truth or falsity "for all mankind."[40] Therefore, Mill's fallibility argument amounts to arguing that since the legitimacy of any coercive interference by the state and society presupposes the false assumption of the infallibility of the state or majority, the interference is groundless. This is, as Sandel argues, precisely what negative liberty intends to suggest.[41]

However, Mill's recourse to the conscience of each individual who "well knows himself to be fallible" marks a gap in his fallibility argument.[42] For, he does not provide us with an argument that dismisses the *possibility* of finding some human beings with infallible knowledge of moral standards. A comprehensive argument based upon fallibility should be able to show that there can be no infallible figure that can decide about moral principles. Yet, Millian liberalism defends itself by rejecting the existence of God who might empower some human beings with infallible knowledge of moral principles. Hence, the role of the secularity of Mill's worldview and morality is crucial to his fallibility argument for the liberty principle.

Utility Argument

Mill's utility argument amounts to suggesting that since some definite valuable benefits can be achieved exclusively in societies that guarantee absolute freedom of thought and speech, their liberty of opinion and discussion should be absolutely assured. These benefits include the correction of our errors, the completion of our true knowledge, and the freshness of our true complete knowledge. The utility argument connects directly Mill's liberty principle with his utilitarian morality. "I regard utility as the ultimate appeal on all ethical questions," suggests Mill, "but it must be utility in the largest sense, grounded on the permanent interests of man as a progressive being."[43] It should be noted immediately that Mill's large conception of utility goes far beyond happiness. Mill's morality, upon which his liberty principle is constructed, sees the ultimate moral standard as the inclusive collection of human interests. The ground for absolute liberty of thought and expression lies in the intrinsic value of the true knowledge attainable only in free societies.

The Correction of Errors
A valuable benefit attainable by freedom of thought and discussion, according to Mill, concerns the correction of our errors. "If the opinion," which it is intended to suppress, argues Mill, "is right, they are deprived

of the opportunity of exchanging error for truth." Taking it for granted that knowledge is a definite social good and resorting to historical findings, Mill expresses his commitment to the improvability of our experimental knowledge in the course of history through free discussion and exchange of views. We know from history that "other people, in less enlightened times, have persecuted opinions now believed to be true." This historical finding apparently shows that man "is capable of rectifying his mistakes, by discussion and experience." According to the exclusive method of inductive experimentalism for discovering the whole truth, a person "can make some approach to knowing the whole of a subject" only through "hearing what can be said about it by persons of every variety of opinion."[44] It is only through trial and error that man can improve his experimental knowledge in a free society where every view can present itself in competition with other views.

The Completion of True Human Knowledge

Not only does free discussion help replace false knowledge with true knowledge, but disagreement and the diversity of ideas presented in free societies also provide a situation in which divergent ideas and doctrines, each of which embodies some parts of the whole truth about human well-being, completes ultimately the knowledge of human beings about the truth. As Mill supposes, contemporary societies are still far away from their destination in which the whole truth is comprehensively explored. One definite requirement for moving in the direction toward the whole truth is absolute freedom of thought and discussion. Given the diversity among human faculties, individuals can potentially contribute to the exploration of different aspects of the whole truth about human well-being. Before the arrival at the final destination where the whole truth lies, the clash among divergent views and doctrines should be embraced as the necessary vehicle for this long journey. Therefore, Mill proposes that "one of the principal causes which make diversity of opinion advantageous" is that "popular opinions, on subjects not palpable of sense, are often true, but seldom or never the whole truth. They are a part of the truth." Yet, Mill conceives of this advantageous diversity and disagreement as a temporary situation when human knowledge is still imperfect. Hence, Mill contends that "only through diversity of opinion is there, in the existing state of human intellect, a chance of fair play to all sides of the truth." Diversity, however, is temporary. "As mankind improve[s]," suggests Mill, "the number of doctrines which are no longer disputed or doubted will be constantly on the increase." Connecting human well-being with the amount of uncontested truths mankind achieves, Mill suggests that "the well-being of mankind may almost be measured by the number and gravity of the truths which have reached the point of being uncontested."[45]

The Freshness of True and Complete Human Knowledge

The last benefit of absolute freedom of discussion, according to Mill, is the freshness of complete and true knowledge in free societies, where false views, by presenting themselves in competition with the true view, strengthen the value of the truth in a comparative analysis. "If the opinion" that is intended to be silenced in illiberal societies, writes Mill, "is . . . wrong, they lose, what is almost as great a benefit, the clearer perception and livelier impression of truth, produced by its collision with error." Thus, "however true" an opinion "may be, if it is not fully, frequently, and fearlessly discussed, it will be held as a dead dogma, not a living truth." For it is not enough for "a rational being" to arrive at the true view; "the cultivation of the understanding" of the true view is also necessary to learn "the grounds of one's own opinions." Otherwise, no one can defend his true view against "at least the common objections." The freshness of our true and complete knowledge depends not merely on learning the rival views as our teachers explain them; rather, it is subject to knowing about all rival views directly from "persons who actually believe them; who defend them in earnest."[46] Hence, it is only in a society with absolute freedom of expression that we can directly learn about competing views to keep our understanding of the truth fresh and living.[47]

However, Mill's conceptualization of harm is deeply secular, and hence unjustifiably ignores the feelings and likings of religious individuals whose feelings should be considered as equal to others. For Mill's liberty principle not only legitimizes scientific criticism of religious values, which is not harmful to religious people, but it also legitimizes blasphemy that causes the severest mental harm to religious people.[48] Hence, as Bellamy observes, Mill's "exclusion of moral offence alone" from his harm principle "provides proof of its value-laden nature," that is, the secular nature of his liberty principle.[49] For, as Skorupski contends, if the "disturbance of other's feelings . . . is intense enough" so as to "harm them," it can "be cited as a ground for prohibition."[50] Likewise, distinguishing between "harm" and "offence," and defining the latter as "an affront to the sense, disgust, shock, shame, annoyance, or humiliation," Feinberg suggests that they are all evil, even when they are not harmful. He argues that an offensive action should be prohibited if the offense involved is serious and outweighs the reasonableness of the offender's conduct.[51]

Yet, a Millian liberal can argue that the immeasurable benefits of freedom of expression for human well-being require sufficient protection be provided against the suppression of free discussion. Admittedly, freedom of expression and political criticism are necessary means for holding authorities accountable with regard to citizens' rights. Furthermore, owing to difficulties with defining mental injury, it should be admitted that putting restrictions on freedom of expression by mental harm might lead to arbitrary interpretations that can deprive citizens of their basic rights, a fact that seems to have led Mill to reject any restriction on freedom of discussion in his ideal liberal society. Yet, as the harm principle demands, freedom goes so far as no definite harm is done to others. Hence, the protection required in the case of bodily injuries is necessary in the case of mental injuries, too.

One way out of this dilemma for Mill would be to rely on his method of inductive experimentalism, which requires that the feelings and likings of real citizens in a given society must be taken into account to define the concept of harm. Thus, as the method requires, the knowledge of the concept of harm should be obtained through collecting data from various citizens living in a given society. Rather than putting himself in the place of all citizens, an experimental political philosopher should examine what harm means to *real* men. The more inclusive this experiment, the stronger the theory.[52] Therefore, Mill's ignorance of the feelings of religious citizens of liberal societies in defining the boundaries of the concept of harm marks his liberalism as deeply secular.

It should be emphasized that Shiite Islam attaches great importance to respecting God, His infallible Messengers, and their infallible successors. It means that while respectful criticism and assessment of religious principles and doctrines are permissible, insulting them is religiously prohibited.[53] Consequently, the reverence of these sacred figures among Muslims is so deep that any disrespect of these sacred figures by others in the presence of Muslims produces intolerable harm, which is much more severe than bodily injury. Therefore, Shiite Islam does not legitimize blasphemy for any reason. This is the clearest case that confirms the theoretical incompatibility between Mill's principle of absolute liberty of expression and Shiite Islamic thought.

The Argument for Limited Liberty of Action

According to Mill, all reasons for rejecting the suppression of opinions and discussion are applicable to individual "independence" in practice so far as it is restricted to self-regarding actions. Hence, if a person "merely acts according to his own inclination and judgment in things which concern himself, the same reasons which show that opinion should be free," such as fallibility, "prove also that he should be allowed, without molestation, to carry his opinions into practice at his own cost." This independence of an individual in adopting his own lifestyle is what Mill calls "individuality." As was indicated above, Mill's view about the liberty of action differs from his view of the liberty of opinion and discussion in that the former is limited by the harm principle. Since, obviously, "no one pretends that actions should be as free as opinions," and since protection from harm by others, and freedom from intervention by others in one's private life "are more vital to human well-being than any other maxims," liberty of action is restricted to the private sphere. Thus, "the punishment of those who violate" the limit of individual freedom of action is "one of the dictates of justice."[54]

The value of self-development and progress is not instrumental to a given end; rather the spontaneous progress of each individual is per se a value. Therefore, "the evil" that should be tackled here "is, that individual spontaneity is hardly recognised by the common modes of thinking as having any intrinsic worth."[55] It seems that Mill's arguments other than the utility argument with regard to the liberty of action are similar to the argument for the liberty of opinions and discussion. Furthermore, the central point on which Mill constructs his justification of freedom of action is self-development and the moral progress of individuals attainable through freedom in the private sphere.[56] Hence, the focus of examination now turns to Mill's distinctive utility argument for the limited liberty of action. It is worth noting that unlike his argument *against* interference with regard to the liberty of opinions and expression, Mill's argument with regard to the liberty of action is *directly for* freedom and not against interference.

Individuality Argument

Mill contends that not only is the independence of each individual to cultivate his potentialities through self-experience an essential instrument for the achievement of the "permanent interest of man as a progressive being," but also that "individual spontaneity" possesses an "intrinsic worth."[57] To capture precisely how Mill argues for individual independence to choose as he wishes in the private sphere, the following formulation is illuminating:

1. Human desires and impulses are a part of an individual's nature so that the amount, the strength, and the variety of his desires contribute directly to his perfection as a human being. Interpreting desires and impulses in terms of "energy," Mill says: "Desires and impulses are as much a part of a perfect human being as beliefs and restraints" such that when we "say that one person's desires and feelings are stronger

and more various than those of another," it merely means that "he has more of the raw material of human nature." However, energy can be used to do evil as it can be used to do good.[58] This is Mill's picture of human nature, by which he seems to be rejecting an alternative religious view that might assert that *all* human desires are evil and hence should be suppressed altogether or subjected to the intellect.

2. Each individual has a distinctive collection of character, traits, desires, beliefs, and tastes. Mill, thus, rejects the uniformity of human nature that might be employed in argument for an Aristotelian morality. "Individuals, classes, nations," suggests Mill, "have been extremely unlike one another: they have struck out a great variety of paths, each leading to something valuable." There is not, therefore, one right path toward human perfection, as Aristotelian morality assumes. Rather, the way toward perfection varies not only from one class to the other, but also from one person to another.[59] Diversity of the paths toward flourishing, thus, is essential to human nature.

3. Essential to human nature is its progressiveness toward its own perfection. This intrinsic feature of human nature provides another ground for diversity and irrelevance of uniformity. Individuals lack a uniform stationary nature, which requires a fixed pattern of perfection for all. According to Mill, every person may have a type of progress different from others. Full personality, according to Mill, lies in naturalness and spontaneity of development of each individual in accordance with his potentialities and endowments.[60] "Human nature is not a machine to be built after a model," proposes Mill, "but a tree, which requires to grow and develop itself on all sides, according to the tendency of the inward forces which make it a living thing."[61]

4. To achieve any end, including one's progress, individuals should be left free to choose from among various options open to them. It is the result of the preceding premises that Mill is hostile to custom, which dictates uniformity to all individuals. Consequently, "the only unfailing and permanent source of improvement is liberty, since by it there are as many possible independent centres of improvement as there are individuals." Since there is not a general pattern for improvement, and given the exclusive reliability of experiment in the discovery of the truth, each individual should undertake a personal experiment to find what is right and what is wrong for him. "Each" person, suggests Mill, "is the proper guardian of his own health, whether bodily, or mental and spiritual," accordingly. Economic and social development, as especial social end, can be achieved only by the growth of a genius minority who can develop their capacities only in a society where

freedom of thought and expression are guaranteed. The freedom they need to unfold their talents includes both "thought" and "practice."[62] However, the role of elites is not to force what they see appropriate to human well-being; rather, they can show the right way to others. Thus, while Mill's theory is antiauthoritarian, it is not absolutely antielitist.[63]

5. In addition to the necessity of liberty for attainment of any end, since human nature is composed of various capabilities and potentialities all of which can be only developed by choice making, liberty in the sense of independence in decision making is a requirement for realization of human development. "The human being['s] faculties of perception, judgments, discriminative feeling, mental activity, and even moral preference," suggests Mill, "are exercised only in making a choice."[64] Hence, the more a person makes choice, the more he materializes his humanity. Here, Mill is committed to the value of liberty as an end, rather than valuing it as a means to other ends. Hence, not only does Mill defend individuality on the ground that liberty is necessary for achieving other human ends, but he also sees liberty as an ingredient of human well-being.[65] He suggests that "it is good there should be differences, even though not for the better, even though, as it may appear to them, some should be for the worse." Diversity of individuals' potentialities will lead to a diversity of lifestyles that should be valued per se. What is more, even for providing supporting circumstances for development of diverse human tastes, uniformity should be dismissed. In this way, Mill explains his interpretation of a happy life as a life that provides each person with the opportunity to satisfy his particular tastes, the prevention of which would harm the person.[66]

6. Human progress in its diverse ways is a *top* interest for each individual. Hence, since utility in its large sense is the ultimate moral standard, human progress is morally valuable. In this way, Mill grounds his liberty principle in his major moral principle of utility. Among diverse human interests are those superior pleasures that are particular to man, such as "the love of liberty," and "personal independence," which account for the liberty principle.[67]

What Mill concludes from the above premises is that no one should interfere in the private sphere, and each individual should be free to make choices required to his well-being. "Over himself, over his own body and mind, the individual is sovereign,"[68] contends Mill.

Britton convincingly maintains that Mill's defense of freedom in the private sphere is based upon his utility principle. As he explains, Mill does not necessitate social interference in the public sphere absolutely. Rather, he prescribes social interference if it contributes to the general welfare. Put another way, if individual action causes harm to others, society can interfere and suppress harmful freedom of action in the interest of the public.[69] Grounding Mill's view of liberty in his basic moral principle of utilitarianism, Levine interprets Mill as suggesting that the justification of interference is subject to the calculation of the advantages of interference against its costs.[70] What constitutes a man's interest as a progressive being is his pursuit of the greatest happiness of the whole society, argues Cowling, rather than the pursuit of his selfish interest. Therefore, since the highest happiness of society materializes only by leaving individuals free to choose as they wish, the very utility principle requires liberty of individuals. In this way, if an assignable damage is done to others, this damage outweighs the damage done by restricting liberty. Otherwise, liberty brings more utility even if it leads to the misuse of liberty.[71] Similarly, Donner bases Mill's liberty principle on his utility principle by broadening the notion of happiness to apply to the concept of self-development and progress by arguing that the exercise of our human faculties will produce happiness. The ground for this interpretation lies in Mill's conception of human nature "as naturally seeking to nurture, expand, and use its higher capacities."[72]

In a different interpretation of Mill's utility principle, rejecting the inclusion within happiness of security and autonomy, Gray interprets Mill as suggesting that "autonomy" and "security" are two top utilities of human beings distinct from "happiness." To Mill, security and autonomy, which account for the principles of justice and liberty, are to be accorded the supreme importance among human interests. Yet, the interests of security and autonomy are not considered by Mill as ingredients of the concept of "happiness"; rather, they are two distinctive human interests located at the top of human interests. Hence, Gray describes Mill's moral and political theory as "*a rights-based political theory grounded in a goal-based moral theory*."[73] By contrast, following Berger, Rosen connects Mill's idea of liberty with his idea of justice, which "provides both a framework of security for non-interference and a ground for the cultivation of individuality." Nevertheless, as Berger warns us, it is dangerous to interpret all of Mill's views about liberty as "an application of his theory of justice."[74]

As this book interprets Mill's Greatest Happiness Principle, Donner and Berger can be justified in affirming that autonomy is an ingredient of happiness. For Mill's ultimate standard of morality is "a happy life," and not instances of happiness. Therefore, a happy life should embody security and autonomy by which each individual can pursue his distinctive plan of life in safe circumstances. In this way, what accounts for liberty is a happy life dependent upon liberty of action, whereas security as the highest interest accounting for justice sets limit to liberty. Hence, in cases of conflict between security and autonomy, in agreement with Wollheim,[75] this book interprets Mill as being committed to ranking security, which accounts for justice, on the top of human interest, and locating autonomy as the second highest interest, which accounts for liberty. When conflict arises between autonomy and security the former should give way to the latter. Hence, liberty is restricted to the private sphere by the requirement of justice.

The real objection to Mill's liberty principle comes from the controversy about the concept of harm, which should set limits to liberty of action. People with divergent conceptions of the good and human interest disagree about what constitutes harm. What is more, even in cases of agreement about what constitutes harm, people disagree about the severity of different cases of harm. Take as an example disagreement about the harmfulness of addiction. Some people assume that addiction is harmful only as far as it damages specific interests. To some others, addiction is harmful per se for weakening personal autonomy.[76] The ambiguity about the concept of harm provokes the common objection to Mill regarding the difficulty of clarifying the precise boundary between the private and the public sphere. As I previously suggested in this chapter, one solution to this objection can be a type of democratic liberalism, which seems to be required by Mill's methodology.

However, the secularity of Mill's freedom of action principle lies firstly in his universal appreciation of individuality, which is incompatible with a Shiite Islamic view that appreciates submission to God as the highest value. According to Tabatabai's interpretation of a verse of the Qur'an, Islam means to submit oneself to God and his will.[77] Moreover, for Shiite Islam, man's potentiality for spiritual progress, in the sense of becoming similar to God, through obtaining his dispositions within the limited capacity of the human being, is the most important end. While spiritual progress accepts a degree of diversity derived from different possessions of the capability of progress, there is only one main path to this type of progress. To Shiite Islam, the path of perfection is drawn between man and God. Mill's philosophy is humanist, constructing its principles on the basic idea of the centrality of man and his desires. By contrast, Shiite Islamic thought is theist and constructs its principles on the basic idea of the centrality of God and conceiving man as dependent on him. Hence, while man is considered as a unique dignified entity in the world, he is conceived of as being dependent on his source of existence and progress.[78] Therefore, while freedom of action is necessary for human development, absolute spontaneity is not acceptable.[79] The disagreement on the idea of spontaneous progressiveness of the human being and the idea of his unique path of spiritual progress toward God is the clearest case that confirms the theoretical incompatibility between Mill's freedom of action principle and Shiite Islam.

Conclusion

This chapter examined the Theoretical Incompatibility Proposition regarding Mill's liberalism and Shiite Islam by looking at Mill's principle of liberty. The depth of the secularity of Mill's liberty principle, which confirms this incompatibility, can be observed in the following points.

(1/a) Mill's conceptualization of harm unjustifiably ignores the feelings and likings of religious individuals whose interests should be protected against harm by others. For Mill's liberty principle not only legitimizes scientific criticism of religious values, which is not harmful to religious people, but it also potentially legitimizes blasphemy that causes the severest mental harm to religious people.

(1/b) By contrast, Shiite Islam attaches the greatest importance to respecting God, His infallible Messengers and their infallible successors. It means that while respectful criticism and assessment of religious principles and doctrines are permissible, insulting them is religiously prohibited. Consequently, the reverence of these sacred figures among Muslims is so deep that any disrespect of these sacred figures by others in the presence of Muslims produces an intolerable harm, which is much more severe than bodily injury.

(2/a) Mill's principle of freedom of action universally appreciates individuality and spontaneous progress as the highest human interest.

(2/b) By contrast, Shiite Islamic view, firstly, appreciates submission to God as the highest value. Moreover, for Shiite Islam, man's potentiality for spiritual progress, in the sense of becoming similar to God, through obtaining his dispositions within the limited capacity of the human being, is the most important end. Hence, the main path to this type of progress is one, and hence while freedom of action is necessary for human development, absolute spontaneity is not acceptable.

PART TWO

Rawls's Mildly Secular Liberalism

CHAPTER 4

Rawls's Methodology[1]

This chapter examines theoretical partial-compatibility between Rawls's liberalism and Shiite Islam by looking at Rawls's methodology. First, his departure from theoretical concern for truth seeking to practical concern for finding a reasonable ground for agreement will be examined. Then, Rawls's idea of political constructivism and his idea of reasonableness, which derive from that practical concern, will be explored. Finally, the technique of reflective equilibrium with the innovative device of the original position, as Rawls's particular method of justification, will be discussed.

As will be demonstrated in this chapter, Rawls departs from theorizing about general philosophy and all issues of moral philosophy. Hence, contrary to Mill, who is in search of the truth in all aspects of human life, Rawls intends only to articulate a conception of justice for the basic structure of liberal democratic societies. In addition, he is searching for reasonable agreement among individuals who follow different doctrines of the good, rather than intending to prove the subject of that agreement to be true. Rawls's methodology amounts to an idealization of the current practices of Western liberal democratic societies, seeking to arrive at a coherent explanation in support of constitutional liberal democracy.

The particular method he invokes in this regard is the technique of reflective equilibrium. According to this technique, we start from some convictions, about which we are more or less secure by intuition. Then we provide a structure of principles that supports these immediate convictions in order to show the underlying assumptions that account for these intuitive convictions. Furthermore, we should provide guidance in those cases about which we have either no conviction or weak or contradictory convictions to manage them in consistency with definite cases.

Although Rawls's methodology is rationalistic and independent from any religious basis, it is mildly secular. The mildness of the secularity of Rawls's methodology lies in the following features. First, he restricts the scope of his argument to the "basic structure of society," rather than all aspects of human life. Hence, by keeping silent with regard to all transcendental issues, he has provided a space in which religious people find themselves absolutely free to choose whatever transcendental convictions they see fit. Second, he restricts the application of his argument to liberal democratic societies, rather than all societies including religious societies. Hence, he paves the way for religious societies to argue for decent religious regimes by following religious goals and values. Third, even in the political domain of liberal democratic societies, what his methodology requires is merely the "reasonableness" of his political conception of justice, rather than its truth. His idea of reasonableness results in the dismissal of only some religions as merely unreasonable, and further in counting some other religions as reasonable. What is more, it will be argued that his methodology would implicitly approve the establishment of religious regimes in religious societies by following the same method of justification. The mildness of the secularity of Rawls's methodology is the clearest aspect for theoretical partial-compatibility of his liberalism with Shiite Islam. As will be demonstrated in this chapter, what Rawls expects of Shiite Muslims is restricted to acceptance of the basic structure of liberal democratic societies by Shiite Muslim minorities who live in those societies, an expectation that can be met, as will be explored in chapter 8, by Shiite Islamic political theory.

The Purpose of Modern Political Philosophy

To begin with, Rawls's methodology can be understood in connection with his idea about the task of modern political philosophy. Explaining the essence of political philosophy, Rawls argues that there are "many ways in which political philosophy may be understood, and writers at different times, faced with different political and social circumstances, understand their work differently."[2] Since Rawls assumes that "the aims of political philosophy depend upon the society it addresses," he is concerned with the most urgent and crucial problem contemporary liberal democratic regimes confront, namely an inevitable plurality of ideas about the good life.[3]

Rawls maintains that the purpose of political philosophy in modern constitutional democracies no longer concerns the pursuit of truth; rather it is aimed at achieving "free agreement, and reconciliation through public reason."[4] Rawls intends to achieve this agreement with recourse to the history of Western societies and their shared experiences about politics.[5] "Justice as fairness," suggests the later Rawls, "I would now understand as a reasonably systematic and practicable conception of justice for a constitutional democracy." Therefore, Rawls goes on to suggest, "its first task is to provide a more secure and acceptable basis for constitutional principles and basic rights and liberties than utilitarianism seems to allow." It is for this purpose that Rawls suggests that his political philosophy "deliberately stays on the surface, philosophically speaking," whereas general philosophy is aimed at the "search for truth about an independent metaphysical and moral order."[6] This "restricted" purpose of political philosophy, obviously, will soften the secularity of Rawls's liberalism by providing citizens of liberal societies with the opportunity to affirm religious conceptions of the good life as "true."[7] In addition, Shiite Muslim societies are justified in establishing the basic structure of their societies in accordance with Islamic principles. These two achievements pave the way for partial-compatibility between Rawls's political liberalism and Shiite Islamic theory of religious democracy.

However, the ground of this shift in the aim of political philosophy to Rawls lies in the permanency of disagreement about the good life, along with the desirability of peace and stability.[8] Put another way, traditional political philosophy is a branch of moral philosophy that constructs and applies the results of its moral theorizing to social structures. By contrast, Rawls suggests that modern political philosophy should build its principles upon shared ethics and values implicit in the common culture of society, avoiding any controversial moral assumptions and metaphysical foundations. The freedom of political philosophy from metaphysical assumptions as well as people's toleration of controversial views about metaphysical disagreements is the only way to attain a stable and peaceful society given the permanent plurality of doctrines about the good life.[9] The aim of political philosophy, hence, is a "practical" agreement and reconciliation among reasonable citizens, and not a "metaphysical or epistemological" one in search for the truth.[10]

It is because of this shift in the purpose of political philosophy that Rawls seeks to "apply the principle of toleration to philosophy itself" through which the concept of neutrality will be an indispensable feature of political liberalism. Consequently, the purpose of political philosophy, according to Rawls, is no longer to articulate "a conception of justice that is true."[11] Rawls does not seek to propose an alternative to any religious or nonreligious comprehensive doctrine of the good. Nor does he expect religious people to convert to liberal doctrine. What he demands of religious citizens residing in liberal democratic societies lies in constructing the terms of social cooperation on some "common ground" that can receive "an overlapping consensus." Religious citizens, as Rawls suggests, can maintain their doctrinal religion while submitting to his political conception of justice as the most reasonable ground for social interaction in Western liberal societies. The possibility of making such an overlapping consensus derives from the alleged "neutrality" of Rawls's conception of justice that provides citizens with divergent comprehensive doctrines the opportunity to agree upon this superior conception independently. This brings us to Rawls's idea of neutrality and the idea of an overlapping consensus.

Regarding the term "neutrality," Rawls notes that "the term neutrality is unfortunate; some of its connotations are highly misleading, others suggest altogether impracticable principles." Then, he distinguishes between two main categories of definitions for neutrality: those interpretations that conceive of it as a neutral procedure and those he refers to as "neutrality in terms of aims."[12] One may suppose that, according to Rawls, liberalism is neutral with respect to morality, that is to say, liberalism is a nonmoral idea. David Paris calls this interpretation of neutrality "external neutrality," by which he means noninvolvement, disinterestedness, or indifference of a person with regard to a situation or a practice.[13] This type of neutrality can be imagined in cases such as physics, which is indifferent, for example, with regard to liberalism and Marxism.[14] It means that physics supports neither liberalism nor Marxism; rather, it is just silent. As will be explored in chapter 7, not only does Rawls explicitly dismiss the idea that liberalism can be procedurally neutral, but he also unequivocally admits that his political conception of justice as fairness is not procedurally neutral.[15] Overall, neutrality in the sense of *amorality* or *indifferent principles* is irrelevant to Rawls's political liberalism.

What Rawls affirms about the neutrality of his political conception of justice as fairness lies in its construction on principles and values that are, as much as possible, "independent" of controversial conceptions of the good life, that is, ideas and principles that are "common ground" or "neutral ground." Since these constructive ideas and principles lead to "a freestanding view" with regard to divergent doctrines of the good life, it "may be shared by citizens" affirming any reasonable doctrine in liberal democratic societies. Put another way, political liberalism hopes to obtain the adherence of "an overlapping consensus of various reasonable religious, philosophical, and moral doctrines."[16]

To put it more explicitly, Rawls hopes that the following four comprehensive doctrines will consider his political conception of justice as superior: (1) Kantian liberalism, (2) the utilitarianism of Bentham and Sidgwick, (3) the theory of value pluralism, and (4) nonfundamentalist historical religions. He hopes that these comprehensive doctrines can develop from within their own sets of convictions an "independent allegiance" to his political liberalism as the basis for "a consensus."[17]

Overall, Rawls's idea of an overlapping consensus amounts to suggesting the following propositions:

1. There are some principles and values that are commonly affirmed by all citizens of liberal democratic societies. These principles and values

can be discovered through elaboration on the public political culture of these societies.[18]

2. The affirmation of these common principles and values do not depend upon commitment to any comprehensive doctrine; that is, they are independently constructible with no recourse to comprehensive commitments.[19]

3. The supposed common principles and values are reasonable premises that are independently capable of producing a reasonable conception of justice as a freestanding view.[20]

4. Not only does the freestanding political conception of justice as fairness derive independently of any comprehensive doctrine of the good, but also "there are many reasonable comprehensive doctrines that understand the wider realm of values to be congruent with, or supportive of, or else not in conflict with" this political conception of justice.[21]

5. Since the political conception of justice as fairness is the most reasonable conception for regulating social interaction in divided societies by divergent comprehensive doctrines and since there is no contradiction between this political conception and any reasonable comprehensive doctrine, this political conception is superior to all comprehensive doctrines.[22]

6. Since the premises leading to the political conception of justice as fairness can be independently affirmed by citizens with no contradiction with their comprehensive doctrines, they have good reasons to submit to political liberalism. Hence, their commitment to the political conception of justice as fairness is built upon the firm ground of "intrinsically moral values,"[23] rather than being merely based upon a vulnerable pragmatic "compromise," or "a *modus vivendi*."[24]

Rawls's expectation of historical religions is that their commitment to the conception of justice as fairness should take precedence over, and should not be "overridden" by, their "transcendent" values such as "salvation and eternal life—the Visio Dei." Therefore, it is true that religious citizens of liberal democratic societies consider their transcendent values as "higher, or superior over, the reasonable political values of a constitutional democratic society," for the latter "are worldly values" that are expectedly "lower" than "those transcendent values." Yet, political liberalism rejects the view "that these lower yet reasonable values are overridden by the transcendent values of the religious doctrine." It is a core expectation of political liberalism that "a reasonable comprehensive doctrine is one in which they are not overridden." Therefore, "it is the unreasonable doctrines in which reasonable political values are overridden." To put it concisely, while political liberalism is silent with regard to the truth of religious transcendent values, it denies their superiority over the reasonable values of political liberalism.[25]

Having positioned their transcendent values as subordinate to the political conception of justice as fairness, reasonable religions should participate in an overlapping consensus on this superior political conception. "In such a consensus," contends Rawls, "the reasonable doctrines," including religions should, "endorse the political conception, each from its own point of view" with good reason. The "plurality of reasonable comprehensive doctrines held by citizens is thought by them to provide further and often transcendent backing" for liberal conception of justice derivable independently from a common ground. Hence, in addition to an independent political argument for the liberal conception of justice as fairness, Rawls expects all reasonable doctrines, including religions, to back his political conception from within their particular comprehensive commitments. He contends that "there are many reasonable comprehensive doctrines that understand the wider realm of values to be congruent with, or supportive of" this political conception of justice. Rawls further argues that since "each comprehensive view is related to the political conception in a different way," it should be "left to citizens individually—as part of liberty of conscience—to settle how they think the values of the political domain are related to other values in their comprehensive doctrine."[26] Thus, it is the task of religious citizens to reconcile the superior principles of political liberalism with their transcendent values to which they are firmly committed. Hence, Rawls intends to find an answer to the question: "How is it possible for citizens of faith to be wholehearted members of a democratic society when they endorse an institutional structure satisfying a liberal political conception of justice with its own intrinsic political ideals and values?"[27]

Put another way, Rawls argues that his main concern is to address successfully the "torturing question in the contemporary world, namely: Can democracy and comprehensive doctrines, religious or nonreligious, be compatible?" Departing from "Enlightenment Liberalism, which historically attacked orthodox Christianity," he grounds his solution in the idea of toleration in two types of justifications. The first is purely political, derivable from an independent political argument, which should be considered as reasonable, leaving aside true/false evaluation. The second solution grounds the value of toleration and other basic values of constitutional liberal democracy in various arguments drawn from different religious and nonreligious ideas that are supposed to be "the true or the right reasons." These two different grounds for toleration are not supposed to conflict with each other. Rather, there are "concordant judgments made within political conceptions of justice on the one hand, and within comprehensive doctrines on the other."[28]

As will be demonstrated in chapter 8, Shiite Muslim minorities living in Rawlsian liberal societies have a moral ground to accept the basic structure of those societies and contribute to their stability. Here a great reconciliation between Rawls's liberalism and Shiite Islam both in theory and practice is achieved. In theory, Rawls neither refutes Shiite Islam, nor does he intend to impose liberalism on Muslim societies. Furthermore, he does not demand in practice anything that contradicts Shiite Muslim minorities' commitment to their religious duties. Likewise, Shiite political theory neither seeks to impose its account of religious democracy on liberal societies, nor does it demand of its followers who live in non-Islamic, but liberal, societies anything that contradicts their duty of civility, as required by Rawls's liberalism.

However, having established that modern political philosophy should search for a secure ground for a stable agreement on the terms of social life, Rawls is led to adopt, as far as possible, a policy of disengagement from controversies over the essence of moral judgments (the idea of political constructivism). Likewise, he attempts to refrain from refutation of different religious and nonreligious doctrines of the good by adopting the criterion of reasonableness for the assessment of solutions to inevitable plurality of doctrines of the good life in contemporary liberal democratic societies (the idea of reasonableness).

The Idea of Political Constructivism

As required by Rawls's practical purpose, with regard to controversy over "realism" and "constructivism," he adopts a neutral stance. He argues that his view is different, first, from Kant's "moral constructivism," and further from "rational intuitionism as a form of moral realism," which can be "found in the English tradition in Clarke and Price, and Sidgwick and Ross, among others."[29] Certainly, however, Rawls's methodology is different from Mill's positivism, which is intended to explore moral rules as "real feelings" in the mind of man. He argues that whether moral judgments report something about the external facts recognizable by theoretical reason, as rational intuitionism suggests, or they are merely constructed by our practical reason, as moral constructivism proposes, a political conception of justice can be worked out by our practical reason. Therefore, Rawls's methodology is silent with regard to the essence of moral judgments and aims at constructing a reasonable political conception of justice for the basic structure of society, irrespective of the truth or mere consistency of this political conception.

According to Rawls, rational intuitionism as far as methodological issues are at stake may be characterized by the following features.

1. Intuitionists ontologically assume that there are some moral values in reality independently of human mind and activity.[30] This is an obvious factual statement about the external world in a sharp stance. For not only does intuitionism assert the existence of the external world, but it also extends the externality to moral judgments.
2. The previous feature logically requires the assumption that the knowledge of moral first principles is achieved by "theoretical reason," which is concerned with the "knowledge of given objects" through a "kind of perception."[31]
3. Furthermore, intuitionism assumes that moral judgments can be assessed as true or false. The criterion for the assessment of moral principles as true/false is their compatibility with that independent order of moral values.[32] Objectivity, hence, should be conceived of as independence of moral values, whether or not individuals reach an agreement about those independent values.
4. Finally, a major assumption connects the recognition of the truth of moral first principles and the "desire to act from them for their own sake," argues Rawls. "Moral motivation is defined by reference to desires that have a special kind of origin: an intuitive knowledge of first principle."[33] Again, externality comes with regard to the human motivation to comply with ethical codes.

In sharp contrast to rational intuitionism is Kant's "moral constructivism," which suggests, as Rawls argues, "the so-called independent order of values does not constitute itself but is constituted by the activity, actual or ideal, or practical (human) reason itself." Therefore, "the intuitionist's independently given order of values," Rawls continues, "is part of the transcendental realism Kant takes his transcendental idealism to oppose."[34] According to Kant's moral constructivism, "the first principles of rights and justice are seen as specified by a procedure of construction," rather than mirroring an independent order of values, as Plato affirms. Nor are the first principles of rights and justice fixed by "psychological constitution of human nature" prior to the procedure of determining the contents of those rights, as Hume suggests.[35]

Rawls intends to take a neutral position with regard to the essence of moral values in order to furnish his theory with the possibility of public justification.[36] Hence, the features of political constructivism are as follows:

1. There is neither assertion nor denial about the existence of an independent order of moral values in reality. Nevertheless, the principles of political justice, and only these principles, "may be represented as the outcome of a procedure of construction" through which "rational agents, as representatives of citizens and subject to reasonable conditions, select the principles to regulate the basic structure of society."[37]

2. The process of making these principles is undertaken by "practical reason," which "is concerned with the production of objects," rather than by "theoretical reason."[38] We are concerned, thus, not with discovering what is out there as moral order, but with making a moral order in our mind, irrespective of their externality.

3. Political constructivism assesses the principles of justice as "reasonable" and "unreasonable," abandoning the true/false assessment without denying or asserting the latter criterion. This is because in modern pluralistic societies "the idea of the reasonable makes an overlapping consensus of reasonable doctrines possible in ways the concept of truth may not." As for the criterion for reasonableness, Rawls suggests that "the correct model of practical reason as a whole will give the correct principles of justice on due reflection" when the "reflective equilibrium is reached." Rawls goes on to add that "as to how we find the correct procedure, the constructivist says: by reflection, using our powers of reason." Put another way, Rawls characterizes all three views—rational intuitionism, moral constructivism, and political constructivism—as having a relevant concept of objectivity. Then, he maintains that as far as political principles of justice are concerned "considered agreement in judgment, or narrowing of differences, normally suffices for objectivity." Furthermore, Rawls argues that "for political purposes, there is not need to go beyond it." On the other hand, "the repeated failure to formulate the procedure so that it yields acceptable conclusions," argues Rawls, "may lead us to abandon political constructivism."[39] Overall, the criterion for reasonableness is the attainment of reflective equilibrium.

4. Finally, the incentive of individuals for compliance with the principles of justice derives from the capacity of persons to understand and act in accordance with justice, along with their capacity to choose a conception of the good, with a further assumption that social life is a fair system of social cooperation among free and equal persons.[40]

What can be significant about Rawls's refraining from taking sides in controversial argument about the essence of moral judgments lies in the acceptability of his constructed political theory as a freestanding view to both sides in morality, that is, rational intuitionists and Kantian constructivists. Rawls seems to be content that rational intuitionists and Kantian constructivists should find his political constructivism congruent with their own views.

The Idea of Reasonableness

Rawls contends that modern political philosophy should aim at providing a secure ground for agreement among individuals who disagree on the conceptions of a good life, rather than exploring the truth about the good life. Thus, with regard to the essence of moral judgments, he keeps this theory silent about moral realism and moral constructivism. Furthermore, he intends to justify the *reasonableness* of his theory of justice, rather than its *truth*. Rawls contrasts between his "coherentism" on the one hand, and intuitionism and "naturalism" on the other. He contends that intuitionism attempts to draw ethical theories on self-evident premises to prove our considered judgments by deductive reasoning, which transfers the truth of premises to their conclusions.[41] As we saw in chapter 1, this is similar to Whewell's and Ross's approach to ethical judgments. Another method in moral philosophy is naturalism, whichsuggests that ethical standards can be given in totally nonethical terms so that they are reformulated in totally nonnormative concepts by precisely defining the ethical terms.[42] As Rawls argues, ethical naturalism is the attempt "to introduce definitions of moral concepts in terms of presumptively non-moral ones, and then to show by accepted procedures of common sense and the sciences that the statements thus paired with the asserted moral judgments are true."[43] Hence, "ethical naturalism is the doctrine that moral facts are facts of nature." For instance, the ethical judgment "murder is bad" or "one should avoid murder" is true because murder can be defined as "the unlawful killing of a human being with malice aforethought."[44] According to Rawls's coherentist methodology, ethical standards can be justified by the criterion of reasonableness and coherency. The method he adopts for this purpose is the technique of reflective equilibrium.[45]

Here, Rawls methodology refrains from dismissing Shiite Islamic morality as a false doctrine of morality. His idea of the reasonableness of his egalitarian political morality is compatible with the truth of Shiite Islamic moral system. This is a great achievement for Rawls's liberal theory that obliges Shiite Muslims, according to the teachings of the Qur'an, to reciprocally respect his liberal theory.[46]

The Technique of Reflective Equilibrium

As has been explained, the technique of reflective equilibrium is Rawls's method of reasoning through which he attempts to justify his political conception of justice as the most reasonable conception for modern pluralistic societies. Here, the present chapter will concentrate on this central part of Rawls's methodology. The technique of reflective equilibrium, according to Lyons, requires that moral principles be matched with our "intuitive" judgments about specific cases, and further determine the rules of controversial cases.[47] According to this technique, we start from some convictions, about which we are more or less secure by "intuition." The moral philosophy should then provide a structure of principles that supports these immediate convictions in order to show the "underlying assumptions" that account for these intuitive convictions, and further to "provide guidance in those cases about which we have either no convictions or weak or contradictory convictions." Hence, the justifiability of moral principles lies in the coherence between our considered judgments and the underlying assumptions that account for those judgments. Cleve calls this method of reasoning coherentism, as opposed to "foundationalism.[48] It is this feature that leads Dworkin to call Rawls's technique of reflective equilibrium a "coherence theory of morality,"[49] and Rorty to call it an "anti-foundationalism" or "idealisation . . . of present practices in the liberal democracies."[50]

Our Considered Judgments and Their Underlying Principles

A useful description of Rawls's idea of reflective equilibrium can be understood by adopting Scanlon's sequential stages:

1. In the first place we affirm some considered judgments about justice.[51] Speaking about moral judgments, Rawls suggests that we have some "considered judgments"—such as injustice of slavery, tyranny, exploitation, and religious persecution, to name but a few—which can be held when we remove all distorting circumstances that may lead us to make mistakes in those judgments.[52] These circumstances should be removed through the following steps: (1/a) a person should concentrate appropriately on all relevant facts about the issue involved—for example, he should not be upset or frightened—and his consideration should not be based on self-interestedness about the issue under judgment;[53] (1/b) the person should be confident steadily about a judgment over time; and (1/c) The judgment involved should be "intuitive with respect to ethical principles."[54] This latter requirement

indicates that the judgment at hand should not be dependent upon the validity of other ethical values.[55]

The rationale for requiring condition (1/a), "the person making the judgment is presumed . . . to have the ability, the opportunity, and the desire to reach a correct decision (or at least, not the desire not to)."[56] Having assumed this potentiality about the nature of man, the first condition determines those harmful situations that may distort man from making a correct judgment.[57]

2. In the next step, we attempt to provide the principles that support those judgments.[58] If "these principles match our considered convictions of justice, then so far well and good. But presumably there will be discrepancies," argues Rawls.[59] When we fail in searching for such corresponding principles that can account for our considered judgments, the third step will fulfill its task of insuring consistency.

3. In the third stage, by going back and forth between a given considered judgment and its supporting principles amending each part as it fits, we attempt to reach a point where there remains no conflict between a given considered judgment and its supporting principles.[60] Therefore, for the purpose of the articulation of a political idea of justice Rawls suggests that "the best account of a person's sense of justice is not the one which fits his judgments prior to his examining any conception of justice, but rather the one which matches his judgments in reflective equilibrium . . . reached after a person has weighed various proposed conceptions and he has either revised his judgments to accord with one of them or held fast to his initial convictions."[61] This is a method for discovering a concept of justice that we have to accept and comply with.[62]

However, since it may well be possible that one can find rival sets of principles each of which can account for our considered judgments about justice, there needs to be a device that preferably approves one set of principles rather than the others. This part of the technique of reflective equilibrium brings Rawls to the idea of the original position as a device for choosing among different descriptions, each of which can account for our considered judgments about justice.

The Device of the Original Position

The device of the original position is a part of the technique of reflective equilibrium as a "whole scheme" of reasoning.[63] Rawls suggests that "justice as fairness can be understood as saying that the two principles" of justice as fairness "would be chosen in the original position in preference to other traditional conceptions of justice, for example, those of utility and perfection; and that these principles give a better match with our considered judgments on reflection than those recognised alternatives."[64] Moreover, in *Justice as Fairness: A Restatement,* to answer the question of how we make our considered judgments about justice in the process of reflective equilibrium more consistent, Rawls resorts to "the idea of the veil of ignorance in the original position."[65] He further argues that the original position is a "modelling" device that determines the "reasonable," "appropriate," and "fair *conditions* under which the representatives of free and equal persons are to specify the terms of social cooperation in the case of basic structure of society."[66] To prevent individuals from bias, the idea of "the veil of ignorance" deprives those engaged in construction of the political conception of justice of any knowledge that may lead them to favor an idea only for their selfish interests. Only by this deprivation can the principles of justice be "the result of a fair agreement or bargain."[67] Hence, the original position acts as a complementary part of Rawls's method of reflective equilibrium. The device of the original position is aimed at nullifying human motives for exploiting social and natural resources to one's own advantages that would certainly contradict justice.[68]

As for the compelling force of this device, Rawls maintains that "the original position of equality corresponds to the state of nature in the traditional theory of the social contract."[69] Yet, contrary to other contractarian theories, this contractarian theory is not only "hypothetical," but it is also "nonhistorical."[70] Hence, since he never claims that anyone has entered in his specific model of contract, it seems as a compelling contract based upon individuals' consent. For, a hypothetical contract "is not a contract at all." Nor does Rawls intend to argue that it would be fair to apply some principles to a person without his consent to those principles only on the basis of his assumed consent in a situation different from what his real circumstances are. Likewise, the original position does not aim at justifying the two principles of justice "on the supposition that, under conditions very different from present conditions, it would be in the antecedent interest of everyone to agree to them," even when the veil of ignorance is lifted and some persons will find that other principles, such as utility principle, would benefit them more than those principles to which they consented under the veil of ignorance.[71] The force of the original position is irrelevant to any account of consent. Thus, when Rawls suggests that "the original position is simply a device of representation,"[72] he does not mean that since the representatives of the citizens of liberal democratic societies made a real contract on their behalf, the citizens' consent have been already obtained. For this representation is merely a hypothesis.

The force of the idea of the original position is connected with the intrinsic force of fairness and its requirements. Therefore, the idea of the original position suggests that a conception of justice worked out in a fair situation is so valid that all individuals innately equipped with a sense of justice when deprived of biased decision making *would and should accept* it. Hence, while it is not just to enforce some principles on the ground that citizens would consent to them in a different situation from their current situation, it is just to enforce those principles on the ground that citizens would admit their justice in a fair situation, which is different from the real unfair situation.[73] Put another way, the original position and the contract made in that imaginary situation are "evaluative rather than legitimising."[74]

With regard to the reliability of reflective equilibrium, Rawls unequivocally affirms that "coherence among considered convictions at all levels . . . is all that required for the practical aim of reaching reasonable agreement on matters of political justice."[75] This unambiguous grounding of reflective equilibrium in coherence argument will subject the methodology to an apparent objection. While obviously incoherence is an indication to the unreliability of an idea, the positive side of the proposition is definitely controversial, that is, mere coherence may not be a sign of reliability. For there is missing the proposition that some premises of a coherent consideration should be "initially credible—and not merely initially believed—for some reason other than their coherence."[76] This is because one might conceive that different persons arrive at different results through the method of reflective equilibrium, each of which is coherent.[77] What the method suggests is merely that reliability requires consistency, though consistency does not necessarily lead to reliability.

It seems that the validity of reflective equilibrium, in addition to the consistency feature, should be grounded in the validity of those assumptions that determine the fairness of the construction process. While Rawls seems to take the validity of these immediate judgments for granted, he describes them not as self-evident premises; otherwise he would be compelled to keep them fixed, with no potential for further revision. Therefore, it would not seem philosophically credible to argue that coherence among our considered convictions is all we need to consensually attain. For the validity of this technique seems to depend partly on factuality of the premises regarding the human talents and character as intuitive judgments.[78] Otherwise, if we assume the opposite view about the human talents and tendencies, Rawls's argument is merely unrealistic. Among these assumptions is the view of a person as having the ability, the opportunity, and the desire to reach a correct decision, as well as the idea of society as a fair system of cooperation among citizens who are regarded as free and equal. The credibility of a conception of justice that includes these assumptions about human nature and society depends on an experimental observation in the course of history and in different circumstances.

Since Rawls's method of reflective equilibrium is intended to validate something that involves a descriptive statement, such as that which asserts that man has a sense of justice and a moral character, he may be charged of ignoring the essence of descriptive statements. For however consistent the idea of citizens as possessing a sense of justice is with other parts of the concept of justice, we cannot assume the idea as valid unless we can show that in reality man desires to act upon justice. Otherwise, if real men desire not to behave in accordance with justice the whole idea will oppose reality and will lack any validity. Therefore, the coherent argument should be conceived as a mere "idealisation" of the present practices, rather than a justification.[79]

The method of reflective equilibrium is employed by Rawls to justify his secular liberal philosophy. Yet, this method is not necessarily secular. The secularity of Rawls's argument and conception, as will be explored in the following chapter, rests on some secular intuitive ideas he adopts as the starting point in his argument. Yet, one can conceivably adopt some Christian intuitive ideas commonly affirmed even in contemporary liberal societies as the starting point. Equally conceivable is the adoption of some Islamic intuitive ideas by Muslim philosophers to search for different political conceptions of justice for contemporary Islamic societies. As far as Rawls's coherentist method is concerned, the latter two theories should be reasonable. Hence, in *The Law of Peoples,* Rawls suggests that "the principles of justice for the basic structure of a liberal democratic society are not . . . fully general principles. They do not apply to . . . the basic structure of all societies. And they also do not hold for the Law of Peoples. Therefore, the limited application of Rawls's methodology approves alternative types of "decent society," which "is the best" arrangement for nonliberal societies that liberals "can realistically—and coherently—hope for."[80]

What is more, he cannot assert that his method of justification can only validate political liberalism for liberal democratic societies. It is a *petitio principii*, or begging the question. Only when other theorists are logically justified to start from some other intuitions known from their public political culture to develop, for instance, a religious regime, can Rawls be a political philosopher equipped with an argument that satisfies the minimum requirements of a healthy argument. Thus, while Rawls's theory of political liberalism explicitly keeps silent about the type of legitimate regimes for nonliberal societies, his methodology is required to potentially justify a religious regime as "just," if applied appropriately. The result would be equal respect between liberal states and reasonable religious regimes.

Overall, both the lack of inherent secularity of his methodology and its restriction to the practical search for a reasonable ground for agreement among citizens of liberal societies with different doctrines of the good provide a firm ground for partial-compatibility between Rawls's liberalism and Shiite Islam. Methodologically, both Rawls's political liberalism and the Shiite Islamic account of religious democracy are mutually disengaged from the subject of each other, and both respect each other's theorization for their subject.

Conclusion

This chapter examined the Theoretical Partial-Compatibility Proposition regarding Rawls's liberalism and Shiite Islam by looking at Rawls's methodology. The mildness of the secularity in his methodology, which confirms this partial-compatibility, can be summarized in the following key points.

1. As was seen, Mill's truth-seeking methodology rejects the Shiite Islamic commitment to intellectual demonstration and revelation. By contrast, Rawls only proposes a method for justification that is concerned with the reasonableness of ideas and doctrines and hence is compatible with Shiite Islamic faith in the truth of God, Messengerhood, resurrection, and the like.

2. As opposed to Mill, the subject of Rawls's theorization is only the basic structure of liberal democratic societies. Hence, by restricting his theorization to the political domain, Rawls has provided a space in which religious people find themselves free to choose whatever transcendent principles they find convincing.

3. Even in the domain of the basic structure of liberal democratic societies, what Rawls's methodology requires is the reasonableness of his political conception of justice—and not its truth—that results in dismissal of other views as unreasonable, and not as false. Here, Rawls successfully abstains from refutation of religious alternative political theories.

4. Not only does Rawls's political liberalism accept *decency* of reasonable religious regimes, but his methodology is also required to approve *justice* of reasonable religious regimes in religious societies that follow the same method of justification in the construction of their basic structure. Hence, Rawls would accept the decency of religious democracy, which Shiite political theory intends to justify for Shiite Muslim societies.

CHAPTER 5

Rawls's Egalitarian Moral Theory

This chapter examines theoretical partial-compatibility between Rawls's liberalism and Shiite Islam by looking at Rawls's egalitarian moral theory, that is, his theory of justice as fairness in contrast with Mill's utilitarian moral theory. The first part will be devoted to a discussion of the features of Rawls's theory of justice. Then, Rawls's definition of the general concept of justice, as well as his particular conception of justice will be explored. Furthermore, this chapter will discuss his argument in defense of his particular political conception of justice. His argument consists of several facts and ideas implicit in the public political culture of liberal democratic societies that altogether lead to his two principles of justice as fairness in lexical order.

Rawls asserts that his theory of justice as fairness is a deontological theory of morality with a particular subject different from teleological theories. His theory belongs to the general category of views about distributive justice, rather than about criminal justice. He claims to have transformed his theory of justice from a substantial, universal, and utopian theory to a neutral, particularist, and feasible conception of justice. His transformed political conception of justice suggests a specific list of basic rights and liberties that all citizens should enjoy equally. He argues also that social and economic inequalities should be attached to positions and offices open to all under conditions of fair equality of opportunity. Finally, these inequalities should serve the least-advantaged members of society. Starting from some ideas and facts that are deliberately adopted from the public political culture of liberal democratic societies, Rawls argues that his particular conception of justice is the most reasonable conception for constructing the basic structure of contemporary liberal democratic societies.

As will be demonstrated, Rawls is totally secular in his conceptualization and argument. First, like Mill, his political morality is humanist, focusing its attention on human beings, rather than God, who is the center of religious thoughts. Second, he constructs his argument and justification upon totally secular premises with no recourse to religion. This is because Rawls postulates that any recourse to religious principles would make agreement among citizens improbable.

Nevertheless, in contrast to Mill's utilitarian moral theory, Rawls's intention to provide a secure ground for agreement among reasonable citizens on the terms of social cooperation led him to soften the secularity of his political morality. First, he successfully refrains from implying any denial or skepticism about God's existence, though his theory is humanist. Second, although he proposes that his political morality is the most reasonable conception for social cooperation, he keeps silent with regard to the truth of religion. Third, since his morality is restricted to the political domain of liberal democratic societies, he explicitly accepts the decency of religious regimes for religious societies. All these features of Rawls's political morality lead to the appreciation of his liberal theory by Shiite Islam. As will be explored in chapter 8, Shiite Islamic political theory recommends a concept of "religious democracy" for Shiite Muslims at home that is compatible with Rawls's theory of decency. In addition, the leading idea for Shiite Muslims abroad is the ethical standard of "the self-restrained Muslim" that is compatible with Rawls's justice as fairness and his idea of "reasonable citizens," though for other reasons than his secular argument. Finally, as opposed to Mill's utilitarian moral theory, the Shiite Islamic idea of justice as impartiality is mainly compatible with Rawls's egalitarian political morality.

The Features of Rawls's Theory of Justice

First, it should be noted that Rawls's theory of justice as fairness is a deontological theory of morality with a restricted subject. Furthermore, his theory belongs to the general category of views about distributive justice, rather than about criminal justice. What is more, his theory has undergone some enhancement, which has enriched it with a more robust basis against its critics. Before exploring Rawls's conception of justice as fairness, the key features of his theory will be examined.

A Deontological Theory of Distributive Justice

The categorization of moral theories, which Rawls prefers, is the dichotomy between "teleological" and "deontological" theories.[1] Following Frankena in *Ethics,*[2] Rawls defines teleological theories as embodying two related ideas. First, teleological theories define the good independently from the right. Furthermore, the rightness of an act is judged on the basis of its maximization of the good. By contrast, deontological theories do not subscribe to both ideas, either by specifying the good in connection with the right, or by defining the right free from its maximization of the good. As a further illumination, Rawls assumes that all rational theories should consider the consequence of actions in defining the right. Put another way, deontology should not be taken as indicating the rationality of judging the rightness of an act irrespective of its consequences.[3]

Having established this dichotomy, Rawls argues that his theory of justice as fairness, as opposed to utilitarianism, is a deontological theory in the sense that justice is not assumed to maximize the good. Then, he characterizes his theory of justice as prioritizing the concept of the right to the concept of the good through the principles of justice, which set limits to the legitimate means to pursue one's own good. Rights, thus, constitute the "framework" within which each individual can legitimately pursue his own specific conception of the good life. A corollary of this priority, argues Rawls, will be the illegitimacy of the breach of any right for achieving an interest when conflict between right and good arises.[4]

According to Dworkin, deontological liberal theories, in the first place, attach supreme importance to rights, which outweighs all considerations of any general end. Second, rights are ascribed to individuals as fundamental presuppositions of political theory. Third, the concept of rights is distinguished from the concept of the good. Therefore, the role of rights is to determine a set of guaranteed entitlements, whereas individuals freely choose any conception of the good. Furthermore, since all ideas of the good life are connected with individuals' choice, no conception of the good can be judged to be superior over the others and hence no conception of the good can be imposed on individuals.[5]

To distinguish the cases of conflict between the right pursued by Rawls's theory of justice as fairness and the good pursued by utilitarianism, Lyons provides us with an illuminating explanation.[6] He suggests that sometimes inequalities in liberty as well as putting restriction on liberty may increase the general welfare, whereas they are not necessary for liberty itself. In this situation, utilitarianism permits this inequality whereas justice does not. Another difference between utilitarianism and justice concerns Rawls's difference principle. This principle requires that after securing for all an equal minimum level of primary goods the further benefits to some is only just if it is to the benefit of the least advantaged in society, which departs from the average welfare permitting the benefit of some at the expense of others. Finally, it may well be possible that while some unjust institutions such as slavery are always rejected by Rawls's principles of justice, utilitarians should logically, according to Rawls, permit this unjust institution if it serves the average welfare.[7]

Rawls's main objection to utilitarianism is that it "does not take seriously the distinction between persons."[8] The ignorance by utilitarianism of the separateness of individuals can be controversially found in the following points: first, in classical utilitarianism, when the total sum of interests is maximized, separate individuals have no intrinsic value. They are important as some channels and locations where pleasures and pains as intrinsic values and disvalues exist. Second, although utilitarianism treats individuals as equal, it is not individualistic and egalitarian. When the utilitarian maxim announces that *everybody is to count for one, nobody for more than one,* equality means that the pleasure and pain of each individual should have equal weight in the calculus of the total sum of utility. It does not require considering each person as an independent end in distribution of the total sum of pleasure. In other words, in calculating the total sum, each counts as one, and not in distributing the total sum. Third, there is no self-evident value in increasing the total sum of pleasure that is not experienced by anyone in society. Society is not one person who can experience the total sum of pleasure. Fourth, classical utilitarianism, if not restricted by an independent distributive principle, mistakenly makes an analogy between one person and society. While it is rational and prudent for one person to order his plans of life by sacrificing a present pleasure for a greater satisfaction later, society is not justified to sacrifice the satisfaction of some for a greater satisfaction of others. So, utilitarianism seems to assume that what is prudent for a single person is prudent for the whole society. In this way, utilitarianism ignores the separateness and the independent worth of individuals.[9]

In addition to the categorization of Rawls's theory under the general group of deontological moral views, his theory belongs to the category of views of distributive justice, rather than of criminal justice. Following Aristotle, philosophers divide justice into two main categories: "retributive justice," dealing with punishment of criminals, and "distributive justice," concerned with the distribution of the benefits and burdens of social cooperation. Rawls's theory of justice is a theory of distributive justice.[10] In this regard, Rawls distinguishes among "perfect procedural justice," "imperfect procedural justice," and "pure procedural justice." Then, he labels his theory of justice both as a theory of distributive justice as well as a theory of pure procedural justice. The conception of allocative justice applies, suggests Rawls, when some goods are aimed to be divided among individuals who have no prior claim on them because those goods are not the product of their cooperation. In this situation, it would be rational to divide these goods on the basis of the "known desires and needs" of the individual. Since Rawls assumes that society is a fair system of cooperation, the benefits and burdens of social cooperation to him should be the subject of distributive justice rather than allocative justice.[11]

The conception of perfect procedural justice, argues Rawls, can be characterized by assuming the existence of an independent criterion for judgment about justice of the outcome, as is the case in justice of dividing a piece of cake belonging to some individuals "equally" among them, along with availability of a specific procedure through which we can assure that the desired outcome be achieved. The conception of imperfect procedural justice applies to those cases where there is an independent criterion for judgment about justice of the outcome, yet the procedure through which we can assure that the desired outcome be achieved is unavailable. An obvious case of imperfect procedural justice is a criminal trial, since the punishment of a guilty defendant independently of any procedure for fair prosecution is definitely known. Yet, however much the procedure of prosecution is fair and properly conducted, the outcome might be wrong. Rawls finally describes pure procedural justice as a conception that applies wherever we lack any independent criterion for judgment about the justice of an outcome, whereas we have access to a fair procedure by which we can assure that the best outcome has been reached, as is the case of gambling. In pure procedural justice the justice of outcome can only be judged if it is reached through the just procedure. Put another way, the outcome is just, whatever it would turn out to be, if a just procedure is adopted and followed properly. Hence, the justice of the procedure would be transmitted to the outcome.[12]

Rawls further enriches his idea of pure procedural justice initially proposed in *A Theory of Justice* (*TJ*) with the idea of political constructivism developed in *Political Liberalism* (*PL*). Combined together, Rawls's theory of justice as fairness is a theory of distributive justice assuming that, first, there is no independent criterion for judging the just division of benefits and burdens of social cooperation. Second, individuals engaged in social cooperation can set a just procedure through the construction of some principles on the basis of which whatever the outcome turns out to be, the justice of principles would be transmitted to the outcome.

A Neutral, Particularist, and Feasible Theory of Justice

Rawls's original work about justice developed in three stages: The initial idea was announced in Rawls's essay "Justice as Fairness," published in 1958. A revised version of the initial theory was developed in "Distributive Justice," published in 1967. Finally, in *TJ*, published in 1971, Rawls introduced his developed theory of justice.[13] By *TJ*, Rawls became an innovator of contemporary political philosophy concerned with justice.[14] It seems that owing partly to criticisms made by communitarians and multiculturalists against his early work, and partly to the need to refine his theory, Rawls has defended and revised some parts of his original work in the last three decades collected in *PL*.[15] What are these developments?

Intending to explain the "fundamental differences" between *TJ* and *PL*, in *The Law of Peoples* (*LP*), Rawls describes his former presentation as a comprehensive doctrine, assuming that all citizens of a constitutional democratic regime affirm the same doctrine. Furthermore, justice as fairness is supposed to have proved superior to a long-dominant doctrine of utilitarianism, as well as another doctrine, namely intuitionism. There is, thus, a contrast between justice as fairness and utilitarianism as the main rival. Conversely, according to Rawls, *PL* introduces the idea of political liberalism to interpret his theory of justice as a mere political conception of justice that all reasonable people in a constitutional democratic regime accept as the freestanding view, while at the same time diverging on comprehensive religious, philosophical, and moral doctrines about the good life.[16]

However, this statement by Rawls needs clarification. He distinguishes between "comprehensive doctrine" and "political conception." He defines the former as including the whole values in human life, that is, as "fully comprehensive." Alternatively, a comprehensive doctrine may include, at least, some nonpolitical values, that is, it may be "partially comprehensive." By contrast, political conception covers only "the main institutions of political and social life," and not the values and virtues of "the whole of life."[17] If this is the meaning of comprehensiveness, justice as fairness has nothing to do with comprehensiveness even in *TJ*, where Rawls is only concerned with "basic structure" and "social arrangements," rather than "practices of private associations" or "the law of nations." Nor is he concerned there with all the values of the basic structure, such as efficiency and liberality, but only with justice.[18] The scope of the application of his theory of justice remains the same in both his major works. As for competition between justice and utilitarianism,[19] Rawls definitely assumes that justice as fairness can be the focus of "an overlapping consensus" among "Kant's moral philosophy with its ideal of autonomy," as well as "the utilitarianism of Bentham and Sidgwick," along with "pluralist account of the realms of values" and finally "religious doctrines with an account of free faith."[20]

What distinguishes Rawls's presentation of the theory of justice as fairness in *TJ* from that in *PL* would seem to be two revisions about the claim of the theory of justice as fairness, along with its completion in one more aspect. While justice as fairness according to the former is a "substantive" view about the highest and ultimate social value in contrast with other views such as utilitarianism, the latter interprets the same principles as "neutral" and consequently with the potential to also be accepted by utilitarians. In *TJ*, Rawls suggests that his theory "is a viable alternative" to "the classical utilitarian and intuitionist conceptions of justice."[21] By contrast, the focal point of Rawls's later work is the "impartiality" of his political conception of justice as fairness articulated with recourse to principles and values that are, as much as possible, independent of controversial conceptions about the good life, founded upon "common ground" or "neutral ground."[22]

Furthermore, justice as fairness would seem to assert "universal applicability" to all societies in the former, whereas *PL* withdraws its claim about universality and presents, instead, the theory of justice as "particular" to Western liberal democracies. In *TJ*, Rawls begins his theory of justice by proposing that "justice is the first virtue of social institutions, as truth is of systems of thought," though social institutions should be conceived as having several different virtues, such as efficiency or liberality and the like. The issue involved, according to Rawls, apparently relates to the domain of "moral theory" aimed to "describe our moral capacity." What follows from this definition of moral theory, Rawls argues, is that his theory of justice as fairness is a moral theory "setting out the principles governing our moral powers."[23] This opening remark seems to demonstrate Rawls's intention to articulate a substantive view about justice as a *universal* moral value. For the answer to a general question about morality should be a general statement applicable to all those who intend to follow moral rules. By contrast, postulating that justice is plausible, Rawls begins his discussion in *PL* by addressing an urgent problem of liberal democratic societies, that is, "how is it possible for there to exist over time a just and stable society of free and equal citizens, who remain profoundly divided by reasonable religious, philosophical, and moral doctrine?"[24] Thus, Rawls's concern is restricted to addressing the "question about a conception of justice for a democratic society."[25] He is not concerned with theorizing an unlikely general theory of justice that can be applicable to all societies.[26]

This shift led Rawls to affirm two distinct theories in a hierarchical order of plausibility. What concerns Rawls in *PL* is the articulation of "a particular theory of justice as fairness" applicable only to those societies that are already liberal democratic. This theory, according to Rawls, should be appreciated as the best approach to justice. Part of his concern in *LP* is the articulation of "a particular theory of decency" applicable to nonliberal societies, which is inferior to the former theory.[27]

In addition to these two revisions about the very theory of justice, the question of "feasibility" is not attended to sufficiently in *TJ*, whereas the major intention of *PL* concerns the development of the theory so as to solve the problem of "stability" and "feasibility" dealt with insufficiently in *TJ*. While *TJ* assumes that all citizens of society may abandon all rivals to Rawls's theory of justice by submitting to justice as fairness, *PL* dismisses the possibility of the common abandonment of utilitarianism, intuitionism, and perfectionism.[28] Thus the impossibility of the agreement of all members of society on one comprehensive doctrine led Rawls to revise his theory of justice as fairness to provide not a rival to other comprehensive doctrines, but an overarching view about justice. Introducing the idea of "political liberalism" in his later work, Rawls interprets his theory of justice as a political conception of justice that all reasonable people in a constitutional democratic regime accept as the freestanding view, while at the same time diverging on comprehensive religious, philosophical, and moral doctrines about the good life. It is a fundamental assumption of *PL* that a well-ordered society in which all the members affirm justice as fairness as their comprehensive doctrine about the good life is unlikely.[29]

Overall, according to Rawls, the "transformation" of his substantive, universal, and utopian theory of justice to a neutral, particularist, and stable political conception of justice does not need so much change either in the components of, or with regard to the ideas leading to the principles of justice. What is required here instead is a mere "reformulation." The only significant change in the ideas invoked to develop the theory of justice as fairness, Rawls argues, concerns the emphasis on the recourse to autonomy as a political notion rather than as a moral notion in Kantian liberal doctrine.[30]

Rawls's Political Conception of Justice

Regardless of any specific conception of justice each of us may hold, Rawls takes it for granted that "each person possesses an inviolability founded on justice that even the welfare of society as a whole cannot override." Only if the prevention from a greater injustice is necessary can justice be sacrificed. This is the logical consequence of the fact that justice is the first virtue.[31] This departure point puts Rawls fundamentally in opposition to Mill whose utility principle attaches prime importance to the general happiness. This opposition is reinforced by the fact that Rawls draws his concept of justice independently of any other concern, such as the general utility. Here, Rawls seems to assume persuasively that every individual self-evidently knows the value of justice and its superiority over all other social values irrespective of its component. No one can explicitly suggest that unjust or discriminatory laws are justifiable. Self-evidence here indicates that no argument is required to admit that justice is good and injustice is evil.

Shiite Islam agrees with Rawls's idea that justice is the first virtue of social institutions, as opposed to utilitarianism. As was discussed earlier in chapter 2, the Qur'an locates justice at the top of human values, and hence asks Muslims to stand for justice even toward their enemies, because justice is required by righteousness.[32] Moreover, the Qur'an explicitly contrasts human utility in the present life with justice, and then asks Muslims to follow the requirements of justice even at the cost of losing their temporary utility.[33]

While there is usually disagreement about what justice means, argues Rawls, each of us has "a conception of justice" determining the proper distribution of benefits and burdens of social life, as well as assigning basic rights and duties to individuals in social interaction. Nevertheless, we all share the idea of "the concept of justice" in the sense of the necessity of such a proper distribution. One more common affirmation about justice concerns the rejection of the "arbitrary distinction" between individuals by social institutions with regard to those rights and duties.[34] Put another way, the general concept of justice connotes some notions such as "the elimination of arbitrary distinctions," "proper share, balance, or equilibrium between competing claims." Consequently, according to Rawls, different theories of justice are attempts to specify arbitrariness and propriety.[35]

As a further illumination, Rawls develops his theory out of the notion of equality. His theory of justice, thus, should be conceived of as being a particular case of that more general concept of justice, which suggests that all social values should be equally distributed except when inequality be to the benefit of all parties. Therefore, injustice should be considered as "inequalities that are not to the benefit of all."[36] It is the benefit of all citizens that justifies inequalities in social values. Hence, as opposed to utilitarianism, Rawls's theory considers the situation and the benefits of every individual independently.

Having established the obvious and superior value of the general concept of justice, Rawls begins to deliver his own conception of "justice as fairness," which is expectedly controversial and needs justification. First, one should not assume that to Rawls justice is equal to fairness. The adoption of this conception is intended to indicate that the conception of justice is "agreed to in an initial situation that is fair. The name does not mean," Rawls goes on, "that the concepts of justice and fairness are the same."[37] To clarify his special case of this broad concept of justice, Rawls suggests his view about justice as two principles in lexical order. Rawls's particular political conception of justice for a liberal democratic society reads as follows:

> **a.** Each person has an equal claim to a fully adequate scheme of equal basic rights and liberties, which scheme is compatible with the same scheme for all; and in this scheme the equal political liberties, and only those liberties, are to be guaranteed their fair value.

b. Social and economic inequalities are to satisfy two conditions: first, they are to be attached to positions and offices open to all under conditions of fair equality of opportunity; and second, they are to be to the greatest benefit of the least advantaged members of society.[38]

The first principle of justice attaches top priority to maximizing the amount of equal political liberties for each individual. Rawls lists the major liberties as the rights to vote and to stand for election, freedom of speech and association, freedom of thought and conscience, freedom of the person including freedom from psychological and physical harm, freedom of ownership and religion, and freedom from arbitrary arrest. These liberties, Rawls maintains, should be guaranteed equally for each individual, so that even in managing the inevitable conflicts between them the same system of arrangement should be applied to all. The second principle deals with inequalities in social position as well as in economic benefits. First, these inequalities should be attached to positions and offices open to all under conditions of fair equality of opportunity and furthermore they should be to the greatest interest of the least-advantaged groups.[39] Put another way, while the second principle does not dismiss differences and inequality in the distribution of economic welfare and social positions as unjust, it requires equal opportunity to obtain economic benefits and to reach social offices, in addition to demanding that any inequality should be to the greatest benefit of the least-advantaged members of society. The lexical order between these two principles, according to Rawls, means that the first is superior to the second, and therefore, no infringement of basic liberties can be justifiable with reference, for instance, to the necessity of promotion of economic welfare. It is only the capacity of one set of liberties to override another set when conflict arises.[40]

As for the subject of justice as fairness, Rawls rules out laws, persons, and actions of individuals or their attitudes as the subject of his theory of justice. Only, Rawls maintains, the basic structure of a society including the political constitution, the principal economic arrangement, such as competitive markets and private property, and finally social arrangements, such as monogamous family, are the subject of social justice. These fundamental arrangements are the subject of social justice because they not only overwhelmingly affect the present life of men, but also "affect men's initial chances in life." Consequently, the two principles of justice might not be appropriate for private associations or the law of nations.[41]

Rawls's theory of justice as fairness intends to mediate between the two conflicting strands of traditional liberalism by respecting both values of liberty and equality. On the one hand, Rawls's theory is liberal for attaching supreme importance to liberty as expressed in the first principle. On the other, his theory is egalitarian for guaranteeing the fair value of political liberties and fair equality of opportunity to obtain social positions and economic benefits, along with requiring that inequalities should be to the greatest benefit of the least-advantaged members of society. Hence, the two principles of justice in its lexical order meet the requirements of liberty and equality simultaneously.[42] Therefore, Rawls's innovation in both aspects of liberal philosophy is considerable. He has not only proposed a new reason in defense of basic liberties for citizens, but also furnished his support of distributive justice in a way that can be reconciled with basic freedoms. As Nagel puts it, Rawls has combined the strong principles of social and economic equality with the strong principles of pluralism and personal freedom.[43]

While Shiite Islam agrees with Rawls's opposition to Mill's utilitarian moral theory, Rawls's particular conception of justice is not acceptable to Shiite Islam. The following section of this chapter aims at showing that Rawls's argument is not justifiable from the Shiite Islamic perspective, a fact that confirms the ultimate affirmation of this book that even Rawls's mildly secular liberalism is not appropriate for Muslims in constructing the basic structure of their society.

Yet, there are sufficient grounds for partial-compatibility between Rawls's political morality and Shiite Islam. As indicated above, while in *PL* Rawls intends to articulate "a particular theory of justice as fairness" applicable only to liberal democratic societies, part of his concern in *LP* is the articulation of "a particular theory of decency" applicable to nonliberal societies, including Shiite Islamic societies. He proposes that a decent Islamic society, which does not accept Rawls's conception of justice as fairness, "is the best" arrangement for nonliberal societies from a liberal perspective.[44] Rawls's recognition of a decent Islamic state requires liberal states "to refrain from exercising political sanctions—military, economic, or diplomatic—to make" decent Muslims change their way of life. Rawls suggests that "liberal peoples must try to encourage decent peoples and not frustrate their vitality by coercively insisting that all societies be liberal."[45] Rawls's particular theory of decency for nonliberal societies reads as follows:

1. Decent societies should lack any aggressive aim by pursuing their national interests through peaceful means.
2. They should respect a "minimal" set of universal "human rights" for their citizens, including: (a) the right to life, (b) the right to freedom from slavery, (c) the right to liberty of conscience and religion, (d) the right to personal property, and (e) the right to formal equality (in the sense that similar cases be treated similarly).[46]

3. There should be some duties and obligations that are publicly recognized by citizens, rather than being merely imposed on them by force.
4. Authorities of a decent society should sincerely believe that a common idea of justice should guide the law.[47]

Hence, there is a broad scope for Shiite Muslim societies to develop their own conception of justice with recourse to their own public political culture. According to Rawls's theory of decency, a conception of religious democracy, which is the preferred political system for modern Shiite Islamic societies, can be legitimate and should be respected by liberal regimes. In brief, Rawls's particular theory of justice as fairness, which disengages from Shiite Muslim societies, does not provide any ground for incompatibility between his political morality and Shiite Islam. In addition, his theory of decency, which engages with Shiite Muslim societies, provides a ground for partial-compatibility between his political morality and Shiite Islamic thought.

Rawls's Argument for His Conception of Justice

Rawls's transformed theory of justice has employed and enhanced some ideas implicit in the public political culture of liberal democratic societies added to some general facts leading altogether to the priority of justice over all ideas of the good. Put more accurately, Rawls intends to fundamentally support "the conviction that a constitutional democratic regime is reasonably just and workable, and worth defending."[48] Hence, he develops his theory of justice to strongly defend liberal democracy.

Employing his method of reflective equilibrium, Rawls deliberately selects some ideas from "a variety of possible organising ideas" found in the public political culture of liberal democratic societies to provide a coherent argument in support of equal freedom along with inequalities in economic benefits and political positions.[49] In what follows, Rawls's transformed theory of justice built upon selected fundamental ideas from the public political culture of liberal democratic societies along with some facts known from the analysis of these societies will be examined. These facts and ideas altogether lead to his two principles of justice as fairness.[50]

The general facts he ascribes to liberal democratic societies are the following:

1. It is impossible to arrive consensually at one conception of the good due to the "burdens of judgement."
2. Therefore, the reasonable pluralism in these societies is permanent.

3. Consequently, the domination of one comprehensive doctrine requires "oppression" of other doctrines.

4. Moreover, we know from experience that stability depends upon justifiability of any conception of justice to the majority of active citizens.

5. Nevertheless, the political culture of a liberal democratic society contains some ideas the resort to which enables us "to work up a political conception of justice suitable for a constitutional regime." These selected ideas, according to Rawls, are sequentially as follows: (a) the idea of society as a fair system of cooperation; (b) the idea of a well-ordered society and its application to the basic structure; (c) the original position as conditions under which the terms of social cooperation should be determined; and finally (d) the idea of the persons who engage in social cooperation as free, equal, and rational-reasonable citizens.[51]

In developing his theory, Rawls adopts some ideas from the mainstream culture in liberal democratic societies.[52] This culture is a civilization that is modern, urban, secular (though definitely incorporating some Christian beliefs), industrialized and with special emphasis on individualism and autonomy.[53] However, the major concern of this book is the degree to which Rawls's political liberalism has softened the secularity of Mill's comprehensive liberalism. Hence, this chapter intends to scrutinize only the secularity of the mainstream culture in liberal democratic societies. By examining the secularity of Rawls's argument for political liberalism, this chapter aims at showing that his theory still belongs to the secular culture, and hence falls short of being justifiable to Shiite Muslims.[54] In his review of Waldron's *Law and Disagreement,* Richard Posner suggests that "not only will deeply religious people refuse to be persuaded that atheists have a superior conception of the good; they will refuse to be persuaded that secular theorists of justice like Rawls have a superior conception of justice."[55] Put another way, Waldron contends that doctrinal pluralism is not the only pluralism to be overcome in modern democratic societies. What is more, "justice-pluralism" and disagreement about a collection of citizens' rights should be dealt with by political philosophy.[56] Hence, *theoretical disagreement* between all variants of liberalism and Shiite Islam is inevitable.

However, Rawls's political liberalism, as a particular theory for liberal democratic societies, might be reconstructed as addressing the following questions justifiable answers to which together build his argument in defense of the political conception of justice as fairness for a liberal democratic society: (1) What is the urgent problem for contemporary liberalism? (2) What is human society? (3) What is a human being? (4) What is the legitimate basis of social cooperation? (5) What is the ultimate end for human society? (6) How should a political conception of justice be worked out? (7) How is the political conception of justice as fairness inferred?

What Is the Urgent Problem for Contemporary Liberalism?

The Fact of Permanent Reasonable Pluralism

The first fact from five facts found in contemporary liberal societies, as Rawls recognizes, is a permanent disagreement about the conception of the good life.[57] As Gray puts it, the determination of the terms of "peaceful coexistence" among proponents of different, and perhaps incommensurable, worldviews is generally the "liberal problem."[58] Here, to ground his theory of justice as fairness in noncontroversial principles as much as possible, Rawls employs the notion of "reasonable pluralism" to be addressed by political liberalism, abandoning some other controversial conceptions, such as pluralism and skepticism. This diversity of comprehensive doctrines about the good life is so permanent that "no one of these doctrines is affirmed by citizens generally. Nor should one expect that in the foreseeable future one of them, or some other reasonable doctrine, will ever be affirmed by all, or nearly all, citizens." According to Rawls, this inevitable diversity of ideas derives generally from the human ability of reasoning. This ground is further reinforced by liberties and rights that are secured by liberal institutions.[59] Hence, what can be reasonable in the situation of the impossibility of agreement over the conception of the good is the search for a just procedure for managing social life and settling disputes over ultimate ends: the superiority of justice over all ideas of the good.[60] As Dombrowski argues, while for the ancient and medieval philosophers the major problem was the conception of the good, for modern philosophers the major problem is doing justice to all in the situation of disagreement about the good.[61] However, the permanency of reasonable plural doctrines about the good life lies in the burdens of judgment.

The Fact of the Burdens of Judgment

In detail, Rawls mentions six sources of disagreement among reasonable individuals: (1) complexity of evidence relating to the issue involved, (2) difficulty in ranking values, (3) shortcomings of concepts, (4) discrepancy of experiences of people, (5) contradiction between various values relating to the issue involved, and (6) the restriction of space in any social institution to accommodate all values that requires balancing various values. These sources of disagreement have produced or will produce some different reasonable doctrines, as well as some other "mad" doctrines about the good.

By reasonable doctrines Rawls means those doctrines that affirm a set of coherent values on the basis of theoretical reason, in addition to ranking them when conflict arises in accordance with practical reason, along with potentiality of slow evolution over time. The task of political liberalism, according to Rawls, is to accommodate only the reasonable doctrines and "to contain [unreasonable doctrines] . . . so that they do not undermine the unity and justice of society." Although "some conflicting reasonable judgments . . . may be true, others false; conceivably, all may be false," Rawls suggests that "these burdens of judgment are of first significance for a democratic idea of toleration."[62] Therefore, political liberalism rejects the legitimacy of coercion in favor of any doctrine assumed to be true.

The fact of permanent reasonable disagreement on conceptions of the good life, as will be explored in chapter 8, is approved by the Qur'an. Therefore, there is no secular element in Rawls's idea of reasonable disagreement derived from the burdens of judgment. Yet, Rawls's starting point, deliberately adopted, marks his theory as particular to modern, urban, industrial and of course secularized societies of the West. Consequently, his solution for this particular problem would restrict the value of his theory to Western societies confronting this particular and urgent question and other *similar* societies.[63] Therefore, some societies may find it more urgent to cope with modernization, urbanization, economic development, and the like, than to deal primarily with diversity of comprehensive doctrines about the good life. It is partly for this particularity that Rawls admits the decency of reasonable religious regimes.[64]

In brief, Rawls intends to overcome the problem of permanent reasonable disagreement on ideas of the good life. For this purpose, he deliberately adopts the fundamental idea of society as a fair system of cooperation among free and equal citizens over a complete life from one generation to the other as the starting point.

What is Human Society?

The Idea of Society as a Fair System of Cooperation

Rawls's idea of society as a fair system of cooperation among citizens consists in its turn of two other fundamental ideas: first, there are citizens in the sense of free, equal, rational, and reasonable persons in society, and second, that their relationship should be conceived of as fairly cooperative. The way Rawls presents this "central" and most "fundamental idea" differs in *PL* from that in *TJ*.[65]

In his early work, borrowing Hume's notion of "the circumstances of justice,"[66] Rawls argues that (1) a society is an association of individuals,

(2) the society members obtain a better life by social cooperation than when they choose to live alone, (3) the chance of obtaining a better life has motivated individuals to assemble, (4) a society is regulated by a collection of binding rules with which its members in most cases comply, and (5) since each individual pursues a larger proportion of social benefits that differs from the same inclination by others, conflicts of interests arise in social life. These assumptions require, as Rawls infers, some principles of social justice that assign rights and duties of each individual in the basic structure of society, and explain the "appropriate distribution of the benefits and burdens of social cooperation."[67] Later, Rawls departs from his earlier view about social life that is an alternative to the Aristotelian view of society as the natural entity resulting from the completion of families and villages with no voluntary entrance.[68]

In his revised idea, he suggests that society cannot be conceived of as being an "association" individuals have entered into voluntarily, as his initial idea *implies*. Rather, he presupposes that human society is viewed as a fair system of cooperation among free and equal citizens over a complete life from one generation to the other.[69] This revised idea is "the fundamental organising idea of justice as fairness, within which the other basic ideas are systematically connected."[70] Far from being a reasoned premise, this central and most fundamental idea about social life is a mere presupposition that Rawls affirms by a supposedly empirical investigation into the ideas implicit in the public political culture of liberal democratic societies. He asserts that in a democratic society citizens "regard" their social life as a system of social cooperation as opposed to a "fixed natural order," or an "institutional structure justified by religious doctrines" and the like.[71]

To elaborate: initially, Rawls argues that social cooperation should be distinguished from "coordinated activity" organized by some rules issued from above. "Cooperation," Rawls explains, "is guided by publicly recognised rules and procedures that those cooperating accept." Furthermore, the fairness of social cooperation lies in the conception of "reciprocity" in the sense that each participant accepts and acts in accordance with the determined social terms provided that others do the same. Finally, cooperation indicates that each cooperating member pursues his own rational advantage through social cooperation.[72]

Shiite Islam partly agrees with Rawls on his central idea of society as a fair system of cooperation. First, as Barry convincingly suggests, there is a necessary connection between the theorization about justice and the rejection of society as a fixed natural phenomenon.[73] Hence, since the Qur'an declares that the ultimate purpose of sending the Messengers by God is that people uphold justice, it implies that the Qur'an conceives of society as a system of cooperation between men.[74] As for the fairness of this cooperation, again the Qur'an confirms Rawls's idea of reciprocity. The Qur'an says: "Shall the recompense of goodness be other than goodness?"[75] Yet, as this chapter proposes in examining Rawls's idea of citizenship, it does not follow that no rule from God should be sent to man for completion of his knowledge and strengthening of his motive.

However, the idea of society as a fair system of cooperation is accompanied by some more basic ideas about the person. This brings us to Rawls's idea of the person as free, equal, reasonable, and rational that this chapter will now discuss.[76]

What Is a Human Being?

The Idea of Citizens as Free, Equal, and Rational-Reasonable Persons
In *LP,* Rawls unequivocally denies that his theory is built upon any account of human nature, though this, Rawls admits, is a common attitude in political philosophy. What he suggests is "a political conception of persons as citizens instead."[77] Put another way, as opposed to Mill who presents an empirical and clear picture of human nature and its potentialities, Rawls merely proposes that we *should* conceive citizens' moral psychology as being constructed such that it supports the political conception of justice as fairness. "We *must* start with the assumption that," says Rawls, "a reasonably just political society is possible, and for it to be possible, human beings must have a moral nature." Furthermore, he suggests that we *must* determine "how citizens need to be conceived . . . and what their moral psychology has to be to support a reasonably just political society over time."[78] Therefore, Rawls asks us to "conceive" citizens for political purposes as free and equal, as well as rational and reasonable persons.[79]

Freedom of the Persons: Rawls maintains that on the basis of his findings people in liberal democratic societies "conceive of themselves" as free in the sense of having three powers: two "moral" powers and one "intellectual" power. The two moral powers are "a capacity for a sense of justice and for a conception of the good," whereas the intellectual power concerns the capacity to reason. On the basis of the possession of these three powers along with participation in cooperative social life over a complete life a person deserves the title of "citizen."[80]

To elaborate: Rawls defines the capacity for a sense of justice as "the capacity to understand, to apply, and to act from the public conception of justice." As can be seen, Rawls remains loyal to the liberal image about morality of the person "in the sense of philosophical doctrine," without which not only "the hope for a regime of liberty may be unrealistic,"[81] but also it would not be "worthwhile for human beings to live on the earth."[82] In *TJ* Rawls asks us merely to "assume that each person beyond a certain age and possessed of the requisite intellectual capacity develops a sense of justice under normal social circumstances."[83] By transforming his utopian theory into a feasible one, in *PL* he maintains that "citizens' sense of justice, given their traits of character and interests as formed by living under a just basic structure, is strong enough to resist the normal tendencies to injustice."[84]

As for the sense for a conception of the good, Rawls defines it as "the capacity to form, to revise and rationally to pursue a conception of one's rational advantage or good" that consists of our loyalties to various groups, as well as our view about our relationship with the world." Furthermore, the "public or institutional identity" of persons that determines their basic rights is fixed, independent, and superior to their specific conceptions of the good. Yet, it should be admitted that their "moral identity" differs by virtue of their attachments and loyalties that may change over time "usually slowly but sometimes rather suddenly." Contrary to communitarians, Rawls here emphasizes that no change to our institutional identity or personal identity that is the subject of social rights will occur when we convert from one religion to another or to atheism. Hence, while our "moral identity" in such a conversion has been changed, it "implies no change in our public or institutional identity, nor in our personal identity."[85]

In addition to possessing two moral powers, another aspect in which citizens in liberal democratic societies regard themselves as free, according to Rawls, is that "they regard themselves as being entitled to make claims on their institutions so as to advance their conceptions of the good," in contrast with slaves who seem not to possess any valid claim. Put another way, citizens in liberal democratic societies can bear rights against their social and political institutions. Finally, citizens 'are viewed as capable of taking responsibility for their ends."[86] Altogether, the two moral powers and the intellectual power, along with the potentiality of bearing rights and responsibilities, constitute the notion of freedom Rawls invokes to justify the principles of justice as fairness.

Equality of the Persons: A further idea is that not only are citizens free, but that each citizen also equally possesses the aforementioned powers and potentiality. "Citizens are equal," suggests Rawls, "in virtue of possessing, to the requisite minimum degree, the two moral powers and the other capacities that enable us to be normal and fully cooperating members of society." It is this equality of citizens that justifies Rawls's final conclusion that "all who meet this condition have the same basic rights, liberties, and opportunities."[87] Hence, differences of individuals in other aspects should be considered irrelevant to citizenship as the subject of social rights and obligations.

However, Rawls's assertion that equality is a conception found in the public political culture of liberal democratic societies has been called into question. Bader's charge against Rawls is that his idealized situation of citizens of contemporary liberal democratic societies in the West ignores the fact of discrimination with regard to sex, gender, race, ethnicity, and class.[88] Likewise, Hampton argues that "the persistence of racial discrimination, sexism, and exploitation betrays a commitment by many to the second-class status of some of their fellows."[89] Thus, these thinkers register doubt over Rawls's assumption about this component of the public political culture of Western liberal democratic societies.

Rationality and Reasonableness of the Persons: One more intuitive idea that Rawls employs to construct his political conception of justice assumes individuals as rational and reasonable to whom the task of determining the fair terms of social cooperation should be entrusted, rather than to God or to aristocrats and the like. Rationality characterizes a person who has adopted a coherent, hierarchical set of available purposes and preferences and a scheme that brings him most of his preferences.[90] Furthermore, rationality has two more features:[91] first, a rational agent is not an envious person who seeks "a loss for himself if only others have less as well." Nor, second, is a rational agent an altruist who seeks to benefit others. Rather, rational agents are those "mutually disinterested" persons each of whom pursues his own benefits with no incentive to harm others.[92]

The "reasonableness" of citizens concerns the way individuals manage their relationship with each other as persons or associations with specific purposes.[93] The first aspect of reasonableness concerns the readiness of persons to "propose principles and standards as fair terms of cooperation and to abide by them willingly, given the assurance that others will likewise do so." The other aspect concerns "the willingness to recognise the burdens of judgment and to accept their consequences for the use of public reason in directing the legitimate exercise of political power in a constitutional regime."[94]

Overall, a rational-reasonable person should be conceived of as having a coherent arrangement to maximize the attainment of his preferences in quantity, quality, and possibility, along with the readiness to accept the consequences of reciprocity and to avoid recourse to state coercion for achieving his specific view about the good life. It is worth noticing that in *TJ,* Rawls defines reasonableness as the readiness of a person to honor others' views with the aim to advance his own benefit in the long run. What motivates the person to reciprocity lies in the instrumentality of honoring others' views to attracting their honors for himself. By contrast, in *PL,* Rawls corrects this "mistake" and defines reasonableness as a separate and independent moral value of fairness to others.[95] This is a major shift with regard to motivation of behaving justly. With this, Rawls replaces his motivational assumption for behaving justly on rationality and mutual advantage in the long run with impartiality and its intrinsically moral worth.[96]

However, Rawls's firm assurance that each member would comply with the fair terms of social cooperation if others comply with these terms has been questioned. The problem with a disinterested and rational agent, as Bellamy and Hollis argue, lies in the rationality of compliance with social obligations. If compliance is not rational in some cases, "'free-riding" devastates the system of social cooperation. It seems that the rational agent benefits from social cooperation both when he does his fair share and when he does not by cheating. Rawls's attempt to overcome this problem by proposing the notion of reasonableness in *PL*—while rational choice theory still provides the rational agent with the choice of cheating and free riding— seems to have failed. The only solution would be to facilitate this idea with a "philosophical psychology or a metaphysical doctrine of the self, which includes [a] Kantian power of reason to override inclination, renders agents less individualistic and more sociable." Hence, since Rawls abstains from constructing his theory on such a metaphysical view about human nature, the problem of obedience among rational maximizer members persists as unsolvable if they notice that cheating and free riding is possible.[97]

Shiite Islam agrees with Rawls's idea of citizenship and the moral personality of man. When the Qur'an asks Muslims to follow the requirements of justice even against their interests, it definitely confirms that man has the capacity for a sense of justice.[98] Furthermore, when the Qur'an asks people to contemplate on the Qur'an, and when it appreciates those who think about the world and the features of the sky and earth, it confirms the human capacity for understanding the conceptions of the good.[99] More explicitly, the Qur'an declares that man has the moral capacity for understanding the conceptions of the good: "By the soul and Him who fashioned it, and inspired it with [discernment between] its virtues and vices."[100] Finally, when the Qur'an expects people to follow religious rules, it implies that those persons can take responsibility for their actions and goals, as opposed to slaves. According to the Qur'an, on the Day of Judgment it is each individual that should stand in front of God and answer His questions.[101] In addition, no one bears the responsibility of others' actions.[102] Hence, if every individual will be responsible on the Day of Judgment with regard to what he does in his earthly life, he should be conceived of as being capable to take responsibility for his actions and ends.

What follows from all these Qur'anic verses is the rejection of communitarianism. For if the community cannot be held responsible for the wrongdoing of its members, the required rights and opportunities for taking responsibility for one's action should be granted to the individual. The individual is free and equal to any other, and he can make decisions as justice requires.

Yet, it does not follow that Godly revelation cannot act as a complementary source for human moral capabilities and his intellectual power. As was discussed in chapter 2, Shiite Islam maintains that Godly revelation acts as a complementary source for morality, by expanding man's natural knowledge and completing his motive to act justly, along with activating the natural endowments by reminding him of his common constitution.[103] Equally agreeable is Rawls's idea that all human beings are equal in possessing these moral capabilities and intellectual power. Yet, it does not follow that God and His knowledge is equal to human beings and their knowledge. It is true, however, that Shiite Islam maintains that the infallible access to the superior knowledge of God was restricted to a very limited time when God's infallible Messengers and their infallible successors were available to human beings. Nevertheless, in other times, human beings still have fallible access to God's superior knowledge as a complementary source, which should carefully be interpreted. Rawls dismisses the relevance of religious principles in determining the terms of social life, even if they are articulated through careful interpretations of God's superior knowledge, to which human beings have fallible access. For this crucial objection, Rawls's argument cannot be justifiable to committed Shiite Muslims and hence they cannot adopt Rawls's conception of justice for constructing the basic structure of their societies.

However, Rawls assumes that persons living in contemporary liberal democratic societies are free, equal, rational, and reasonable citizens. Faced with the problem of permanent, reasonable plurality of comprehensive doctrines about the good life, citizens seek to determine some principles for their social cooperation. Rawls's complementary idea for these citizens in determining the terms of social cooperation brings him to the liberal principle of legitimacy.

What Is the Legitimate Way of Social Cooperation?

The Fact of Oppression
Given the inevitability of reasonable disagreement about the good, according to Rawls, the adoption of one comprehensive doctrine by the state from among the conflicting ideas would require the use of oppression over citizens.

The history of the Middle Ages demonstrates that preserving one shared religion requires state suppression of heresy. The same necessity holds, suggests Rawls, when the state chooses a comprehensive liberal doctrine, such as those of Kant and Mill. Hence, achievement of a peaceful cooperation would dismiss the possibility of uniformity. It is the desirability of securing a peaceful and stable society that requires the free and willing support of majority of political active citizens. What Rawls invokes at this stage demonstrates his commitment to "the liberal principle of legitimacy" according to which the "exercise of political power is proper and hence justifiable only when it is exercised in accordance with a constitution, the essentials of which all citizens may reasonably be expected to endorse in the light of principles and ideals acceptable to them as reasonable and rational."[104] Put another way, as the corollary of assuming persons as free and equal citizens engaged in social cooperation, the oppressive use of political power is illegitimate.

However, it is worth noticing that the original principle of legitimacy is based upon the actual consent of *each* person who is affected by the state policies. Hence, Waldron proposes that "all aspects of social world should either be made acceptable or be capable of being made acceptable to *every last individual.*"[105] Likewise, Nagel suggests that the "ultimate aim of political theory," including liberal political theory, is "to justify a political system to *everyone* who is required to live under it," rather than being acceptable only to a *selected portion* of reasonable citizens.[106] Hence, Rawls's exclusion of unreasonable citizens from the principle of legitimacy in his liberal political theory should be conceived of as being essentially similar to alternative illiberal theories that legitimize the employment of the state coercive power over those who do not consent to it.[107]

Rawls's formulation of the liberal principle of legitimacy shows another secular element in his argument, and hence cannot be justifiable to Shiite Muslims. By grounding the legitimacy of the employment of the state coercive power in citizens' consent, Rawls opposes the Shiite Islamic view of dual legitimacy, which also stipulates God's consent to the basic structure of society and major policies pursued by the state. It should be noted that those religious citizens who have subscribed to the view of dual legitimacy attempt to discover God's consent by careful interpretation of religious texts, which they believe originated from God's revelation. Therefore, not only does Rawls's formulation of legitimacy exclude from the citizenry unreasonable people whose consent should be required, but he also ignores some alternative religious views of legitimacy that are supported by some religious citizens.

However, Shiite Islam disagrees with Rawls on the fact of oppression and its consequences. It is true that the Qur'an recommends peaceful methods of inviting people to religion: "Invite to the way of your Lord with wisdom and good advice and dispute with them in a manner that is best."[108] More explicitly, the Qur'an rejects the moral legitimacy of imposing any religion on individuals: "There is no compulsion in religion."[109] According to this verse, there should be no compulsion on individuals with regard to submitting to any religion.[110] Since the intellect is only susceptible to rational reasoning, the coercive imposition of doctrines on individuals is *inconceivable*. Furthermore, since Islam is supposedly supported by rational reasons accessible to every individual, there will be no *need* for coercion and compulsion of its principles.[111]

Yet, while the Islamic state should refrain from oppressing citizens with other convictions, a type of religious democracy for societies with a majority of Muslims can be legitimate. Interestingly, Rawls's theory of decency admits the possibility of such a decent religious regime in which while Islam is the dominant religion, other religions are also tolerated. Hence, neither Rawls's argument nor his conception of justice is justifiable to Shiite Muslims in constructing the basic structure of their societies.

However, what follows from the illegitimacy of the oppressive use of political power lies in the prohibition of the pursuit of one conception of the good life by the state. Therefore, the only possibility in contemporary liberal democratic societies is the pursuit of just institutions through which different conceptions of the good find room to present and develop themselves. This brings Rawls to the idea of a well-ordered society not only as the ultimate end, but also as the best we can expect given the current situation of liberal democratic societies.

What Is the Ultimate End for Human Society?

The Idea of a Well-ordered Society

One more idea in Rawls's argument is "the idea of a well-ordered society as a society effectively regulated by a political conception of justice."[112] Faced with the permanent reasonable disagreement on the conceptions of the good and assuming society as a fair system of cooperation among free, equal, and rational-reasonable citizens, as well as the illegitimacy of the oppressive use of political power, political liberalism restricts its ultimate purpose to securing a well-ordered society.

The idea of a well-ordered society as the ultimate goal of political liberalism in its "general meaning" has the following "idealised" features: (1) all citizens not only accept the same conception of justice whatever it be, but they also mutually recognize this knowledge and acceptance; (2) its basic social and political institutions are not only organized so as to satisfy the publicly recognized conception of justice, but this situation is also publicly known; and (3) citizens normally abide by the requirements of the publicly known and recognized conception of justice.[113] Thus, all citizens generally comply with the institutions of the society that they believe to be just.[114] What distinguishes Rawls's theory of justice from other liberal theories of justice, thus, lies in his affirmation that his particular conception of justice as fairness provides "a sufficient as well as the most reasonable basis of social unity available" to liberal societies.[115] Rawls concludes from all the facts and ideas discussed above that in contemporary pluralistic societies with some liberal values, the ultimate end political liberalism should aim at is the "articulation" of a conception of justice which regulates the basic structure of society.[116] This liberal view of justice, as the only reasonable option in the situation of disagreement on the conceptions of good life, is not acceptable to Shiite Islam. Since Shiite Muslims maintain that religion is true, the ultimate end of social cooperation cannot merely be the articulation of a conception of justice that regulates the basic structure of society. Rather, the ultimate end should be the pursuit of the true way of life in a just way. Justice is the guideline for pursuing the true way of life, by recognizing human fallibility and meeting the requirements of impartiality. Interestingly, this conclusion corresponds to Rawls's theory of decency, as was shown earlier.

However, the final step in the articulation of the political conception of justice as fairness would be the articulation of those conditions in which that conception should be fairly worked out. This final step brings Rawls to the idea of the original position.

How Should a Political Conception of Justice Be Worked Out?

The Idea of the Original Position

The device of the original position in Rawls's technique of reflective equilibrium plays a decisive role in choosing from among various alternative suggestions about the conception of justice. At this stage, Rawls attempts to argue that those free, equal, and rational-reasonable citizens who intend to construct a political conception of justice should be located in a situation where all incentives other than seeking justice are removed from them. "One of our considered convictions I assume," argues Rawls, "is this: the fact that we occupy a particular social position is not a good reason for us to propose, or to expect others to accept, a conception of justice that favours those in this position." Rawls adds "the fact that we affirm a particular religious, philosophical, or moral comprehensive doctrine with its associated conception of the good is not a reason for us to propose, or to expect others to accept, a conception of justice that favours those of that persuasion."[117] The task of the philosopher here is to bring us to agree on those conditions required for fairly constructing a conception of justice.

It is worth noticing that most parts of the conditions of the original position in Rawls's transformed theory are discussed as ideas and facts implicit in the public political culture of those liberal democratic societies elaborated above. The major part of the original position, which is quite decisive, is the idea of "the veil of ignorance." The role of the veil of ignorance is to provide each individual with the opportunity for "self-clarification" to fairly determine the conception of justice.[118] The original position is proposed to eliminate the possibility of choosing those principles the rationality of which relates to some purpose other than justice. For instance, it is rational to propose or accept rules that determine reducing various kinds of taxes depending on how wealthy a person will be.[119]

To achieve its goal, the veil of ignorance is designed to deny each party knowledge of (1) his specific social status, (2) his natural assets and capabilities, (3) his intelligence and power, (4) the conception of the good he might adopt, (5) his psychological specificity including his aversion to risk and his optimism or pessimism, (6) the specificities of economic and political situation of his society, and finally (7) the generation to which he belongs.[120] Knowledge of all these would be harmful to a fair judgment about the conception of justice citizens intend to determine. Therefore, the terms of social cooperation should be constructed by free, equal, rational, and reasonable citizens located behind a thick veil of ignorance about those facts and statuses, the awareness of which normally undermines the fairness of their judgment.

Rawls's idea of the original position is a plausible way for modeling the necessary conditions for fair decision making and is acceptable to Shiite Islam.[121] A saying by the Prophet of Islam states that "you should dislike for others whatever you dislike for yourself and like for them whatever you like for yourself. This will make you a just arbitrator and a fair judge."[122] Hence, by entering the original position, a person can successfully contribute to determining the fair terms of social cooperation. Yet, when the individual enters the original position he need not forget that there can be a true way of life, which cannot be equal to false ways of life. It seems that Rawls unconvincingly neglects this latter point. Rawls is neither skeptical nor relativist; rather, he is silent about the truth and leaves these controversies to comprehensive doctrines. While Shiite Islam agrees with Rawls that individuals should determine the terms of social cooperation in an impartial situation, it seems that they should have in mind that the truth is not equal to falsity. While the result will be freedom of conscience and religion, there is no ground for separation of religion and the state. For the majority, who maintain that they follow the true way of life, can establish the state in accordance with their convictions. Yet, on the basis of fairness the majority let minorities pursue their own ways of life, though not with equal access to public funds. Again, we arrive at Rawls's theory of decency, not his theory of justice.

How Is the Political Conception of Justice as Fairness Inferred?

Rawls argues that the derivation of the first principle of justice, equal freedom, from the original position and the veil of ignorance is "obvious." He suggests that "the parties start with a principle requiring equal basic liberties for all, as well as fair equality of opportunity and equal division of income and wealth." Regarding the second principle, he draws our attention to the "economic efficiency and the requirements of organisation and technology." He presupposes that (1) economic efficiency necessarily requires inequality in wealth, (2) efficiency of organization of social and political institutions requires differences in authority, and (3) these inequalities "make everyone better off in comparison with the benchmark of equality," and (4) given that rationality removes envy from the persons, there remains no psychological ground for opposing rational inequalities in wealth and power.[123] Hence, the result of the aforementioned premises is equal basic liberties for all, equal opportunity for each member to achieve social and political offices, and an economic system that increases the life chances of the worst-off members of society.

To clarify: Rawls maintains that under the condition of uncertainty in the original position rational agents would choose the "maximin" strategy in the sense of avoiding the worst possible outcome.[124] The term "maximin" derives from the term *maximum minimorum*, meaning "to maximise the status of the least members."[125] Maximin strategy is "the choice which *maximizes* the *minimum* pay-off," through which the person adopts the alternative "which gives him the smallest losses if everything goes wrong."[126] The alternative utilitarian rule of "expectation-maximising," instead, requires that we consider all outcomes and weigh the likelihood of each, and "choose the course that carries the highest probable-utility." While Rawls admits that the latter approach is naturally more rational than the former, it is because of some particular features of the original position that we follow the conservative maximin strategy. First, since the knowledge of likelihood is impossible or insecure, the measurement of alternative outcomes against each other and choosing the highest probable-utility is unachievable. Furthermore, since individuals know that they have a conception of the good to secure, they care more about securing their conception of the good, and care little about other benefits that they could obtain by choosing the maximum rule.[127] Hence, the risk-averse parties to the original position would decide to minimize the worst-off outcome.[128] This argument also accounts for the lexical order between the two principles. Since everyone is risk-averse, one prefers to secure the minimum share equally to the others, rather than jeopardizing that minimum with the hope to obtain a greater share of economic and social advantages.[129]

This is a brief sketch of the derivation of the two principles of justice as fairness from the facts and ideas discussed above.[130] In the following chapter, I will examine Rawls's principle of equal basic liberties and the way he derives it from the argument mentioned above in depth, leaving the examination of the second principle of justice to further research for two reasons. First, this book is concerned with the secularity of liberalism and its reconcilability with Shiite Islam whose view of liberty can be explored more clearly and with more determinacy. Second, it is Rawls's first principle regarding equal basic liberties that is broadly accepted in the contemporary United States and other liberal societies, whereas his principle of equal opportunity and difference principle are either contested or unaccepted, at least in contemporary United States.[131] Therefore, not only does Rawls's principle of equal basic liberty represent Western liberalism sufficiently, but it also proposes a subject on which there is a clear Islamic view for comparison.

Conclusion

This chapter examined the Theoretical Partial-Compatibility Proposition regarding Rawls's liberalism and Shiite Islam by looking at Rawls's egalitarian political morality. The mildness of the secularity of his political morality, which confirms this partial-compatibility, can be summarized in the following points.

(1/a) Like Mill, Rawls maintains that the right to determine the terms of social cooperation belongs to human beings, though he refrains from an explicit declaration that God has no right to set moral rules for human beings.

(1/b) Shiite Islam explicitly maintains that God has the right to help human beings to determine the principles of the true way of life in a just way.

(2/a) Unlike Mill, Rawls does not announce that God should follow his (Rawls's) conception of social justice, thought he (Rawls) expects religious people to subordinate their transcendent doctrines to his (Rawls's) principles of justice.

(2/b) Shiite Islam agrees with Rawls that justice is the supreme social value and should override utility. Yet, it combines human transcendent happy life with the requirement of justice in the temporary world.

(3/a) Unlike Mill, Rawls refrains from engaging with observation about the ultimate conception of the good life and confining it to the happiness in the earthly life. He successfully restricts his theorization to the articulation of a reasonable conception for the basic structure of liberal democratic societies. Hence, what he expects of Shiite Muslims is confined to the concept of reasonable citizenship.

(3/b) Shiite Islam appreciates Rawls's disengagement from the ultimate conception of the good life and his abstinence from rejecting Islam as untrue or even as an unreasonable doctrine of the good life. The concept of the self-restrained Muslim, which Shiite Islam requires from its followers abroad, corresponds to Rawls's concept of reasonable citizens.

(4/a) Rawls's particular theory of justice as fairness disengages from Shiite Muslim societies. However, his theory of decency, which engages with Shiite Muslim societies, provides a space where Shiite Muslim societies can construct the basic structure of their own.

(4/b) Shiite Islam appreciates Rawls's theory of decency, which potentially confirms the establishment of religious democracy for Shiite Muslim societies. However, Rawls's argument for his theory of justice is not justifiable to Shiite Muslims in most parts, and hence cannot lead Muslim societies in constructing the basic structure of their own.

CHAPTER 6

Rawls's Liberty Principle

This chapter examines the Theoretical Partial-Compatibility Proposition regarding Rawls's liberalism and Shiite Islam by looking at Rawls's principle of liberty. First, Rawls's particular conception of civil liberty will be discussed. Moreover, the development of Rawls's principle of liberty from maximal equal liberty to a fully adequate scheme of equal basic liberties will be subjected to critical examination. Finally, his particular list of equal basic liberties will be explored.

As for his conception of civil liberty, Rawls suggests that liberty is the permissibility of doing or not doing something and this requires legal prohibition on interference by others. He suggests that a person can be said to be free to the extent that he is permitted legally to decide about doing or not doing something, and to the extent that government and society are obliged legally not to interfere with his action. In this way, dismissing the common dichotomy introduced by Berlin between negative and positive liberty, Rawls seems to affirm only one conception for liberty comprising noninterference as well as the ability to do what one wishes.

Rawls's particular principle of liberty is characterized by four ideas: (a) the greatest possible liberty, (b) the superiority of liberty over all other ends and rights, (c) the equal entitlement of all citizens to liberty, and finally (d) a preferred list of basic liberties. He departs from the idea of the greatest possible liberty in his later writings and attempts to expound different aspects of the other three ideas.

By persistently showing his commitment to the superiority of liberty over all other goods and rights, Rawls seems to have failed to account for the restriction of basic liberties by the harm principle. As for equal entitlement to basic liberties, he affirms the equal worth of political liberties only and legitimizes inequalities in the real worth of other basic liberties. The combination of these two ideas seems not only practically unsustainable, but also morally insignificant. The most important charge against his preferred list of basic liberties concerns its dependence on a particular conception of the good, which may not be shared by religion.

Rawls's liberty principle is unjustifiable on the basis of Shiite Islamic thought for his narrow conceptualization of human progress, as well as his insufficient attention to the issue of blasphemy. Shiite Islam disagrees with Rawls's humanist picture of man and proposes that the path toward progress is one that is determined by human nature. In addition, Rawls's explicit affirmation that the freedom of speech is only restricted by security and social order, which is not threatened by free speech in developed societies, is not acceptable. Absolute freedom of speech ignores the violation of Muslims' integrity by blasphemous speech.

Yet, theoretically he positions the right to freedom of conscience and religion at the top of human values. In addition, he devotes the strongest part of his argument to supporting the equal right to freedom of conscience and religion. However, Rawls's abstinence from any refutation of religion does not persist throughout his philosophical theorization. For the defense of his preferred list of basic liberties has led him to invoke the Millian idea of the desirability of diversity and individuality, which implicitly indicates that all monist doctrines, including religions, are evil, no matter how reasonable they would be in accordance with his idea of reasonableness. Here, Rawls slips toward perfectionist theories of liberalism and loses the major merit of his theory.

The Conception of Liberty

Reluctant to engage with definitional controversy about the conception of liberty, Rawls "simply assume[s]" that liberty can be understood by considering three "items" in this regard. In the first place, there should be an "agent" described as being free who is the bearer of freedom. One more item of freedom concerns those "restrictions" and obstacles from which the agent is free, that is, the absence of deliberate interference by others. And finally, a free agent should be provided with opportunity of making choice as he wishes. Hence, the mere absence of external interference is not sufficient for the conception of freedom. The agent should also be able "to do or not to do" something.[1]

Put another way, Rawls suggests that a person can be said to be free to the extent that he is permitted legally to decide about doing or not doing something, and to the extent that government and society are obliged legally not to interfere with his action. He defines liberty in terms of the permissibility of doing or not doing an action, the other side of which requires legally society and government be obliged not to interfere.[2] Like

Mill, Rawls seems to include in his simple definition of liberty what Berlin calls negative and positive liberty. Hence, Jeffrey Paul seems wrong to assume that Rawls defines freedom "negatively" as the "freedom to do certain things unrestricted by a variety of potential constraints."[3] There are not, according to Rawls, two conceptions for liberty pointing to different types of freedom. Freedom is simply the ability to do or not to do something requiring the absence of all external interferences by government and society in the way of realization of a free man's wish. The rejection of the dichotomous conception of liberty requires the interpretation of the conflict between negative and positive liberty as a rivalry between different cases of liberty and "the relative values of the several liberties when they come into conflict."[4]

The Principle of Liberty

Rawls's first principle of justice articulates the republican ideal of citizenship, according to which "all citizens share the identical set of common citizenship rights."[5] This principle expresses the core liberal commitment to the significance of liberty derived from the value of equality of citizenship.[6] If there is no hierarchy in individuals' relationship on the basis of which some can impose their will on others, each will be free to manage his own personal affairs as he wishes. As was discussed earlier in this book, liberalism in general is a theory of liberty. It was established that Mill's specific liberalism values individual liberty in the aspects of thought and expression absolutely, while restricting liberty of action through the harm principle. With regard to freedom of action, thus, Mill's liberal theory prioritizes the value of no harm over the value of liberty. Although Rawls shares the liberal concern with the priority of liberty, what characterizes Rawls's theory of liberalism lies in his commitment to four ideas about liberty as follows: (1) the idea of the greatest possible liberty or basic liberties; (2) the idea of the superiority of liberty not only over all human ends, but also over all other rights and primary goods; (3) his specific idea of equal liberty or basic liberties for each person; and finally (4) his preferred list of basic liberties and the relationship among different rights and liberties.

Rawls provides us with three different formulations of his principle of liberty in his writings, departing from some of these ideas and modifying some others in his later formulation of the principle. To capture precisely Rawls's specific theory of liberty, a comprehensive examination of the above four ideas in their chronological development is undertaken in the following part of this section. As will be demonstrated, Rawls's particular principle of liberty is the focal point for the assessment of the secularity of his liberalism, as well as the degree to which he has succeeded in softening Mill's comprehensive liberalism.

The Idea of the Greatest Possible Liberty

One controversial idea about liberty, which Rawls suggests in his earlier formulation of the principle of liberty in "Justice as Fairness," derives the value of maximizing liberty from its value. Liberty is so worthwhile a liberal value that the more liberty is provided, the more basic human value is achieved. Therefore, while primarily what justice requires is equal liberty for all, suggests the early Rawls, "if, however, a greater liberty were possible for all without loss or conflict, then it would be irrational to settle on a lesser liberty." Hence, Rawls calls the first principle of justice in his early article as the principle of "the greatest equal liberty" indicating that "each person participating in a practice, or affected by it, has an equal right to the most extensive liberty compatible with a like liberty for all."[7]

Although Rawls modifies the formulation of his idea of liberty in *TJ*, he maintains his commitment to the value of maximum liberty. "Each person," contends Rawls in his last formulation of the principle of liberty in *TJ*, "is to have an equal right to the most extensive total system of equal basic liberties compatible with a similar system of liberty for all."[8] Therefore, while Rawls shifts from the idea of liberty as such to the value of a certain collection of basic liberties determined by a list, he still proposes that this collection of basic liberties should be advanced to the most possible portion for each person.

The idea of the greatest possible portion of liberty, or basic liberties, has been questioned by O'Neil on the ground that a maximal set of liberty assumes wrongly the possibility of identifying a set of liberties which is "larger" than another set of liberties in the sense of containing the "most member' of liberties. O'Neil rejects this possibility on the ground that we can always "show that any given set of liberties was as numerous as any other merely by listing the component liberties more specifically."[9] Therefore, the greatest liberty in the sense of the most numerous collection of liberties is inconceivable.

One further possibility of identifying a set of maximal liberties would be to assume that there can be a set of liberties that includes all liberties in other sets with some additional liberties particular to itself, that is, there can be a dominant set of liberties. O'Neill also dismisses this supposition with recourse to the possibility of assuming two incompatible liberties for a set of persons, such as the freedom of association, which justifies the dismissal of gay teachers, and freedom from homophobic discrimination, which prohibits such dismissal, as Gray suggests.[10] The idea of incommensurability of different liberties undermines the possibility of identifying a set of dominant liberties.

Another interpretation of the most extensive liberties, according to O'Neill, is to assume that there can be a set of core liberties shared by all co-possible sets of liberties, which is larger than any other set of basic liberties. She, also, rejects this interpretation by denying the possibility of identifying a set of core liberties that can be shared by all co-possible sets of liberties. For it is always possible to form a "counterpart set of liberties" that shares no liberty in those sets of which it is the counterpart. For instance, if we form a set of liberties, which includes the liberty to vote, it is possible to assume a counterpart set of liberties, which include the liberty to prevent others from voting. Hence, one cannot identify a set of core liberties that can be shared by all co-possible liberties and considered as the largest set of basic liberties.[11]

However, Rawls's shift from the value of liberty as such in "Justice as Fairness" to the idea of "basic liberties" in *TJ* does not lead him to modify his idea of the greatest possible liberty. He suggests that it is a specific collection of basic liberties that should be maximized. Yet when he addresses some objections to the first principle of justice as fairness in *PL*, he explicitly departs from the idea of maximum liberty. For, firstly, "we cannot maximise the development and exercise of two moral powers at once." Furthermore, "it would be madness," Rawls goes on to admit, "to maximise just and rational actions by maximising the occasions which require them." Therefore, he replaces the idea of the greatest liberty with "a fully adequate scheme of basic liberties."[12]

The Idea of the Superiority of Liberty

One more idea, which characterizes Rawls's specific theory of liberty, strongly attaches absolute superiority to liberty, or basic liberties. Although Rawls is not explicit about the superiority of liberty over all other human goods and rights in his early article, the issue is forcefully stated both in *TJ* and in *PL*. To Rawls, a collection of basic liberties has priority not only over various human ends, but also over other basic rights and primary goods, such as the access to public offices. The priority of liberty, which should be guaranteed by the constitution, over other values pursued by legislatures "is reflected in the priority of the constitutional convention to the legislative stage." This idea is vigorously demonstrated in what Rawls calls "the priority rule" in which Rawls suggests that the "principles of justice are to be ranked in lexical order." Hence, "liberty can be restricted only for the sake of liberty." The first principle of justice as fairness is prior to the second and hence no infringement of basic liberties can be justifiable with reference, for instance, to necessity of promotion of economic welfare. Only one set of liberties can override another set when conflict arises.[13]

The idea of the superiority of liberty and its self-containment apparently shows Rawls's attempt to realize the liberals' aspiration to position liberty at the top of human values.[14] As was shown in chapter 3, Mill rules out denies the self-containment of liberty by prioritizing the harm principle over the liberty principle: liberty should be valued so far as it does not harm anyone. Rawls's commitment to the superiority of liberty is not what Rawls departs from even in his last formulation. "The priority of liberty," suggests Rawls in *PL,* "implies in practice that a basic liberty can be limited or denied solely for the sake of one or more other basic liberties." This self-containment of basic liberties rejects the justifiability of "reasons of public good or of perfectionist values" to restrict any basic liberty.[15]

However, Rawls's unambiguous emphasis on the absoluteness of the superiority of liberty over all other human goals and rights by the idea of lexical order as well as the self-containment of liberty is not consistent with other ideas to which he is still committed. By an unequivocal expression, Rawls not only admits the necessary restriction of liberty of conscience, as an obvious case of basic liberties, for the sake of "public order and security," but also suggests that this restriction is what *everyone* agrees with.[16] Even if public order and security are valued for their crucial instrumentality in enabling citizens to pursue their interests and to fulfill their obligations necessary for the enjoyment of individual liberty, public order and security are different concepts from liberty. Thus, Rawls should admit that the value of security and public order is higher than that of individual liberty and it is the superiority of security and public order over liberty that legitimizes the restriction of the latter by the former. The definite superiority of security over liberty destroys Rawls's appreciation for superiority of liberty and its self-containment, and brings his theory of liberty in line with Mill's theory of liberty, which compromises liberty by the harm principle.

It is, also, the superiority of security and public order over liberty that accounts for conditionality of the priority of liberty upon "reasonably favourable conditions," which support the exercise of basic liberties, such as "the political will," the "level of economic advance" of the society involved, public culture of managing institutions skilfully and democratically, and so forth. Rawls contends that, for instance, these conditions are met in the present United States. Therefore, the superiority of liberty in practice over all other human values can be held in a country such as the United States where liberty might not threaten security, which is the highest value. Put another way, while in cases of conflict between liberty and security the former should give way to the latter, in contemporary US politics and social development the superior value of security is not threatened by liberty. "For practical purposes," proposes Rawls with regard to the absoluteness of freedom of political speech, "in a well-governed democratic society under reasonably favourable conditions," such as the contemporary United States, "the free public use of our reason in questions of political and social justice would seem to be absolute."[17] This latter comment by Rawls is also not only another indicator of the particularity of his theory of justice as fairness to the industrial, urbanized, and developed societies of the West with a long tradition of democracy and the rule of law, but also of his intention to justify retrospectively the political system of contemporary United States.

One more objection to Rawls's priority rule derives from the definite restriction of liberty by the harm principle, from which no theory of liberty can escape. Rawls can argue that the physical damage caused by the exercise of one's liberty might really damage others' ability to use their liberty. Alternatively, "the knowledge that such harmful actions were not prohibited might create conditions of apprehension and uncertainty among potential victims which would grossly inhibit their actions." This interpretation requires that in balancing the value of liberty and the negative value of harm, serious harm or suffering originates from liberty of action. Otherwise, the restriction of liberty for the mere expectation of receiving harm is not reasonable.[18] Consequently, Rawls's priority rule cannot sufficiently account for restricting harmful actions for the sake of liberty. Rather, it is the independent undesirability of injuring others that restricts liberty. Furthermore, we can intuitively find that the undesirability of psychological oppression derives from the mental injury it causes to the individual; it doesn't derive from disabling him from using any basic liberty. We deprecate physical and mental damages not for their disabling part in our prospective conduct, but for the very damage we received in the past, even if no more such conduct is conceivable in the future. For instance, the damage to the mental or physical health of a powerful person to whom a mere apprehension of restriction of his liberty in the future is inconceivable is as condemnable as damage to a powerless individual who is apprehensive about his liberty in the future.

However, it is Rawls's idea of the superiority of liberty over all other human values that directly targets religion and its principles. As was discussed in chapter 3, to Shiite Islam, positive freedom of spiritual progress, which is attainable through moving toward God, is the highest end, and hence should be superior over other cases of freedom. In addition, freedom should be restricted by the principle of harm, which should include psychological harm caused by insulting God or His Messengers in front of Muslims. These two objections to Rawls's principle of liberty are the clearest cases that reject the justifiability of Rawls's principle of liberty to Shiite Muslims and confirm the impossibility of full-compatibility between his liberalism and Shiite Islam.

The Idea of Equal Liberty for All

Liberty as the manifestation of justice, which intuitively embodies the idea of equality, should be provided equally for all. To put it another way, Rawls's success in the elaboration of some values, which should be provided for each person equally in the strict sense, is crucial for meaningfully labeling his theory as a theory of justice. In Rawls's theory of justice as fairness, liberty is a value that should be provided for each person equally in the strict sense. Pointing to the centrality of equality of liberty in the first principle of justice as fairness, Rawls argues that "justice requires only an equal liberty," accepting inequalities in some other aspects.[19] However, in his later works, Rawls distinguishes between liberty and the worth of liberty and allows inequality of the worth of liberty. In the last formulation of the first principle in *TJ*, Rawls writes: "Each person is to have an equal right to the most extensive total system of equal basic liberties compatible with a similar system of liberty for all."[20] Despite his emphasis on the equality of basic liberties for all in this formulation, he later legitimizes inequality in the worth of liberty.

Rawls's idea of the "worth of freedom" consists of three components. The first component, which Pogge calls "legal freedom," is "public recognition" of certain rights for individuals. The second component, combined with the first one, called "effective legal freedom" by Pogge, is the protection of those recognized collection of rights. Finally, the third part, combined with the other two parts, called the "worth of freedom" by Rawls and "worthwhile freedom" by Pogge, is the availability of the means of taking advantage of effective legal freedom to all citizens.[21] The equality of liberty required by Rawls's first principle of justice goes so far as to necessitate effective legal freedom for all citizens, whereas inequalities at the stage of distribution of the means that enable citizens to take advantage of their effective legal liberties is legitimate.

Therefore, justice is compatible with various levels of citizens' enjoyment of worthwhile liberty. "Freedom as equal liberty," argues Rawls in *TJ*, "is the same for all," although "the worth of liberty is not the same for everyone." The ground for difference in the worth of liberty lies in the difference in citizens' access to "authority and wealth, and therefore greater" or lesser "means to achieve their aims." The most justice as fairness can provide for citizens with the "lesser worth of liberty" is to compensate for this difference by attempting "to maximize the worth to the least advantaged," rather than eliminating differences. "This defines the end of social justice."[22] Hence, while difference in the worth of liberties is inevitable, justice as fairness endeavors to *maximize* the worth of liberties for those with less means, rather than trying ineffectively to *remove* differences of worthwhile liberties.

Aiming to point to the legitimacy of inequality in the worth of liberty in the last formula of the first principle of justice, Rawls proposes that "each person has an equal claim to a fully adequate scheme of equal basic rights and liberties, which scheme is compatible with the same scheme for all; and in this scheme the equal political liberties, and only those liberties, are to be guaranteed their fair value."[23] Here, he is clear that the "worth" or the "fair value" of liberty should be protected equally for each citizen only with regard to political liberties, whereas in other aspects inequality of citizens in their ability to take advantage of their recognized and legally protected liberties is legitimate. It is, as Daniels suggests, a common attitude of liberal theorists to support some degree of equality in the political sphere and to justify considerable inequalities in wealth, income, and powers between individuals, as well as different classes. He contends that liberal theorists generally affirm that considerable social and economic inequalities are compatible with political equality.[24] Daniels's objection to Rawls's idea of unequal worthwhile liberties points to the practical impossibility of political equality combined with social and economic inequalities, as well as the moral insignificance of mere legal equality.

With regard to scientific inconsistency between the two principles of justice, he argues that Rawls does not show that from the viewpoint of social sciences large inequalities in social position and economic benefits always fail to satisfy the second principle. He also does not suggest that from the moral point of view there should be some limits on large inequalities in social and economic shares. What accounts for the latter affirmation lies in the rejection of envy in the original position that allows considerable inequalities. Hence, Rawls should agree to large social and economic inequalities, which are not compatible even with equality in political liberties, as we know from social sciences. Daniels suggests that (1) inequality in economic power will result in inequality between poor and wealthy "to select candidates, to influence public opinion, and to influence elected officials." Hence, the equality of political participation will be damaged. Furthermore, he proposes that (2) as far as equal right to a fair trial is concerned, the poor have less access to better legal counsel, as well as less ability to influence laws, which determine what the crimes are. Moreover, (3) since the wealthy have more power to influence the media, formal equality in expressing one's opinion will be shifted to the interest of the wealthy. To the latter case should be added that (4) the greater ability that the wealthy citizens possess to influence what is taught in schools, reinforces their privilege in advancing their own interests.[25]

Overall, inequality in economic possessions and social positions nullify the usefulness of formal and legal political liberty so long as citizens' interests are concerned. Thus, Daniels rejects the effectiveness of Rawls's stipulation of public funding for political parties and pubic debate to counteract the influences of the wealthy. For the mechanisms of political control by the wealthy, argues Daniels, are so complicated, as we know from social sciences, that a simple public funding will be ineffective.[26]

While Rawls is not blind to these objections, he merely connects them with political sociology with which his political philosophy aiming at "describing an ideal arrangement" is not concerned. It is obvious that connecting the inconsistency between the two principles of justice to political sociology does not protect his theory from the dilemma of impracticability. The precise objection is that given the situation in real life, the two principles of justice are not practically achievable simultaneously. Rawls, admittedly, attempts to consider "the normal conditions of human life" in his theory, and his whole argument starts from considering the real situation of man and his real potentialities, such as self-interestedness.[27] Thus, his escape from the normal conditions of human life in this case is inconsistent. This objection is reinforced if we consider his shift from utopianism in *TJ* to a feasible theory of justice for contemporary liberal democratic societies in *PL*. For any feasible endeavor to solve a current problem in a given society it should attend to the real surrounding circumstances of that society. Otherwise, the theory is a mere reflective exercise for describing an ideal arrangement for a society located in an ideal situation.

With regard to the moral worth of a mere formal equality of political liberties and rights accompanied with considerable social and economic inequalities, Daniels asks what value is equal liberty when individuals are not equally able to exercise their freedoms.[28] By contrast, Shiite Islam can agree with Rawls on equal effective liberty with an emphasis on the availability of "sufficient resources" for all reasonable doctrines of the good, although not on equal resources and opportunity. As Rawls argues, the representatives in the original position do not risk the most significant aspect of their life, that is, their thought and religion. If religion and conscience are so important that they decide to guarantee a principle that enables them to fulfill this most significant aspect of their life, that principle is not equal liberty of conscience in the sense of a mere legal immunity. Nor is it necessarily the availability of equal resources and opportunities for all doctrines. Rather, it is the principle of equal legal protection, along with the availability of sufficient resources for all reasonable doctrines of the good life to be promoted.

Rawls convincingly attaches great importance to the position of religion behind the veil of ignorance. He suggests that since religion is a value that no one is ready to compromise on, the immediate and the first principle that comes out of the original position is equal freedom of conscience.[29] Furthermore, he distinguishes between neutrality of "aims" and neutrality of "effects" and ascribes to his liberal state neutrality of aims and not neutrality of effects, which is impossible. "It is surely impossible," Rawls convincingly argues, "for the basic structure of a just constitutional regime not to have important effects and influences as to which comprehensive doctrines endure and gain adherents over time."[30] Therefore, religious ways of thinking would be disfavored by a Rawlsian liberal state.[31] In other words, liberal institutions are expected to provide "supportive circumstances" for secular ways of life and "unsupportive or undermining circumstances" for religious ways of life by the vast investment of public resources in this-worldly well-being of citizens in general. Consequently, fewer resources remain for equal development of the transcendental concerns of religious people. Yet, there should be sufficient resources for the promotion of all reasonable doctrines of the good.

Why should there be sufficient resources and not equal opportunity for all? We should reconstruct Rawls's original position by noticing that in the original position every participant knows that *he may turn out to be a person with firm commitment to the truth of a religion.* Obviously, no one may see truth as equal to falsity. The idea of equal respect or value of doctrines can be only drawn on an account of skepticism, whereas the original position is the situation of uncertainty and not skepticism. Person *A* does not know whether he will be among the minority or the majority. In both cases, he may believe in the truth of his comprehensive doctrine. What he impartially expects when he is among the majority is to enjoy extra resources to expand the true doctrine that the majority support. To him, there is no ground to provide equal opportunities for the true doctrine and untrue doctrine to promote because truth is not equal to falsity. Yet, since person *A* may turn out to be among the minority, which is assumed by the majority to follow a false doctrine of the good, he should guarantee the minimum requirements for maintaining and promoting his doctrine.

Therefore, we should distinguish between "sufficient resources" for maintaining and promoting one's own religion and "extra resources" in the sense of "supportive circumstances" for strengthening and expanding a given doctrine. It seems that the impartial decision, which can be made in the original position, confirms only the former and certainly not the latter. This comes close to Rawls's idea of unequal worth of liberty.

A List of Basic Liberties and Rights

The value of whatever that can be called liberty seems to be Rawls's primary idea in "Justice as Fairness" where he introduces his provocative theory for the first time. Yet, what would seem fair to Rawls is that being basically concerned with distinguishing between permissible inequalities and prohibited inequalities, he intends to elaborate on those cases in which inequality can be justified. Thus, at this stage it is only important that he emphasizes that in contrast with wealth, social positions, and political offices, liberty should be equally provided for all citizens. However, Rawls's later formulation invokes the idea of a collection of basic liberties determined by a list in place of the value of liberty as such. The departure from the value of liberty as such to the idea of a list of equal basic liberties, along with his previously mentioned dismissal of the maximum scheme of basic liberties have completed a shift in Rawls's theory of liberty.[32] Rawls's list of equal basic liberties suggested roughly in *TJ* includes only the "important" cases with the implication that the list is not comprehensive. Yet, when he intends in *PL* to choose a precise list of equal basic liberties incorporating only the essential cases he arrives at a similar list. However, his list of various basic rights and liberties includes the following:

1. Political rights, including the right to vote and to stand for election for political offices, as well as liberty of political speech and association.[33] As was indicated above, this category is the only collection of basic rights whose "fair value" should be equally guaranteed for all citizens.
2. Personal liberties or civil liberties, such as liberty of conscience and thought, as well as liberty of nonpolitical speech and association.[34] This category, as will be demonstrated below, has received the strongest justification from Rawls's argument both in *TJ* and *PL*.
3. Security rights, as this book calls them, including what is required by the "integrity of the person," such as freedom from psychological oppression as well as from physical assault and dismemberment; furthermore, they include those rights protected by the rule of law, such as freedom from arbitrary arrest and seizure, as well as the right to hold private property.[35] Rawls, also, incorporates in this category the right to private property as a necessary instrument to individual

independence and self-respect, leaving aside the controversial issue of the ownership of the means of production between democrats and socialists.[36] "The two principles of justice," contends Rawls, "by themselves do not settle" decisively "the question of private property in democracy versus socialism."[37]

Defining freedom in the general sense as the ability to do an action, Martin argues that freedom from physical injuries cannot be properly viewed as freedom. He divides Rawls's list of basic liberties into two groups: "(a) liberties in the strict sense and (b) the avoidance of certain injuries at the hands of others." Hence, according to Martin, whenever Rawls talks about basic liberties, we should take him to mean both groups of liberties.[38]

Connecting "equal political liberty" with democracy and "equal personal liberty" with liberalism, Gutmann argues that Rawls never speaks about democracy directly, except in one passage in *TJ* and not even once in *PL*. She assumes that Rawls explains nothing about the relationship between political liberties and personal liberties and how they are fixed in the "complete scheme of equal liberty," although they are included in his first principle of justice as fairness. While to the liberals equal political liberties are instrumentally valuable to achieve personal liberties, democrats conceive of personal liberties as being instruments to political liberties in the sense of autonomy and collective self-government. As far as Rawls's theory of liberty is concerned, Gutmann suggests that equal political liberties and personal liberties are "co-original" in Rawls's system of thought. For on the one hand, without basic personal liberties, citizens lack the power to criticize their government and participate in public decision making to pursue justice. On the other, it is political liberties that enable citizens to shape their laws and the terms of their social cooperation such that each can enjoy personal liberties to choose their way of life. As Gutmann understands it, Rawls's principle of equal basic liberties "incorporates the protection of *both* personal and political liberties and gives priority to the entire system of basic liberties, not to personal over political liberty, or vice versa."[39]

According to Gutmann, in the case of conflict among different liberties, rather than making trade-offs between political and personal liberties, Rawls's method is to assess the importance of each liberty, whether political or personal, in accordance with the view of representative citizens in the original position. Hence, on the one hand, he gives priority to freedom of religion and conscience when it conflicts with freedom of participation in public decision making. On the other, in *PL*, he defends putting restrictions on campaign contribution for the sake of guaranteeing equal political liberties by criticizing the United States Supreme Court in Buckley vs. Valeo.[40]

Yet, Rawls would appear to tend to give priority to personal liberties over political liberties when conflict arises. "The role of the political liberties" in practice, suggests Rawls, "is perhaps largely instrumental in preserving the other liberties." Consequently, they are logically supposed to be next to personal liberties in cases of conflict. "But even if this view is correct," Rawls suggests, "it is no bar to counting certain political liberties among the basic liberties and protecting them by the priority of liberty."[41] What he intends to emphasize here is the justifiability of their incorporation in one list, rather than aiming to rank them at the level of personal liberties. Put another way, while Rawls categorizes all basic liberties in his first principle of justice side by side, he considers political liberties as instrumentally valuable and personal liberties as independently valuable. Therefore, with recourse to his idea of the instrumentality of political liberties for personal liberties one can infer the superiority of the latter over the former in cases of conflict, even though Rawls does not directly announce this. What is more, he sees no inconsistency between equal political liberty and the restriction of "the scope of the principle of participation" by constitutional devices, such as "bicameral legislature, separation of powers mixed with checks and balances, a bill of rights with judicial review." These constitutional devices, by setting restrictions on participation rights, seek to guarantee other liberties, such as "freedom of speech and assembly, and liberty to form political associations. Hence, it is certain that Rawls locates personal liberties and other political liberties over the political right of participation. Liberalism, according to Rawls, takes precedence over democracy. As for the superiority of all personal liberties over all political liberties, he advances no general rule, except for announcing the instrumentality of the latter to the former. With regard to security rights, apparently, he should affirm their precedence over the other two categories, as our intuition implies. The precedence of security rights over political rights, however, is mentioned by Rawls as the justification of setting limits on the latter. Rawls suggests that "the less extensive freedom of participation is sufficiently outweighed by the greater *security* and extent of the other liberties."[42] Although this extract does not necessitate thoroughly all political rights giving way to security rights, its implication to Rawls's idea is undeniable.

However, the major objection to Rawls's collection of basic liberties concerns those rights required by integrity of the person and the rule of law, such as protection from psychological oppression and physical assault, as well as freedom from arbitrary arrest, which can hardly be labeled as liberties.[43] Protection from assault and oppression fit best the harm principle. As was seen in Mill's case, he distinguishes explicitly between the concept of liberty and the concept of harm and restricts the principle of liberty by the harm principle. To maintain the superiority and self-containment of the principle of equal basic liberties, Rawls incorporates the requirements of the harm principle in his liberty principle. If he could convincingly incorporate the concept of no-harm into his collection of basic *liberties,* he would tackle the difficulty with maintaining his commitment to the superiority and self-containment of basic liberties by balancing liberty and no-harm in the whole scheme of basic liberties.

However, Rawls's attempt to incorporate what this book calls security rights into his list of basic liberties is destined to failure. For he defines liberty in terms of the permissibility of doing or not doing an action that requires other persons and government be legally obliged not to interfere. Rawls makes no attempt to apply his conception of liberty to the third category of rights, except for using the term "freedom" in describing them. In his list of freedoms of the person is included "freedom from psychological oppression and physical assault," as well as "freedom from arbitrary arrest and seizure."[44] It is true that the general term "freedom" can be used in cases of harm by assuming that when person *A,* for instance, refrains from doing harm to person *B* the latter can be said to be free from being harmed. Yet, Rawls's particular conception of "liberty" in the sense of permissibility of doing or not doing something with legal protection against interference by government and other citizens cannot be logically applied to these cases. For in the case of protection against arbitrary arrest there is nothing that can be described as permissible for bearers of the right to do. Rather, what the bearer of the right possesses is "legal immunity" from being harmed. The result is unfortunate for Rawls who seems to argue that liberty can be restricted only for the sake of liberty, because in cases of a clash between individual liberty and harmful actions by others liberty should give way to a different concept, that is, the value of no-harm overrides the value of individual liberty.

The superiority of the conception of no-harm over the conception of liberty can resolve the dilemma of balancing some conflicting claims that belong to these two categories. For instance, the competition between liberals' view about freedom of speech including insulting religious sacred figures and religious believers' notion of a right not to be offended in this way is considered by Bellamy as a competition between two incommensurable liberties.[45]

The Argument for the Principle of Liberty

What has been discussed so far concerns Rawls's particular conception of liberty as a distinctive theory of liberalism. In the remaining part of this chapter his argument in support of this particular theory of liberty will be explored. Two distinctive sets of argument can be recognized in Rawls's discussion about the superior value of liberty. The first argument, developed in *TJ* and with a further modification in some chapters of *PL,* is based on the inevitability of diversity in contemporary liberal democratic societies, which should be tackled. In another Millian approach in Lecture VIII of *PL,* his argument invokes the desirability of diversity, which should be protected and promoted.

The Argument from the Inevitability of Diversity

Rawls's transformed argument for the superiority of equal basic liberties, examined in detail in chapter 5, can be summarized as follows:

1. Since, owing to the fact of the burdens of judgment, diversity of doctrines of the good in contemporary liberal democratic societies is an *inevitable* fact, the pursuit of agreement on one doctrine of the good is unattainable.
2. Since the dominance of one doctrine of the good is only achievable with recourse to coercive means, which presupposes the wrong assertion of the privilege of one doctrine among all and requires unjustifiable suppression of other doctrines, the state should avoid the pursuit of one comprehensive doctrine of the good.
3. Since the state should avoid the pursuit of one doctrine of the good, the best we can expect is the establishment of a just and stable society, that is, a well-ordered society organized on the basis of the commonly recognized principles of justice according to which the benefits and burdens of social life are appropriately distributed.
4. Since citizens of liberal democratic societies conceive themselves as free and equal persons, they should consensually accept the principles of justice with which they would be expected to comply.
5. Since the conceptions of justice are diverse, the only probable agreement on a conception of social justice can be achieved by constructing a political conception of justice acceptable to citizens affirming various conceptions of justice, as well as divergent doctrines of the good.
6. Since the conception of justice should be constructed, rather than being perceived, the justice of the terms of social cooperation depends on the fairness of the procedure by which equal and free citizens engage in determining them.
7. Since the fairness of the procedure for establishing the terms of social cooperation requires the removal of those circumstances under which prejudice might enter into the construction of the conception of justice, the constructors should decide behind a thick veil of ignorance about those cases of knowledge that might affect their fair judgment.[46]

8. Since each constructor of the terms of social cooperation located behind the veil of ignorance sees it as equally probable that after the lifting of the veil of ignorance he appears as a member of religious majority or religious minority, the adoption of one religion as dominant will risk enjoying less-than-sufficient liberty of conscience if he would be among the minority.[47]

9. Since taking risks with regard to the most significant aspects of individual life is perfectly unreasonable, the risk-averse members to the original position would attach superior importance to the equal liberty of conscience and religion.[48]

In *TJ*, the most Rawls convincingly infers from the above premises, if fully admitted, is proving the exclusive reasonability of equal liberty of conscience. "The question of equal liberty of conscience," infers Rawls, "is settled." Or else, he admits that "the strength of religious and moral obligations as men interpret them seems to require that the two principles be put in serial order, at least when applied to freedom of conscience." Yet, he asserts that the "reasoning in this case can be generalized to apply to other freedoms, although not always with the same force."[49] Hence, what Rawls is expected to forcefully deliver is to show how the representatives of citizens located behind the veil of ignorance would adopt an adequate scheme of basic political and personal liberties, as well as security rights guaranteed equally for all citizens. Yet, in *TJ*, he does not show how other rights and liberties derive from the original position, as freedom of conscience does.[50] This gap is the focus of Rawls's discussion in Lecture VIII of *PL*, which brings us to his second argument for liberty and its priority over all other goods and rights.

So far, Rawls's argument for his liberty principle is mildly secular. As was examined in the previous chapter, some of Rawls's premises are not acceptable to Shiite Islamic thought and hence his argument is not justifiable to Shiite Muslims in constructing the basic structure of their societies. Yet, he restricts his theorization to liberal democratic societies and refrains from refuting religion. Moreover, he positions the right to freedom of conscience and religion at the top of human values. Furthermore, he allocates the strongest part of his argument to supporting this case of civil liberty. So far, his liberty principle is *mildly* secular. Yet, this great achievement, as will be demonstrated below, cannot remain fully safe for Rawls.

The Argument from the Desirability of Diversity

In addressing Hart's objection, Rawls proposes two methods for choosing a particular list of basic liberties. One way is to examine the constitutions of those liberal democratic regimes that have worked well in protecting citizens' liberties and rights, and to choose the shared protected liberties and rights. The successful protection of a certain collection of liberties and rights in several constitutional regimes, thus, can be a persuasive reason for adopting that collection.[51] An alternative justification is an analytical method in which we examine which set of basic liberties is essentially required for "adequate development and [the] full exercise of the two powers of moral personality over a complete life." Employing his conceptions of the person and society, Rawls contends that his theory of justice as fairness can show why his list of equal basic liberties should be preferred to other traditional alternatives.[52]

Moving away from his central commitment to keep silent with regard to various conceptions of the good, in Lecture VIII of *PL* Rawls subscribes to the idea of the desirability of diversity as a particular idea of the good life. Here, Rawls supports a core notion that Mill's comprehensive liberal theory affirms the desirability of diversity. Thus, he is no longer affirming merely the reasonableness and the inevitability of diversity of comprehensive doctrines of the good life. The search for a just and stable society, in which inevitable diversity of doctrines of the good life should be accommodated, now is changed to the appreciation of diversity and individuality. Like Mill, Rawls suggests that "liberalism accepts" supremely "the plurality of conceptions of the good" within the limit set by the principles of justice as an inevitable "fact of modern life." Furthermore, liberalism "tries to show both that a plurality of conceptions of the good is desirable and how a regime of liberty can accommodate this plurality so as to achieve the many benefits of human diversity."[53]

If diversity is desirable and advantageous, as Rawls explicitly affirms here, all "necessary" requirements for its achievement and promotion are valuable. What explains his proposing some values as "primary goods" in Lecture VIII of *PL* lies in their crucial instrumentality for empowering "persons to pursue their determinate conceptions of the good and to develop and exercise their two moral powers," which are intrinsically valuable in accordance with liberalism. The grounds for determining these crucial instrumental values are "the normal circumstances of human life in a democratic society."[54] Once more, the particularity of Rawls's liberal theory to the liberal democratic societies is reinforced by his search in Western human life and its normal circumstances for a list of primary goods that encompasses his preferred list of equal basic liberties.

Primary goods, as necessary instruments of self-development and protection of diversity of conceptions of the good, include (1) the basic liberties specified in Rawls's list, (2) freedom of occupation and movement, (3) equal access to social and political offices, (4) income and wealth, and finally (5) the social bases of self-respect. The argument for his specific list of superior basic liberties proceeds by suggesting that not only "basic liberties are indeed primary goods," but also that the first principle of justice as fairness, which guarantees them, is superior to the second principle, which protects most of the other four categories of primary goods.[55]

Rawls's idea of primary goods brings his liberalism in line with Mill's comprehensive liberalism. Here, he adopts one controversial doctrine about the good life from among rival doctrines. Then, he argues that the means to achieve that end is to determine a collection of necessary conditions as primary goods. A good life, which must be accepted as good by all citizens, is a life in which each individual can promote his power of forming, revising, and following any conception of the good life that he happens to affirm independently. Any doctrine that pursues uniformity of the conception of the good even without the invocation of coercive means should accordingly be conceived of as evil and not merely as unreasonable. For what contradicts "primary goods" should definitely be considered as evil. It is the replacement of the notion of basic rights and liberties with the notion of primary goods that destroys the great merit Rawls's liberal philosophy had previously achieved. Although Rawls's liberal state still recognizes equal basic liberties for religious and nonreligious citizens residing in liberal democratic societies, all those religions seeking a uniform pattern of the good life for all humanity even through peaceful ways of inducement, propagation, education, and the like are labeled as evil by his liberal philosophy.

However, in addition to the argument from the original position, Rawls grounds the value of liberty in the requirement of the person's capacity for a sense of justice and his capacity for a conception of the good. Rawls argues that whatever a person's conception of the good happens to be, he can largely benefit from a just and stable scheme of social cooperation, which can more confidently be provided by the two principles of justice as fairness with its superior principle of equal basic liberties. Thus, the equal basic liberties are enabling rights for citizens to pursue their various conceptions of the good, which supposedly possess intrinsic value. Furthermore, the primary value of self-respect can best be achieved and encouraged through the equal basic liberties provided by the first principle of justice rather than any alternative list of liberties. What is more, it is in a well-ordered society organized in accordance with the two principles of justice with its superior principle of equal basic liberties that any one can actively participate in social cooperation through which to promote his talents by collective efforts.[56]

To be precise, Rawls derives equal political rights and liberties as well as freedom of thought from the requirements of "the full and effective exercise of citizens' sense of justice." Moreover, since these rights can be materialized only in a representative democratic regime, some political rights, such as freedom of political speech and press, as well as freedom of assembly, should be also protected.[57] Rawls's reference to the freedom of political speech and press, as well as freedom of assembly in a further expression implies that by equal political rights he has in mind participation rights, such as freedom to vote and to stand for election to public offices.

As for the derivation of civil liberties, such as liberty of conscience linked with freedom of association, Rawls grounds them in their crucial instrumentality to the full exercise of the person's capacity for a sense of a conception of the good. Put another way, only when freedom of conscience and association is guaranteed for all can citizens enjoy the necessary conditions for self-development in the sense of "forming, revising, and rationally pursuing a conception of the good over a complete life" through deliberate understanding.[58] Here, Rawls shows his tendency toward Millian comprehensive liberalism by grounding the idea of freedom of conscience in the conception of individuality and the desirability of diversity of doctrines. Like Mill, Rawls suggests that a positive conception of the good is only what we have made "our own" conception, that is, the Millian idea of spontaneity and individuality.[59]

Finally, the inclusion of what this book calls security rights relating to the integrity of the person and the rule of law in Rawls's list of equal basic liberties derives from their crucial part in properly safeguarding the other basic liberties.[60] Yet, Rawls does not discuss this crucial role in detail. From what he explains in *TJ*, the ground of the rights relating to the rule of law can be understood. For the violation of the rule of law leads to uncertainty of the boundaries of liberties, which in turn restricts liberty "by a reasonable fear of its exercise."[61] And this latter consequence violates the superiority of liberty over all other human values. As for those rights relating to the integrity of the person, he explains nothing. This is because, as this book argues, these rights can hardly be called "liberties" capable of being included in a list of basic liberties. Rather, they are rights relating to the harm principle. This is true, at least, according to Rawls's simple definition of liberty, as discussed earlier in this chapter. Hence, Rawls is required to admit that some other values superior to the value of liberty can set limits to the basic liberties.

Overall, the criterion for inclusion of any liberty in the list of equal basic liberties lies in the essential necessity of that liberty for self-development, individuality, and the promotion of a diversity of doctrines of the good in liberal democratic societies. Therefore, the elaboration of a list of equal basic liberties distances Rawls from his central commitment to the neutrality of his liberal theory with regard to conceptions of the good and brings him in line with Millian comprehensive liberalism with its focal emphasis on individuality and self-development. What can be inferred from this argument is that like nonliberal regimes, all liberal regimes construct a particular conception of the good life, a fact that undermines the possibility of constructing a neutral set of basic liberties that all reasonable citizens should accept.[62]

However, Rawls admits that while the whole scheme of equal basic liberties is superior to all other human values in the sense that no other value can limit the set of basic liberties, one basic liberty can limit another. He further admits that there is not initially a fundamental coherence among the liberties in the basic set of liberties. Hence, "the basic liberties," argues Rawls, "may be limited when they clash with one another, none of these liberties is absolute." Nevertheless, he contends that "a fully adequate scheme of basic liberties" can be elaborated by "adjustment" of each liberty to arrive at one coherent scheme. To arrive at this coherent scheme, the more significant liberty, which should take precedence over the less significant liberty when clashes among basic liberties arise, is judged by the criterion of the weight of its essential instrumentality to protect and promote "the full and informed and effective exercise of the moral powers."[63]

Here, the objection, which Gray addresses to Rawls's list of equal basic liberties, invokes the idea of the incommensurability of values. He argues that people differ as to what set of liberties is basic and how the basic liberties are to be weighed against each other. Although Rawls attempts to give a general rule by which to adopt basic liberties, "incompatible applications of his principles," contends Gray, "can be justified by different conceptions of the good." Gray emphatically argues that Rawls's preferred list of basic liberties "cannot avoid conflicts among the liberties that it singles out as basic." He argues that in Britain and most other European countries, freedom of political speech is "rightly curbed" when intended to be used for promotion of racism. Judges in the United States have always dismissed endeavors to forbid racist speech. What justifies restriction of racist speech in European legislations lies in the necessity of protecting political freedom of speech of minorities against whom racist speech might be used. As another case of conflict between two freedoms, which requires putting some restriction on either side to settle the conflict, Gray points to the freedom of association, which justifies the dismissal of gay teachers, and freedom from homophobic discrimination, which prohibits such dismissal.[64]

Gray suggests that neither the American solution nor the European solution for the conflict between two freedoms of speech can be rightly judged to be better or worse, nor are they the same in value. "They may simply be different in that they embody incompatible solutions of conflicts among incommensurable values." For in the case of conflict between freedom of racist speech and freedom from racist abuse no liberal value can settle the conflict. The solution, thus, lies in appeal to some specific conception of the good society in a specific liberal society based on its particular history and circumstances. Gray emphasizes that the conflict among liberal freedoms is not caused by the imperfection of human society. Rather, the full exercise of all liberal freedoms is not even logically conceivable. He concludes that since the conflict among different liberal freedoms is deeply subject to the incommensurability of values, the only way to settle this type of conflict is to rank freedoms on the basis of the relative "importance" of different human interests protected by these freedoms. This in its turn will demand that we appeal to our specific conception of the good.[65]

The main objection from the Shiite Islamic point of view concerns settling the conflict between security rights and civil rights. In particular, when freedom of speech and protection against psychological oppression, such as blasphemous speech, which is guaranteed by the integrity of the person conflict, Shiite Islam maintains that the former should give way to the latter. By contrast, Rawls supports absolute freedom of speech. This is one major objection by Shiite Islamic thought to Rawls's list of equal basic liberties.

Conclusion

This chapter examined the Theoretical Partial-Compatibility Proposition regarding Rawls's liberalism and Shiite Islam, by looking at Rawls's liberty principle. The mildness of the secularity of his liberty principle, which confirms this partial-compatibility, can be summarized in the following points.

(1/a) Like Mill, Rawls's idea of absolute freedom of speech legitimizes blasphemous speech, which violates Muslims' integrity. While Rawls is expected to give priority to security rights, including freedom from psychological oppression, his idea of absolute freedom of speech, which includes blasphemy, seems unjustifiable.

(1/b) By contrast, Shiite Islam attaches the greatest importance to respecting God, His infallible Messengers and their infallible successors. Consequently, any disrespect of these sacred figures by others in the presence of Muslims produces the severest psychological oppression to them and should be prohibited.

(2/a) Rawls's first argument for his liberty principle, which resorts to the inevitability of diversity and the rejection of imposition of one comprehensive doctrine on all, successfully refrains from refuting religion and hence is mildly secular.

(2/b) Shiite Islam agrees with Rawls's first argument and maintains that diversity of doctrines is perpetual and inevitable. Hence, liberty of conscience and religion is the most reasonable principle in this condition.

(3/a) Rawls's second argument for his liberty principle resorts to the Millian idea of the plausibility of diversity and spontaneous progress. This Millian idea of individuality and spontaneous progress is deeply secular.

(3/b) By contrast, Shiite Islamic view understands submission to God as the highest value. Moreover, man's potentiality for spiritual progress, by moving toward God is the most important end. Hence, while diversity should be tolerated in practice, absolute spontaneity is not theoretically acceptable.

On the whole, it seems that Rawls's final version of the liberty principle is as deeply secular as Mill's liberty principle, and hence is not theoretically compatible with Shiite Islamic teachings. For this reason, this chapter proposes that Rawls's liberal theory is only *partially* compatible with Shiite Islam.

PART THREE

The Liberal State and Shiite Muslim Citizens

CHAPTER 7

Toleration of Shiite Muslims by the Liberal State

This chapter examines the Practical Reconcilability Proposition with respect to the liberal state and Shiite Muslim citizens by looking at how the former tolerates the latter. The next chapter will be devoted to examining this proposition by looking at the grounds on which the liberal state is acceptable to Shiite Muslim citizens. First, an examination will be made to create a list of the protections, freedoms, and opportunities that the Millian liberal state appears to offer Shiite Muslim citizens. Then, a similar exploration will be made with regard to the protections, freedoms, and opportunities that the Rawlsian liberal state appears to provide for Shiite Muslims. It should be emphasized that my concern is not with real liberal states at a given time. This would be an empirical judgment that would require undertaking surveys regarding some specific liberal societies. Rather, since this book is a philosophical research, I am concerned with what Millian and Rawlsian ideal liberal states are expected to provide for their citizens.

As will be shown, Rawls's list of protections, freedoms, and opportunities for Shiite Muslims is broadly similar to Mill's list. One significant point that results from this comparative examination is that what Rawls's neutral liberal state offers to Shiite Muslims is little more than what Mill's secularist liberal state offers them. The major privilege of the list of protections, freedoms, and opportunities that the Rawlsian state provides to Shiite Muslims is the availability of religious schools with public funds to Shiite Muslim children. However, this major privilege is the logical requirement of Rawls's argument, although he does not express this result explicitly.

Shiite Muslim Citizens and the Millian State

As was suggested in the introduction, all possible state-religion relations can be categorized into three types: religionist states, secularist states, and neutral states. The Millian liberal state is secularist, seeking the domination of this-worldly human interests in liberal societies as the true way of life. Yet, as opposed to intolerant secularist states, Mill's liberal secularist state guarantees certain liberties and opportunities for religious individuals. In what follows, an examination will be made with regard to the precise toleration that the Millian liberal state practically offers to religious citizens residing in societies ruled under his secularist state. This exploration paves the way for the analysis of the degree to which the Rawlsian liberal state broadens comparatively its toleration of religious citizens and hence can be more acceptable to Shiite Muslim citizens.

First, as discussed in chapter 3, the Millian liberal state should guarantee for each citizen, religious or nonreligious, an absolute right to liberty of conscience, thought, and feeling.[1] On the basis of this absolute freedom, Shiite Muslim citizens of a Millian liberal society can uphold their religious convictions and loyalties with no fear of prosecution.

A further liberty offered to Shiite Muslim citizens of a Millian liberal society concerns the right to absolute liberty of expression.[2] According to this case of liberty, the followers of all supernatural religions, including Shiite Islam, possess the right to express their religious convictions openly in liberal societies, as long as this expression does not lead to any harmful action. This liberty, also, provides religious leaders with an opportunity to propagate Islamic norms and principles to strengthen them in their followers, as well as to defend the faith of Islam against its critics.

Furthermore, as for actions, Mill's principle of liberty prevents the state and other citizens from intervening in the performance of religious ceremonies so long as no harm to other individuals results from the religious actions.[3] Therefore, Shiite Muslim citizens of Millian liberal societies are guaranteed the freedom to form their private life, as their religion requires. The domain of public life and politics, however, should be entrusted to secular principles. On the basis of this right, Shiite Muslims in such societies can perform daily prayers in public places, schools, offices, and universities. Similarly, Muslim women can wear a headscarf, *hijab,* in public places with no pressure from others who follow a different way of life.

Shiite Muslims possess another more important right to liberty of association, on the basis of which they can form various groups and unions with the aim of safely promoting their religious values. Shiite Muslim leaders can propagate Islamic basic convictions and seek to strengthen religious loyalties and commitments in their followers who voluntarily join these groups and unions. Likewise, since Mill does not restrict the educational system to the government, Muslim leaders as well as parents can form complementary educational associations for raising Muslim children in accordance with Islamic values. Mill assumes that "one of the most sacred duties of the parents" is to provide a child "an education fitting him."[4] This complementary communal education, according to Mill, should be privately funded by parents, rather than being dependent upon public funds.[5] In all these associations, an Islamic milieu can maintain the religious spirit in Shiite Muslims, protecting them from the harmful effects of the mainstream secular environment.

However, the morally and legally recognized absolute freedom of conscience and speech and freedom of action and association are not distributed equally between religious and nonreligious individuals in practice. Hence, the public "circumstances" surrounding a religious individual who lives under the rule of the Millian liberal state can be considered not only as "unsupportive," but also "harmful" with regard to the promotion of religious spirit. The evidence of this harmful circumstance is the major investments of the state in the promotion of this-worldly interests. In the first place, the this-worldly principle of "utility would enjoin," contends Mill, "that laws and social arrangements should place the [this-worldly] happiness," or more generally "the interest, of every individual, as nearly as possible in harmony with the [this-worldly] interest of the whole."[6]

What reinforces this harmful circumstance is Mill's view of the national educational system through which the state, as its highest objective, promotes certain this-worldly moral and intellectual standards free from religious supervision.[7] Since Mill assumes that the majority of people lack the desire and sufficient knowledge to cultivate man's potentialities, he supports state intervention in public education. This national educational system is secular. According to Mill, since public education should be for all and since people differ in their commitment to one religion or another, or are agnostic or atheist, public schools should be purely secular, covering this-worldly issues that all people share. Furthermore, he argues that religious indoctrination is not consistent with releasing individuals' potentialities to develop themselves on the basis of their own intellects and desires. Hence, he disapproves of any doctrinal teaching of religion in public schools.[8] He maintains that since the state is obliged to ensure that children's opinions are not influenced through education, the teaching of religions in public schools is permissible only if it is free from persuasion. Thus, the teaching of religious convictions, values, and history is permissible if it merely describes the history of religions and their principles and values, rather than encouraging children to accept them as true.[9]

What deepens, further, the secularism of Mill's public education lies in his central commitment to the secular moral system of utilitarianism, which obliges the state to promote the general happiness in its this-worldly sense by peaceful methods including the national educational system as the most influential means:[10] "education and opinion, which have so vast a power over human character," according to Mill, should be employed to educate each citizen in accordance with the principle of utility.[11] Therefore, he maintains that the Religion of Humanity, the principle of utility, deserves to be taught as a religion by all educational means to "take the hold of human life, and colour all thought, feeling and action."[12]

Another indicator of the depth of the secularism of Mill's educational system is his idea of individuality. As far as this idea is concerned, compulsory liberal education is aimed at developing the capacity for autonomy and individuality through strengthening the values of critical inquiry, reason, and sympathetic reflection in children.[13] What follows from Mill's idea of individuality is the necessity of children's exposure to various ideas and doctrines and their being able to independently choose from the ideas and doctrines. According to Shiite Islamic moral system, the exposure to various doctrines contradicts the parents' duty to inculcate in their children religious convictions and to promote a commitment to religious morality in them.[14]

Overall, a Millian liberal state not only refrains from the coercive imposition of nonreligious values on religious citizens, but also provides the necessary conditions for Muslims to keep and promote their religion. Yet, its aim in the promotion of this-worldly interests by governmental peaceful investments provides better circumstance for secular individuals to promote their doctrines. However, in reality, most Western liberal societies provide public funds for religious schools and hence Muslim children are unharmed by this aspect. As Brian Barry reports, nowadays most liberal democratic societies, with the significant exception of the United States, provide public funds for religious schools on different bases.[15] For instance, according to Christine Barker, a specific character of state-religion relationship in Germany is "the religious education of children in school" set out in the constitution. What is significant in this relationship lies in the authority of the churches to determine the contents of religious education in school, though under state supervision. Therefore, it is parents who decide to send their children for such religious education, and children who are over 14. In a controversial case, the court of Berlin emphasized that it is the religious communities who are entitled to decide the contents of religious education and not the state authorities. In her concluding remarks, Barker suggests that the German experience about religious education in school "is one from which much can be learnt."[16]

This chapter will, now, examine the degree to which the Rawlsian liberal state is different from the Millian liberal state.

Shiite Muslim Citizens and the Rawlsian State

Rawls's argument for his principles of justice as fairness is purely secular with no recourse to religious principles. Yet, as it is possible that a secular political philosophy advocates an intolerant or tolerant secularist state, it is conceivable that it supports a neutral state that aims at maintaining the minimum social order, leaving the pursuit of any comprehensive doctrine to groups within society.[17] As will be discussed later in this chapter, although Rawls's liberal state is alleged to be neutral with regard to competing doctrines of the good, it should be categorized as a tolerant secularist state. At any rate, what can be important here concerns the real protections, freedoms, and opportunities the Rawlsian liberal state provides to religious citizens, including Shiite Muslims. Equally important is exploring the extent to which the Rawlsian liberal state provides more opportunities to Shiite Muslims in comparison with Mill's secularist state. As chapter 8 will demonstrate, Shiite Islamic political theory embodies principles and values that correspond to Rawls's idea of reasonable doctrine. Thus, what Rawls's political liberalism offers to all reasonable doctrines of the good should be applied to Shiite Islam.

In the first place, in a Rawlsian society, Shiite Muslim citizens should enjoy a safe life, free from psychological oppression, physical assault, arbitrary arrest and seizure, as well as the right to hold private property. Furthermore, the Rawlsian liberal state provides each Shiite Muslim citizen with the right to liberty of conscience, thought, and religion.[18] Consequently, Shiite Muslim citizens of a Rawlsian society can perform daily prayers in public places, such as schools, offices, and universities. Similarly, Muslim women can wear a headscarf, *hijab,* in public places absolutely free from any social pressure from non-Muslims.

Moreover, Shiite Muslim citizens of a Rawlsian society possess an "internal life" with assured "liberties of thought and speech, and the right of free association." Rawls's "political liberalism fully agrees" with the "full and open discussion in the background culture," or in "the culture of civil society,"[19] of which Shiite Muslims are a part. These rights enable Shiite Muslim citizens to form various assemblies to safely promote their religious values. Shiite Muslim leaders can confidently propagate Islamic basic convictions among their followers and strengthen religious commitments by all peaceful means in their followers who voluntarily join these assemblies.

The most important opportunity in this regard is that Shiite Muslim leaders as well as parents can form complementary educational institutions for raising Muslim children in accordance with Islamic values in a perfectly Islamic milieu. These complementary educational institutions can nullify, more or less, the unsupportive or harmful effects of the mainstream secular environment. "Private educational efforts," suggests Amy Gutmann, "to cultivate religious devotion" are "of course permissible" in accordance with Rawls's political liberalism.[20] Stephen Macedo suggests that Rawls's political liberalism "avoids saying anything about how religion is to be studied: that is left to churches and other private groups."[21] Hence, complementary educational institutions are private institutions conducted by religious leaders and parents. Therefore, as Gutmann concludes, parental religious education "should not be publicly subsidized by schools."[22]

It is worth noticing, however, that Rawls strongly disagrees with the dichotomy of the public/private spheres if the latter means space that is exempt from the application of the principles of justice as fairness. "If the so-called private sphere is alleged to be a space exempt from justice," argues Rawls, "then there is no such thing." Rawls's liberal state attempts to protect the "equal rights of women and the basic rights of their children as future citizens [which] are inalienable . . . wherever they are."[23] Yet, this legal protection does not prevent Shiite Muslim leaders and parents from inculcating Islamic values in children through any peaceful means available in civil society. This is what Rawls's full agreement with full and open discussion, and equal liberty of speech, thought, and association requires.

So far, there seems to be no noticeable difference between the Millian liberal state and the Rawlsian. Hence, to the question whether the Rawlsian liberal state is secularist or neutral, this book answers that it is secularist. "Political liberalism," admits Rawls, "agrees with many other liberal views" in a central commitment to the idea of "the separation of church and state." Moreover, his liberal state is secularist in the sense that "the discourse of governmental official, especially chief executives and legislators," as well as "judges" and "candidates for public office" should be conducted in accordance with "public reason." According to Rawls, although public reason is not secular "in the sense of a nonreligious comprehensive doctrine," it is secular "in the sense of a purely political conception," which is presented independently from religion, as it is independent from secular comprehensive doctrines. The Rawlsian liberal state "allows us to introduce into political discussion at any time our comprehensive doctrine, religious or nonreligious." However, we are obliged to "give properly public reasons to support the principles and policies our comprehensive doctrine is said to support."[24]

Furthermore, as far as the effects of his liberal state for religionism and secularism are concerned, Rawls is explicit that his ideal liberal state is not neutral. Rawls distinguishes between neutrality of "aims" and neutrality of "effects," and ascribes to his liberal state neutrality of aims and not of effects.[25] Rawls concedes that a liberal state benefits a liberal way of thinking rather than, for instance, strong religious commitments. He grounds the definite tendency of the liberal state to favor a liberal way of thinking in the impossibility of neutrality of effects. "It is surely impossible," suggests Rawls, "for the basic structure of a just constitutional regime not to have important effects and influences as to which comprehensive doctrines endure and gain adherents over time."[26] Thus, a religious way of thinking would be disfavored by a Rawlsian liberal state.[27] On the other hand, a Rawlsian liberal state guarantees citizens affirming different reasonable religions "equal opportunity" and unbiased circumstances in order that each can freely advance and pursue his reasonable religion. Rawls contends that his political conception of justice "hopes to satisfy neutrality of aim in the sense that basic institutions and public policy are not to be designed to favor any particular comprehensive doctrine."[28]

Overall, the neutrality of Rawls's liberal state with regard to religionism and secularism is confined to abstaining from deliberately disfavoring any reasonable religion, as also abstaining from deliberately disfavoring any reasonable secular doctrine. Consequently, within a Rawlsian neutral liberal state, "Christians, Jews, Muslims, Buddhists, atheists, agnostics, Macedonians, Albanians or Serbs may all equally freely pursue the way of life proscribed to them by their religion or national characteristics."[29] However, unreasonable religions, as well as unreasonable secular doctrines, are deprived of this weak sense of neutrality. "No society," proposes Rawls, "can include within itself all forms of life."[30]

A major way of disfavoring religious ways of thinking can be liberal education. Rawls explicitly distinguishes between the comprehensive liberalisms of Kant and Mill, which intend to "foster the values of autonomy and individuality as ideals to govern much if not all of life," and his political liberalism, which "has a different aim and requires far less."[31] As Gutmann explains, "Political liberalism does not try to cultivate individuality or autonomy through public education, any more than it tries to cultivate religious devotion."[32] Rawls's educational system is concerned with the following purposes: (1) the educational system should familiarize individuals with their civil and political rights, including their right to "apostasy"; (2) education should prepare individuals for social cooperation as "self-supporting" members; and finally, (3) education should promote political virtues,[33] which are the minimum standards for "creating and sustaining a fully just society."[34] These virtues include "the virtues of civility and tolerance, of reasonableness and the sense of fairness." Therefore, the educational system of the Rawlsian liberal state is entitled to discourage doctrines that can only survive by controlling the apparatus of government and implementing effective intolerance.[35] Furthermore, it can block all "repressive and discriminatory practices in any realm," including in the realm of public education.[36]

As was just shown, Rawls stipulates that the educational system should familiarize individuals with their civil and political rights, including their right to "apostasy." In this affirmation, he is not clear how the educational system should familiarize them. Rawls might intend that the required familiarization should be done by merely presenting his argument from the inevitability of diversity to students that does not contradict Shiite Islamic principles. Alternatively, he might mean that students should be presented with his argument from the plausibility of diversity and spontaneous progress, which contradicts Shiite Islamic values. Thus, Rawls is not clear whether familiarization of children with their rights should include a skeptical way of thinking, or a mere explanation about the necessity and advantages of mutual respect and toleration of others. Equally ambiguous is the stance of Rawls's educational system with regard to compulsion of mixed schools, mixed swimming pools, and sex education, or the permission of adding religious materials to the public curriculum. Rawls is also unclear whether or not his ideal liberal state should subsidize religious schools, as it subsidizes secular schools.

However, the Rawlsian educational system need not be deeply secular. Hence, according to Macedo, the followers of reasonable religions would have the right to withdraw their children from public secular schools and educate them in private religious schools, provided that the state "regulate[s] private schools to insure that civic basics are taught."[37] Granted that Shiite Islam passes the test of reasonableness, if Muslims demand to educate their children in private Muslim schools where boys and girls are educated separately, if they want to hold collective prayer each day in those schools, if they ask female students to cover their hair in those schools, if they attempt to inculcate the belief in God, His Messengers, and the hereafter in the students of those schools through additional modules, no infringement of equal basic liberties occurs.

From a historical point of view, what gave rise to liberal thought was the desire to find a secure ground for the virtue of toleration.[38] Therefore, as William Galston convincingly argues, the liberal state needs only to secure the promotion of the virtue of toleration by its educational system.[39] It should guarantee that those who are educated in religious schools promote this virtue on a firm ground, whatever that ground turns out to be. Otherwise, to impose a particular liberal way of toleration on all citizens is merely to impose a particular way of life on those who disagree with liberalism. Thus, liberalism would turn out to be another illiberal doctrine. Furthermore, it should be noted that children are not eligible to decide for themselves. Thus, others should decide on their behalf. If the liberal state assumes an exclusive right to educate all children in secular schools, it is merely an imposition of a particular way of life on those who cannot voluntarily accept it while they are not adults. By contrast, if parents want to educate their children in accordance with their way of life, the liberal state should show a high level of toleration toward a rival way of life.

However, as was suggested in chapter 6 on Rawls's liberty principle, what logically results from Rawls's idea of the original position is the equal legal right to freedom of conscience, as well as sufficient resources for maintaining and promoting one's religion. While this chapter rejects the demands of multiculturalists for equal effective opportunity and legal recognition, it maintains that sufficient resources should be provided for all reasonable doctrines of the good life. Hence, Shiite Muslim minorities should be provided with sufficient resources to keep and promote their religion. This includes public funds for religious schools that meet the general standards of education.

Therefore, in an atheist or a Christian society, Muslim minorities should possess the legal freedom to pray wherever necessary by their religion. For instance, there should be a prayer room in universities where Muslims study. Yet, there is no need to provide a few Muslim students with the opportunity to publicly call for prayer at prayer times, because this may disturb others who do not believe in Islam. Similarly, since wearing a headscarf is an important religious duty for Muslim women, they should be allowed to wear the headscarf in public places. Yet, there is no need to provide them with the opportunity to propagate the use of headscarves, as there is propagation for alternative dress codes. Another example is the unisex swimming pool. Since Muslims do believe in *hijab,* forcing Muslim students to go to a unisex swimming pool contradicts their legal right to freedom of religion. Yet, a non-Islamic society is not morally obliged to subsidize single-sex swimming pool in order to enable Muslims to have a leisure facility as others have. For deprivation of a swimming pool does not violate any religious duty.

This latter requirement, if accepted, is the major advantage of the Rawlsian liberal state in comparison with the Millian liberal state, which funds only secular public school. However, the liberal state is justified in supervising all schools, secular or religious, to ensure that there is no threat to the common tolerance, peace, and stability of society. Also, the state should ensure that no cruelty results from communal education to children. That is the most a political liberalism needs, or is justified, to undertake with regard to education. This view about public education is compatible with Kukathas's view about basic human rights, which include the right to join a community and withdraw from it and the right against cruel behavior.[40]

Conclusion

This chapter examined the Practical Reconcilability Proposition regarding the liberal state and Shiite Muslim citizens by looking at protections, freedoms, and opportunities that the liberal state provides to Shiite Muslims.

As has been shown, the Millian liberal state is secularist, seeking to promote nonreligious purposes through the state apparatus, though tolerating religious doctrines. Freedom of conscience, thought, and religion; freedom of expression; freedom of association; and freedom of action are unequally distributed between religious and nonreligious citizens in the Millian liberal state. The major inequality concerns the public funds of secular education, whereas religious schools, as complementary educational institutions, have no public funding.

Furthermore, like the Millian liberal state, in the Rawlsian liberal state, freedom of conscience and religion, as well as freedom of speech and association, along with freedom of action is unequally distributed between religious and nonreligious citizens. Yet, Rawls appears to approve of public funding for religious schools, in which children whose parents have submitted to any reasonable religion are educated. This is the unique major advantage of the Rawlsian liberal state in comparison with the Millian. Yet, Rawls is not explicit about this major privilege that is the logical result of his argument. What is important is that nowadays almost all Western liberal societies, except the United States, agree with religious schools for minorities with public funding. Therefore, Shiite Muslim citizens of Western liberal societies enjoy required protections and freedom, as well as sufficient opportunities for maintaining and promoting their religion safely.

CHAPTER 8

Acceptability of the Liberal State to Shiite Muslims

Chapter 7 examined the Practical Reconcilability Proposition regarding the liberal state and Shiite Muslim citizens by looking at how the former tolerate the latter. As a complementary discussion, this chapter explores the other side of this practical reconcilability by looking at the grounds on which Shiite Muslim citizens accept the liberal state.

Part One and Part Two of this book attempted to show in detail that neither the comprehensive nor the political theories of liberalism are justifiable in the view of Shiite Islam, and hence Shiite Islam does not legitimize the construction of the basic structure of Shiite Muslim societies in accordance with secular liberalism. Theoretical disagreement between liberal philosophy and Shiite Islam is indisputable. Nevertheless, I have shown that while there is disagreement between Rawls's mildly secular liberalism and Shiite Islam, they are compatible in a sense. Hence, I have supported the Theoretical Partial-Compatibility Proposition regarding Rawls's liberal theory and Shiite Islamic political theory on the grounds that both are particularistic, and that their demands do not contradict each other.

However, at the practical level, there is a wide scope for reconciliation between liberal states and Shiite Muslim citizens of Western liberal societies. On the one hand, this practical reconcilability is due to the tolerance that the liberal state shows toward diverse doctrines of the good life in varying degrees. On the other hand, this practical reconcilability results from the distinction made by Shiite Islam between ethical theory and political theory. While the latter applies only to majorities of Shiite Muslims living in Islamic territories, the former is the leading idea for all Shiite Muslims irrespective of their place of residence. The duties and obligations Shiite Islamic ethical theory sets for its followers can be fulfilled in Millian and Rawlsian liberal societies.

The focal point here is the development of a moral viewpoint that could be recommended to Shiite Muslim citizens of Western liberal societies in their interactions with the secular liberal state. The argument will introduce two basic moral principles: the principle of particularity and the principle of possible individual self-restraint. The principle of particularity of the Shiite state to a society with a majority of Shiite Muslim population rejects the legitimacy of the coercive establishment of a Shiite Islamic state in non-Islamic societies where a minority of Shiite Muslims resides. Moreover, "the principle of possible individual self-restraint" in non-Islamic societies obliges Shiite Muslim citizens of liberal societies to accept the basic structure of these societies in return for the protections, freedoms, and opportunities that they receive there. The result is a moral viewpoint about the acceptability of the Millian and Rawlsian liberal states to Shiite Muslim citizens of Western liberal societies in varying degrees.

The Principle of Particularity of the Shiite State

The argument for the principle of particularity of the Shiite state proceeds by distinguishing between the Islamic collective goal and the individual goal. Since there is a set of collective values that can be achieved only through the state apparatus, Shiite Muslims are obliged to pursue the substantiation of these collective values through a Shiite state. Furthermore, the restricted application of Islamic laws to those who have freely adopted Islam as their faith dismisses the legitimacy of a Shiite minority's attempt to establish the Shiite state with the purpose of imposing Islamic laws on non-Muslims. On the other hand, the idea of public election legitimizes the establishment of the Shiite state in a society with a majority of Muslims in the pursuit of the implementation of the shared values. The result of all these ideas would be the justifiability of the Shiite state for a society with a majority of Shiite Muslims, along with the illegitimacy of such a state for a society with a minority of Shiite Muslims. Therefore, when Imam Khomeini speaks of the necessity of establishing a legitimate form of religious rule, he confines his theory to an Islamic country where Muslims reside. In fact, what concerns him is restricted to the promotion of the religiosity of the Islamic rules in Muslim societies.[1]

What follows is a close examination of the ideas that lead to the principle of particularity of the Shiite state to a society with a majority of Shiite Muslims. The main purpose of this section is to argue for the restricted application of Islamic political theory to Islamic societies, rather than providing a convincing argument for the necessity of religious rule to secular thinkers.

The Idea of Dichotomy of Islamic Goals

Resorting to some verses of the Qur'an, the main source of Islamic values, a distinguished Shiite philosopher, Murtaza Mutahhari, argues that the ultimate goal of Islam consists of an individual and a collective goal.[2] The individual goal is spiritual progress, as the ultimate individual value, whereas the collective goal consists in establishing the Islamic account of social justice. Thus, though there are two goals Islam advises its followers to pursue, they are closely interrelated.[3]

As for the collective goal of Islamic values, which is the central focus for "Shia political theory," the most direct evidence is a verse of the Qur'an that reads: "Indeed, We sent Our Messengers with the clear signs, and We sent the Balance so that men might uphold justice."[4] This verse, according to Tabatabai, a prominent philosopher and interpreter of the Qur'an in the contemporary Shiite world, explicitly points to the collective goal of religion—social justice among human beings in their social interactions.[5] Thus, Islam embodies a social theory, seeking to establish a particular conception of social justice. Put another way, part of the goal of Islam, as Imam Khomeini suggests, consists of providing "stable peace" and "social justice" as the collective goal.[6]

As for the individual goal of Islam, which is the focus of attention for "Shia ethical theory," addressing the Prophet the Qur'an says: "It is He who has raised up from among the common people a Messenger from among them, to recite His signs to them and to purify them, and to teach them the Book and the Wisdom."[7] According to this verse, the Prophet has the mission, first, to recite the Qur'an and then to interpret the Qur'anic principles and values to his followers. What is more, he is tasked with promoting virtues in Muslims to lead them toward human perfection.[8] In comparison with the collective goal, individual ethical perfection is so significant that a distinguished Shiite thinker suggests that the ultimate goal of Islam is individual ethical perfection through education and training.[9] Likewise, Imam Khomeini argues that the individual ethical perfection is more significant than the collective goal.[10] In a more straightforward expression, Tabatabai argues that the ultimate purpose of human life is individual progress, and hence social life should be conceived as a means to attain that individual purpose.[11]

The Idea of the Shiite State

Admittedly, there is controversy as to whether the legitimate state, which rules over a Shiite Muslim society, should meet some specifically religious standards distinct from secular regimes.[12] For instance, Mahdi Ha'eri, a contemporary Shiite scholar, suggests that Islamic regimes of all kinds should be democratic, receiving their legitimacy from the ruled.[13] By contrast, Abdullah Jawadi Amoli, another contemporary scholar, argues that the only legitimate Islamic regime is a type of perfect guardianship.[14] As indicated in the Introduction, by Shiite Islam this book refers to the theory that justifies the Islamic Republic of Iran in its ideal form. Hence, apart from those basic principles and values that are characteristic to all Twelver Shiite Muslims throughout the world, in controversial and sensitive cases, this book constructs its arguments largely on views and ideas developed by two thinkers: Imam Khomeini, the political theorist and founding leader of the Islamic Republic of Iran, and Muhammad Hussein Tabatabai, the most prominent philosopher and interpreter of the Qur'an in the contemporary Shiite world. As will be shown here, even the most prominent advocate of Islamic rule in the contemporary Shiite world, Imam Khomeini, accepts the dichotomy of Islamic political theory and Islamic ethical theory. While the latter is a universal theory, the former should be conceived as being particular to a society with a majority of Shiite population committed to Islamic values and principles.

However, like other political theories, Islamic political theory seeks to show what good government is, and how an Islamic society should be governed. Undeniably, every human society should be governed by a form of political system in handling its public affairs for one reason or another. The urgent need for security and peace, the assurance of private property and prosperity, the establishment of a just social structure, the promotion of individual virtues, and the like are usually mentioned as grounds for the establishment of civil society and the state.[15] Therefore, taking for granted the irrelevance of anarchical theories, it is clear that an Islamic society for one reason or another needs a state.[16] In brief, the implementation of Islamic values and the pursuit of Islamic collective and individual goals require the establishment of the Islamic state.[17]

Since Islam intends to present its own conception of the good life for Islamic society, the recourse to the state apparatus is inevitable.[18] The purposes of the Islamic state can be encapsulated as providing "stable peace," "social justice," and "promotion of citizens' virtues."[19] Therefore, the ground for the Shiite state lies in two major aspects: the pursuit of Islamic conception of social justice as the collective goal and the provision of "supportive circumstances" for the "individual ethical perfection" of Muslim citizens.[20]

As for the necessity of the Islamic state with regard to the Islamic collective goal, one ground requiring the Shiite state concerns a specific conception of "distributive justice," the achievement of which is subject to the state apparatus. Islamic values in economic issues support a welfare state aimed at meeting citizens' requirements in the public domain, such as prosperity, cultural needs, health services, and the like. Admittedly, however, these public purposes and goals might not be realized unless a modern state chooses them as its policies. Therefore, the specific Islamic values about distributive justice require the establishment of an Islamic state by which those values should be implemented. A further aspect of Islamic values that requires the establishment of the Islamic state, according to Imam Khomeini, concerns national security and the protection of Islamic society against foreign intervention and control. Evidently, apart from the purposes it has in common with all other states, an Islamic society has some particular foreign policies, such as those that give priority to strengthening of its ties with Islamic societies over other countries. Hence, the specific Islamic values with regard to foreign policies require the establishment of the Islamic state by which an Islamic society can pursue its particular foreign policies. Moreover, an Islamic society has a distinctive view about "criminal justice." The particular conception of the good life that Islam proposes for a Muslim society necessitates that some actions be criminalized, the corollary of which would be enforcing some punishment for criminals in those aspects.[21]

Apart from the pursuit of the Islamic collective purposes discussed above, the establishment of the Islamic state for individual flourishing requires, as Imam Khomeini contends, the decisive influence of circumstances on human characters. As Imam Khomeini proposes, all individuals are born with a similar set of basic tendencies. However, what makes individuals diverge in conviction and affirmation lies in differences of the circumstances in which they grow up and interact with each other, along with the ideas to which they are exposed.[22] The influence of circumstances is so decisive, suggests Imam Khomeini, that they can convert someone from one set of convictions to a conflicting one. Hence, an Islamic conception of the good may justifiably attempt to provide some sort of "supportive circumstances" in order to enable citizens to preserve their convictions and commitment to Islamic values. And further, it may help them to promote their potentialities in accordance with the requirements of their constitution.[23]

The Idea of the Restricted Application of Islamic Laws

In the first place, the Qur'an confirms that disagreement about the truth is "inevitable." Hence, the Qur'an maintains that the unification of people under one religion is "impossible,"[24] for which only "uninformed" people might aspire.[25] In the deepest analysis, admitting the perpetuity of disagreement on the conception of the good and religion, the Qur'an attributes this perpetual disagreement to God's will. Addressing the Prophet, the Qur'an proposes that "had your Lord wished, He would have made mankind one community; but they continue to differ."[26] Therefore, according to the Qur'an, it is God who did not want to unify people under one religion by compulsion. Rather, He has created human beings with free will in order for them to choose their way of life and religion.[27] The natural consequence of free will is, admittedly, disagreement on the conception of the good life.[28] Since disagreement on the conception of the good and religion is a necessary attribute of human beings with free will, it has been and will be inevitably perpetual in human society.[29]

The moral consequence of inevitable disagreement on religion, according to the Qur'an, will be freedom of religion. Since the unification of human society under one religion is inconceivable, it cannot be legitimate. Thus, the Qur'an rejects the moral legitimacy of imposing any religion on individuals: "There is no compulsion in religion."[30] According to this verse, there should be no compulsion on individuals with regard to submitting to any religion.[31] Put another way, since the intellect is only susceptible to rational reasoning, the coercive imposition of doctrines on individuals is *inconceivable*. Furthermore, since Islam, supposedly, is supported by rational reasons accessible to every individual, there will be no *need* for coercion and compulsion of its principles.[32]

Therefore, although Islamic laws have a universal basis, they apply particularly to those who have freely submitted to the faith of Islam. In Islamic jurisprudence, the term "excused" is used to describe non-Muslims with regard to their disobedience of Islamic laws. To clarify: Islamic jurisprudence distinguishes between two stages of law making. At "the establishment stage," considering the common human constitution and its requirements, a law is universally made for mankind. At this stage, there is no "moral responsibility" for anyone to comply with a given law. However, this universality of established Islamic laws only holds if the common human constitution and the "essence of an action" regardless of circumstances are at stake. The moral responsibility with regard to universal laws, however, is assumed when the "surrounding circumstances" and "specific attachments" of each individual are taken into consideration. It is only with these considerations that a law applies to individuals. "The application stage" of Islamic laws, according to Imam Khomeini, is reasonably restricted only to Muslims and certainly not to those who affirm different conceptions about the good. Since non-Muslims do not believe in the truth of the faith of Islam they might not reasonably be expected to approve the validity of its values and laws as necessary for moral responsibility. Hence, they can reasonably be "excused" with regard to disobedience of these universally precious laws.[33]

This innovation regarding the restricted application of Islamic laws to Muslims, apparently, has a decisive part in the development of Shiite political theory.[34] At the same time, it protects Islamic values from any sort of "scepticism," which assumes that "no point of view is privileged, no description is true, and no assessment of value is valid." Nor does it result in "permissiveness" or arbitrariness, which suggests that "all points of view are equally privileged, all descriptions are true and all assessments of value are equally valid."[35] In this way, Islam maintains two significant ideas. First, Islam introduces the true way of life to mankind.[36] Second, it supports toleration of people with wrong convictions by recognizing human fallibility. Therefore, Islamic tolerance is Socratic.

Referring to the Socratic notion of respect for others while criticizing their views, Hampton proposes that "implicit in genuine philosophical argumentations is respect for one's opponent," whereas at the same time the disputant might not respect the ideas of his interlocutor by attempting to show his wrongness. She further claims that this type of toleration of others, and not others' views, according to Mill is what "liberalism was all about."[37] The crucial point here is that secularism and liberalism are not the unique political theory of toleration. The religious intolerance, which has led to the secularization of politics, should be subjected to careful scrutiny.[38] "Peaceable religions" can develop a firm ground for toleration of others while maintaining their firm commitment to the truth of their basic convictions.[39]

Therefore, the Shiite Islamic view of toleration differs in essence from Lord Scarman's prudential view that suggests that toleration can be grounded in the considerations of public order and stability. John Locke supported this view with regard to the economic advantage of tolerating French Huguenots in Britain. The problem with this view is that it permits suppression whenever it serves social order and stability.[40] Hence, the prudential argument for toleration lacks any moral ground for toleration. Likewise, the Shiite Islamic view is different from the Popperian falsificationist view, which draws the morality of toleration from an epistemological necessity. The morality of toleration, for Popper, lies in its instrumentality in providing an open society in which criticism eliminates present errors with regard to the truth, and hence confirms those hypotheses that withstand more severe tests.[41] Therefore, rational discussion, criticism, and toleration of disagreement would be the only means to correct our mistakes and to approach nearer to the truth.[42]

The Shiite Islamic argument for toleration is different from Locke's rationalist view of toleration. Aimed basically at guaranteeing toleration of various sects of Christian believers in his time, Locke's argument in *A Letter Concerning Toleration*[43] for religious toleration supposes the "irrationality" of the recourse to coercive means to secure religious belief and commitment. Persecution seeks to achieve something unachievable by coercive means. As Waldron expounds, Locke tries to prove the impossibility of the coercive imposition of religious beliefs by two ideas. First, he suggests that coercion acts through changing our will and decision. Second, he proposes that belief is beyond will: belief comes and goes without our will. The change in our belief happens, not as a result of our doing, but rather as the result of the work of "light and evidence" on the understanding.[44] What distinguishes Locke's rationalist view of toleration lies in his concern about the *obligation* of toleration among the *sects of Christian faith,* as well as his affirmation of the *irrationality* of intolerance. By contrast, modern views of toleration, including Mill's and Rawls's, focus on the *moral wrongness* of intolerance, the *worth of diversity* in human society or the inevitability of disagreement, and the *rights of the victims* of intolerance.[45]

As opposed to all these views, the Shiite Islamic view of toleration articulated above combines the affirmation of the truth of Islamic values and the crucial influence of circumstances on understanding and accepting the truth. Hence, it recognizes *human fallibility* with regard to the understanding of, and the submission to, the truth. Not only is intolerance conceived of as *irrational,* but toleration is also considered as a *moral obligation* of those who have submitted to Islam with regard to non-Muslims.

The Idea of the Electiveness of Top Authorities

One further idea with regard to Shiite political theory connects necessarily the legitimacy of the Shiite state with the electiveness of its top authorities in the contemporary Shiite world. What accounts for this idea lies in a specific Shiite conviction about leadership and its different degrees, suggesting a dichotomy between "perfect-guardian rule" and "quasi-guardian rule." The major ground accounting for this difference lies in acknowledging different degrees of virtue and knowledge of Islamic laws reasonably stipulated in the leader of the Shiite state. This variation is drawn on the capability of the concept of leadership for classification into two ranks: while the "first rank Imam"[46], supposedly, possesses the superior knowledge of the human good, as well as being infallible, the "second rank Imam" possesses a normal knowledge of Islamic laws as well as virtues inferior to infallibility. The first rank Imam is commonly called an "infallible Imam," whereas the second rank Imam is called a "self-restrained Imam."

Unlike the self-restrained Imam, the infallible Imam does not need public acceptance to be legitimate, whereas the former needs public acceptance as the complementary source of legitimacy along with religiously approved competency. As Shiite Muslims generally believe, there have been such infallible Imams with Godly revealed superior knowledge.[47] Explaining Shiite Muslims' beliefs, Imam Khomeini argues that "Messengers of God and their Successors possess an eminent position in spirituality called the sacred spirit with the help of which they have access to the perfect and comprehensive superior knowledge." He further argues that one consequence of that superior knowledge is their infallibility.[48]

The only problem with this form of rule lies in the difficulty of proving the existence of, or discovering, such a person who genuinely possesses superior knowledge and infallibility. However, religious people who have followed the idea of perfect-guardian religious rule have not ignored this problem. First of all, they have rationally stipulated that only God is competent to recognize his infallible representatives who possess Godly revealed knowledge. Furthermore, to distinguish those authentic Godly appointed Imams from any person who might deceitfully assume this high position they argue that any infallible Imam can only be followed if his Imamate is proved by a type of miracle.[49] Explaining the general conviction of Shiite Muslims, M. R. Muzaffar, a distinguished contemporary thinker, argues that "we believe that when God the Almighty appoints a Messenger for people He should introduce him to people by determining a sign to his Messengerhood. . . . This sign is what is called the miracle."[50] Likewise, with regard to a successor of a Messenger, Muzaffar affirms that "the Imamate of a person is only acknowledged by a Messenger's or a previous Imam's report about his appointment by God."[51] This principle is the focus of the consensus by all Shiite scholars as well as ordinary Shiite Muslims.[52] As for Imam Khomeini, he suggests that "the Prophet of Islam is appointed by God . . . and after him the Imams[53] who were the supreme leaders among people were appointed by God."[54]

However, since such an ideal rule governed by an infallible figure with superior knowledge of the human good is unavailable in the contemporary Shiite world, the need for the election of top authorities of the Shiite state is crucial to its legitimacy. Within the system of Shiite convictions, the subjection of top authorities of the Shiite state to public election is the logical consequence of the fact that the leader of Shiite society is not appointed by God in person. Regarding the necessity of public election for the appointment of members of the body that intends to determine the basic structure and values of Shiite society, Imam Khomeini contends that "if the Constituent Assembly is valid it is caused by people's vote; the criterion is the people's vote. Therefore, sometimes people vote directly and on some other occasion, they choose representatives to make decisions on their behalf. In both cases, the right belongs to people themselves."[55]

The election of top authorities in Shiite society is so important a value that Imam Khomeini argues explicitly that even the supreme leader should be chosen by the people themselves, not to mention the president and other authorities at the lower level. *Wilayati Faqih,* or the supreme leader, proposes Imam Khomeini, "is an individual whose morality, patriotism, knowledge and efficiency are clear to the people and the people themselves choose this person."[56] Acknowledging the election of top authorities as a basic human right, he maintains that "people themselves should rule on questions of laws and administration or other matters of their government."[57] Positioning the parliament at the top of governmental institutions, Imam Khomeini points to the manifestation of the people in the parliament: "The Parliament lies at the top of all other institutions and the Parliament is the people who have been embodied."[58]

As a complementary part of the argument for the idea of electiveness of top authorities, dismissing a narrow assumption that restricts the engagement in public decision making to an elite minority, Imam Khomeini generalizes the sovereignty to the public. "Elections are not confined to anybody," suggests Imam Khomeini, "the clerics, the parties and the groups. Elections belong to all people. People have their fates in their own hands." Furthermore, he emphasizes the importance of the equality of citizens' votes. "In elections," contends Imam Khomeini, "every citizen is equal to every other citizen no matter who he is; whether the President, the Prime Minister, a farmer who works on the farm, or a businessman engaged in economic activities. In other words, each of them has equally one vote."[59] Hence, Imam Khomeini grounds the idea of the Shiite state in the democratic value of public election according to which all citizens of Islamic society equally participate in appointing top authorities of their society.

The underlying idea that accounts for the democratic value of equal political participation derives from a Qur'anic verse and a prophetic tradition regarding the equality of all human beings. In the most explicit expression, a famous saying by the Prophet of Islam emphasizes that "all people from the era of Adam and Eve up until the present time are equal like the teeth of a comb."[60] Furthermore, the Qur'an quotes God as saying: "Indeed We created you from a male and a female, and made you nations and tribes that you may identify with one another. Indeed the noblest of you in the sight of Allah is the most Godwary among you."[61] In the interpretation of this verse, Tabatabai repeatedly puts emphasis on the idea of "the initial situation of equality" among all human beings, derived from having the same parents. "Men are equal with each other in being human," suggests Tabatabai, "and there is no privilege for any one over others. Thus, no one has any intrinsic right to exploit or dominate over others."[62]

The derivation of the idea of the initial situation of equality among all human beings from having the same parents, according to a saying by the Prophet, is reinforced by the fact that all human beings have been created by the same God.[63] Therefore, what accounts for the initial situation of equality of all individuals lies in three ideas. First, all human beings have been created by the same God. Second, all men have ultimately been born of the same parents. And, finally, all human beings are equal in possessing the modicum of humanity that entitles everyone to social obligations and rights.[64]

Overall, the idea of dichotomy of Islamic goals along with the idea of the Shiite state justifies the establishment of the religious state for a society with a majority of Muslims. On the other hand, the idea of the restricted application of Islamic laws to Muslims along with the idea of majority support for the Shiite state dismisses the relevance of such a religious state for a society with a minority of Shiite Muslims. As has been discussed, Shiite Islamic political theory approves of the establishment of a religious democracy for Shiite Muslims at home. In brief, religious democracy, in its Shiite proceduralist account, combines two phases for the settlement of public affairs in lexical order. In the superior phase the common concern of a Shiite community is explicated with recourse to the legitimate interpretation of Islamic laws by all Shiite adults with potentially equal eligibility. In the inferior phase individual preferences of all community members are aggregated with equal weight within the framework set by the explication phase.[65] This account of religious democracy, as was discussed above, is a type of tolerant religionist state that chiefly recognizes freedom of conscience and religion.[66]

The next principle shows that the demands of Shiite Islam from Shiite Muslims abroad are confined to the concept of "the self-restrained Muslim." This corresponds to Rawls's concept of the reasonable citizen, as well as to Mill's concept of the free and harmless individual.

The Principle of Possible Individual Self-Restraint

The argument for the principle of possible individual self-restraint proceeds by distinguishing between Shiite political theory and Shiite ethical theory. Since the latter is relatively independent from the Islamic state, the commitment to Shiite Islamic ethics is possible even in nonreligious societies. According to the idea of the human constitution, the tendency toward religion is naturally present in man, enabling him to understand, accept, and practice religious values more probably than other doctrines. The idea of Islamic teaching connects the activation of this natural tendency with exposure to religious teaching, be it socially, communally, or domestically delivered. Finally, the idea of nonobstructive circumstance dismisses an assumption that the harmful circumstance in nonreligious societies is obstructive with regard to the Islamic ethical goal. Hence, it is conceivable that Shiite minorities that reside in nonreligious societies maintain their commitment to their religion with regard to their ethical goal, provided that freedom of religion, religious teaching, and freedom of action are guaranteed in such societies. From what has been argued in chapter 7, it is evident that both Millian and Rawlsian societies guarantee for Shiite Muslims this collection of liberties in different degrees. Therefore, as Millian and Rawlsian liberal societies tolerate or respect minorities of Shiite Muslim residents, the latter have a moral obligation to respect the basic structure of these societies.

As a complementary principle, possible individual self-restraint in some non-Islamic societies legitimizes the residence of Shiite Muslims in those non-Islamic societies where freedom of religion, as well as Islamic teaching, along with freedom of action are legally guaranteed for them, a situation that is found in Rawlsian and Millian liberal societies in varying degrees. In what follows, the ideas accounting for this complementary principle will be examined.

The Idea of Common Human Constitution

Islamic ethical theory firmly rejects a liberal idea of the person as an empty entity with only the capacity for decision making.[67] Human nature is so constituted as to demand him to take a specific route to his excellence. The person has a destination that can be discovered by reference to his constitution and natural tendencies. Therefore, the person is not indifferent with regard to the various conceptions of the good such that the only reasonable principle would be to let him choose as he wishes. The main ground for this idea lies in the following Qur'anic verse: "So set your heart on the religion as a people of pure faith, the origination of Allah according to which He originated mankind There is no altering Allah's creation; that is the upright religion, but most people do not know."[68] According to this verse, as Tabatabai interprets it, man has a specific nature pushing him to move in a specific way toward a specific destination. All human beings have one common nature dictating to them one general conception of the good, though diversity in details is inevitable.[69] Furthermore, another verse of the Qur'an indicates that knowledge of good and evil is incorporated in human nature and is discoverable by practical reason: "By the soul and Him who fashioned it, and inspired it with [discernment between] its virtues and vices."[70]

Thus, the Qur'an suggests that not only is there just one general destination for mankind that can be discovered by reference to the dictates of his nature, but also that the knowledge of good and evil by which humanity can develop their nature in order to arrive at their ultimate excellence is granted to them by their creation. Their practical reason, therefore, can show them the way toward their deserved excellence.[71] Of course, religious teachings expand what man can understand by his practical reason, especially with regard to balancing different values against each other when they clash.

Therefore, according to Imam Khomeini, the common human constitution dictates a certain religious way of life.[72] What is situated at the center of his proposition here relates to connecting man's constitution and his ultimate goals. Human nature, as he maintains, is so constituted as to determine some specific values and virtues to promote and crystallize man's natural tendencies and potentialities. This view is similar to MacIntyre's Aristotelian view, which connects human nature with its *telos,* according to which what moves man toward his *telos* should be considered as good and what prevents him from moving toward it as bad.[73] This Shiite Islamic view about human nature resembles the Millian view in that both are objectivist and realist, whereas Rawls's view is objectivist and constructivist.[74] However, the verses of the Qur'an, which are the most reliable source of morality to Muslims, for whom this viewpoint is developed, support the mentioned Shiite Islamic view of human nature.[75]

The Idea of Islamic Teaching

Having established the Islamic idea of the common human constitution, what is required necessarily to substantiate this human tendency toward flourishing is the absence of oppression against this tendency, along with the availability of religious teaching. The Qur'anic idea of common human constitution should not be taken to suggest the sufficiency of human practical reason for humanity's progress toward its deserved end. Due to contingencies of time and space leading to variation in traditions and customs, disagreement on doctrines and conceptions of the good life would be inevitable. What humanity needs to crystallize its common constitution, according to Tabatabai, is a common doctrine of the good life in harmony with the common human constitution. The role of religion in human progress and flourishing, therefore, lies in completion of the knowledge and tendencies man naturally possesses. This completion is substantiated, first, in expansion of the natural knowledge of the good and evil by religion. Furthermore, religion completes the motive to self-construction toward the deserved excellence.[76] Finally, by reminding humankind of his common constitution facilitated with the knowledge of the good and evil, religion activates the natural endowments. The purpose of the Qur'an, thus, can be summarized as reminding, rather than original teaching:[77] "We have not sent down the Qur'an upon you for you to be unprosperous, but only as a reminder to him who fears."[78]

As to how religion seeks to fulfill its role in the completion of common human constitution, what the Qur'an suggests as the effective and legitimate method lies in various forms of "peaceful discussion."[79] Addressing the Prophet with regard to the legitimate methods of Islamic teaching, the Qur'an says: "Invite to the way of your Lord with wisdom and good advice and dispute with them in a manner that is best."[80] Depending on the interlocutors' position, ranging from intellectuals, through ordinary people, to those who employ rhetorical argument against Islam,[81] this verse emphatically demands that the Prophet resort only to different forms of peaceful discussion in order to convince them of the truth of Islam, or to defend it against its critics. While the legitimate method of peaceful discussion effective with regard to intellectuals is "rational reasoning," for ordinary people it is a "good preaching" that can convince them of the worth of Islam. A third method of peaceful discussion advisable in dealing with rhetorical disputants is "the best kind of argument" with the aim of dismissing the interlocutor's rhetoric.[82]

Overall, the idea of Islamic teaching suggests that although the common human constitution is furnished with the basic means required for self-construction and progress toward the deserved excellence, it should be activated and completed by various methods of peaceful discussion. Hence, what Muslims need in crystallization of their common constitution, as far as individual self-restraint is concerned, lies in personal freedoms, along with exposure to Islamic teaching.

Hence, in a liberal society, Muslim parents' chief demand is availability of religious schools where they can educate their children in accordance with Islamic values in a religious milieu. The demand follows parents' requirement to transmit basic religious convictions and values to their children by inculcation during the decisive period of childhood. What reinforces the necessity of the employment of educational system in this period is the fact that individuals in this period lack the capability of reasoned understanding in respect of human values and social interaction. Hence, inculcation through the educational system is the only peaceful means for the maintenance of religious commitment in children. However, after being educated in Muslim schools, there would be no problem for Muslim adults to study in universities where they are exposed to various

nonreligious doctrines and ideas. They are adults and can decide for themselves. In addition, parents have no right, or religious duty, to impose on their
adult children a particular way of life. Therefore, studying in nonreligious
universities is no problem.

The necessity of providing religious schools to Muslim children and the
superfluity of providing religious universities to them is what I call a policy
of "insulation," as an alternative to the policy of "isolation" and the policy of
"integration." The policy of integration attempts to integrate Muslim children in the mainstream culture through denying them sufficient funds for
studying in Muslim schools. By contrast, the policy of isolation assumes that
no interrelations should be established between Muslim communities and the
mainstream secular society. According to this policy, Muslims are allowed to
live in a non-Muslim country, but in isolation and not with the people of
that country. The policy of insulation is the mean between these two
extremes. It requires inculcating basic religious convictions in Muslim children in religious schools up to the 14, while allowing adults to communicate
peacefully and respectfully with non-Muslims.

As was discussed in chapter 7, religious teaching is more available in
Rawlsian liberal societies than in Millian. For in a Rawlsian society parents
can withdraw their children from public schools and educate them in religious private schools probably with public funds. By contrast, the Millian
educational system allows them to educate their children in complementary
educational institutions, which are fully religious, while they study in public
secular schools.

The principle of possible individual self-restraint in liberal societies
depends further on "the idea of non-obstructive circumstance" in liberal
democratic societies. This I will now discuss.

The Idea of Non-Obstructive Circumstance

The circumstances of religious societies are clearly supportive of the ethical
goal of Islam. Yet, the Islamic conception of self-construction does not
necessarily depend upon the presence of such supportive circumstances,
unavailable as they are in nonreligious societies. Although the achievement
of the Islamic ethical goal by a Muslim living in an Islamic society, in which
spirituality is the dominant value, is "more probable," it is also "achievable"
in some kinds of nonreligious societies where freedom of religion is morally
and legally recognized. What accounts for the achievability of maintaining
one's religion in some nonreligious societies lies in the Qur'anic law of
migration, which has two sides: "the precept of permissible immigration"
and "the precept of obligatory emigration." According to the precept of

permissible immigration, it is possible for Muslim minorities residing in nonreligious societies to keep their commitment to religion.

As for the Islamic laws about the precept of permissible immigration, Najafi, a prominent Shiite jurisprudent during the last two centuries, maintains that as far as he could discern the views of other Shiite jurisprudents he found no controversy about this precept. The source of this consensual precept, as Najafi demonstrates, is so many verses of the Qur'an.[83] This precept permits a Muslim minority to migrate to non-Islamic societies provided that they can maintain their convictions and exercise their religious duties. These duties include those personal actions that need no resort to the state apparatus, such as prayer, fasting, pilgrimage, promotion of human virtues, and the like. What he further stipulates is that they should be able to exercise their religious duties "overtly," requiring that in such societies, for instance, Muslim women should be able to follow an Islamic code of dress, *hijab*, in public places.[84]

The permissibility of residence in non-Islamic societies, according to Tabatabai's interpretation of the Qur'an, depends upon (1) the freedom of religion, as well as (2) the availability of religious teaching, along with (3) the freedom of action to practice Islamic ethical duties.[85] However, the other side of this law, "the precept of obligatory emigration," requires Muslim minorities to leave non-Islamic societies and settle in other places if they are not offered personal freedom to maintain and practise their religion there.[86]

In brief, the consensual law of migration with its two sides is sufficient evidence of the core point of Islamic ethical theory. The permission of residence in non-Islamic societies indicates the achievability of Islamic ethical goals in non-Islamic societies, provided that personal freedom and Islamic teaching are guaranteed for Muslims. For if the achievement of the goal pursued by Islamic ethical theory were unconditionally subject to the availability of the Islamic state, the immigration of Muslim minorities to non-Islamic societies would not be permissible at all. Therefore, the Islamic laws of migration do evidently show the relative independence of ethical self-restraint from the Islamic state.

It should be noted that Shiite Muslims have no demand with regard to public holidays. Since they are not obliged to congregate for Friday or *Eid* prayers, they do not demand leaving their jobs at certain times of certain days. Nor are they obliged to perform daily prayers congregationally at a certain time. Therefore, the commitment to their religious duties does not require any exemption from pubic laws regarding working hours. One other point in this regard is that they are not allowed to join the army of a non-Shiite society, not to mention Western non-Islamic societies. This is because the law of military conflict is very restricted in Shiite Islamic jurisprudence such that many military conflicts are illegitimate. Hence, Shiite Muslims are not religiously permitted to contribute to prohibited wars.[87] However, it seems that a Millian or a Rawlsian society does not necessarily demand the participation of a specific group in a specific public service. In contemporary modern and industrial societies organized in accordance with the division of labor, there is no obligation for each citizen to participate in all public services. Hence, freedom of religion should enable citizens to choose their job and public activities.

In brief, the principle of particularity of the Shiite state to a society with a majority of Shiite Muslim population rejects the legitimacy of the coercive establishment of a Shiite Islamic state in non-Islamic societies where a minority of Shiite Muslims resides. Moreover, the principle of possible individual self-restraint in non-Islamic societies obliges Shiite Muslim citizens of liberal societies to accept the basic structure of these societies in return for the protections, freedoms, and opportunities that they receive there.

What reinforces this acceptability is the Islamic ethical code of "constructive reciprocity." The duty of constructive reciprocity set by the Qur'an obliges Muslims to first respond to all good behavior by similar behavior. "Shall the recompense of goodness be other than goodness?" asks the Qur'an.[88] This verse indicates that the appropriate response by a Muslim to a good action is a good action, irrespective of the religion or moral perfection of the person who does good to them.[89] This Qur'anic verdict confirms the theory of natural duty of gratitude in discussions of political obligation, as proposed by Socrates and supported by A. D. Walker.[90] As the complementary side of the duty of "constructive reciprocity," the Qur'an still requires Muslims to respect those who do not respect them: "Repel ill [conduct] with that which is the best."[91] This verse demands that Muslims respond to any probable lack of respect from non-Muslims not only by abstinence from reciprocal disrespect, but also by respecting their opponents' convictions and principles as the best way of constructive reciprocity.[92] Therefore, Shiite Muslim citizens of Western liberal societies are obliged to respect the basic structure of liberal societies in return for the protections, freedoms, and opportunities from which they benefit in those societies.

Conclusion

This chapter examined the Practical Reconcilability Proposition with respect to the liberal state and Shiite Muslim citizens. It explores the grounds on which Shiite Muslim citizens accept the liberal state. The following points confirm the Practical Reconciliability Proposition.

1. This chapter distinguishes between Shiite political theory as the leading idea for Shiite Muslims in an Islamic and Shiite ethical theory as the leading idea for them abroad.

2. Shiite Islamic political theory is particularist and its view of religious democracy is confined to a society with a Shiite Muslim majority. Hence, there is no ground for a minority of Shiite Muslims in liberal democratic societies to have political demands.

3. What Shiite Islam demands of its followers abroad is confined to the concept of the self-restrained Muslim, which is compatible with Mill's idea of the free and harmless person, as well as Rawls's concept of the reasonable citizen.

4. Shiite Islam recognizes and appreciates the value of tolerance on the grounds of human fallibility, which is compatible with its assertion to proposing the true way of life.

5. The duty of Shiite Muslim citizens of liberal societies to be self-restrained Muslims can be fulfilled in Millian and Rawlsian liberal societies, by freedom to practise daily prayers and to wear the headscarf in public places. In addition, they can choose jobs that are religiously permissible.

6. According to the ethical code of constructive reciprocity, Shiite Muslim citizens of Millian and Rawlsian liberal societies are obliged to respect the basic structure of those societies in return for the protections, freedoms, and opportunities that they receive in those societies.

Conclusion

The Questions of This Research

This book has attempted to examine the extent to which liberalism and religion can be reconciled. This is exactly Rawls's concern in his theorization about liberal philosophy. Rawls's attempt has been made from a liberal standpoint, whereas this book is a parallel attempt from a religious standpoint. To properly answer the question of reconcilability of liberalism and religion, three points should be determined in advance. Which theory of liberalism is at stake? Which religion is adopted for comparison? What do we exactly mean by reconciliation? I chose Mill's traditional comprehensive liberalism and Rawls's contemporary political liberalism as two representatives of liberal philosophy. As the representative of religion, I adopted Shiite Islam. Furthermore, I distinguished among theoretical justifiability, theoretical compatibility, and practical reconcilability. Hence, I am concerned with three issues: theoretical justifiability of liberalism in the view of Shiite Islamic thought; theoretical compatibility between liberalism and Shiite Islam; and finally, practical reconciliation between the liberal state and Shiite Muslim citizens.[1] I have addressed the following questions in detail.

1. Is Mill's liberalism justifiable in the view of Shiite Islamic thought?
2. Is Mill's liberalism theoretically compatible with Shiite Islamic political theory?
3. Is Rawls's liberalism justifiable in the view of Shiite Islamic thought?
4. Is Rawls's liberalism theoretically compatible with Shiite Islamic political theory?
5. Is the Millian ideal liberal state practically reconcilable with Shiite Muslim citizens, and vice versa?
6. Is the Rawlsian ideal liberal state practically reconcilable with Shiite Muslim citizens, and vice versa?

Chapters 1–3 are devoted to the investigation into questions 1 and 2, and my answer has been "no." Chapters 4–6 are devoted to the investigation into questions 3 and 4; my answer to question 3 has been, again, "no," whereas my answer to the question 4 has been "partially yes." Chapters 7–8 are devoted to the investigation into the questions 5 and 6, and my answer has been "yes."

My examination has three significant theoretical findings as follows:

1. *Theoretical Incompatibility Proposition:* Mill's liberal theory is *deeply* secular, and hence is incompatible with Shiite Islamic political theory.
2. *Theoretical Partial-Compatibility Proposition:* Rawls's liberal theory is *mildly* secular, and hence is partially compatible with Shiite Islamic political theory.
3. *Practical Reconcilability Proposition:* The Millian liberal state as well as the Rawlsian liberal state should tolerate, and should be reciprocally acceptable to, Shiite Muslim minorities.

In addition, my research has two practical recommendations for Shiite Muslims at home and abroad as follows:

1. Shiite Muslim majorities at home have to refrain from constructing the basic structure of their societies in accordance with liberal theory.
2. Since liberal societies tolerate Shiite Muslim citizens, the latter should reciprocally accept the basic structure of the former.

In what follows, I revisit these questions and answers in brief.

Theoretical Incompatibility Proposition

I have shown that Mill's deeply secular liberalism is unjustifiable in view of Shiite Islam. Although Shiite Islam agrees with Mill that general philosophy, as well as political philosophy, should seek the truth, truth in the view of Mill's philosophy is different from truth in the view of Shiite Islam in the following aspects. Mill's view, which asserts that inductive experimentalism is the unique method for scientific explanation and investigation about the truth, is not justifiable in the view of Shiite Islam. Rather, Shiite Islam maintains that proof can be provided by revelation and intellectual demonstration, as by inductive experiment. Shiite Islam disagrees with Mill's view that the ultimate moral standard is subjective, and hence cannot be assessed as true/false. Conversely, Shiite Islam holds that since the common human constitution determines a particular spiritual path toward human progress, even the ultimate moral standard is a factual statement that shows the cause-effect relation between that ultimate moral standard and human progress.

Shiite Islam disagrees with Mill's proposition that God has no right to set moral rules for human beings. By contrast, according to Shiite Islam, although the knowledge of good and evil is incorporated in human nature and is discoverable by practical reason, religion and Godly revelation act as complementary sources for morality. Shiite Islam disagrees with Mill's suggestion that even if God intends to reveal something about morality, he should follow Mill's idea of utilitarianism in its earthly sense. By contrast, according to Shiite Islam, Muslims are obliged to follow the requirements of justice even to the cost of losing their temporary utility. Shiite Islam disagrees with Mill's confinement of the notion of happiness to the domain of the earthly life. By contrast, Shiite Islam holds that while the ultimate end for human conduct is happiness, the worth of the happiness in the present temporary life is inferior to the happiness of the eternal life where there will be all that man desires. Shiite Islam obviously disagrees with Mill's idea of the Religion of Humanity as a necessary and sufficient substitute for supernatural religion. By contrast, Shiite Islam introduces divine religion as a necessary part of the good life on earth, by which man can establish a plausible life in his temporary life and move toward an eternal happy life.

Shiite Islam disagrees with Mill's principle of freedom of speech and his conceptualization of harm that potentially legitimizes blasphemous speech, which causes the severest emotional harm to religious people. By contrast, Shiite Islam expands the notion of harm to emotional harm and prohibits insulting God, His infallible Messengers, and their infallible successors in the presence of Muslims. Shiite Islam disagrees with Mill's principle of freedom of action, which universally appreciates individuality and spontaneous progress as the highest human utility. By contrast, Shiite Islam appreciates submission to God and moving toward Him in a spiritual journey as the highest value, although it admits that freedom of action is necessary for human development.

Overall, Mill's liberalism is unjustifiable in the view of Shiite Islam. Nor is his claim that his political philosophy is universally applicable to all developed societies compatible with Shiite Islam, which prescribes a type of religious democracy for Shiite Muslims at home. Yet, his expectation of Shiite Muslim citizens of liberal societies that is confined to the concept of "the harmless person" is compatible with what Shiite Islam demands of his followers abroad, that is, the concept of "the self-restrained Muslims."

Theoretical Partial-Compatibility Proposition

I have shown that Rawls's mildly secular liberalism is unjustifiable in the view of Shiite Islam. Yet, there are some features in Rawls's political philosophy that decrease the disagreement between his theory and Shiite Islam. In what follows, the grounds for partial-compatibility between Rawls's philosophy and Shiite Islam will be summarized. Shiite Islam disagrees with Rawls's view, which suggests that political philosophy should pursue a method for justification, one that is merely concerned with the reasonableness of ideas and doctrines. By contrast, Shiite Islam maintains that political philosophy, like general philosophy, should seek to discover the truth while recognizing human fallibility and managing the inevitable disagreement on the truth in a fair way.

Rawls's view, which restricts the right to determine the terms of social cooperation to human beings, is not justifiable in the view of Shiite Islam. By contrast, Shiite Islam explicitly maintains that God has the right to help human beings to determine the principles of the true way of life justly. Rawls's particular conception of justice is not justifiable in the view of Shiite Islam, which combines human transcendent happy life with the requirement of the true way of life determined in a just manner.

Rawls's idea of absolute freedom of speech, which legitimizes blasphemy, is not justifiable in the view of Shiite Islam, which severely prohibits it. Rawls's first argument for his liberty principle, which resorts to the inevitability of diversity and rejects the imposition of one comprehensive doctrine on all, is justifiable in the view of Shiite Islam. Yet, his second argument for his liberty principle, which resorts to the Millian idea of the plausibility of diversity and spontaneous progress, is not justifiable in the view of Shiite Islam. By contrast, Shiite Islam suggests that the only way for human progress is moving in the direction that leads to God.

Shiite Islam appreciates Rawls's claim of the reasonableness of his political theory, which successfully abstains from the refutation of religious basic convictions. Shiite Islam recognizes Rawls's disengagement from observation about the ultimate conception of the good life and its confinement to the happiness in the earthly life. Shiite Islam acknowledges Rawls's refraining from declaring that God should follow Rawls's conception of social justice. Also, Shiite Islam agrees with Rawls that justice is the supreme social value and should override utility. Shiite Islam appreciates Rawls's restriction of the subject of his theorization to the basic structure of liberal democratic societies, and his disengagement from the way in which Muslim societies construct the basic structure of their own.

Overall, Rawls's liberalism is unjustifiable in the view of Shiite Islam, and hence Shiite Muslims are not religiously permitted to construct the basic structure of their societies in accordance with Rawls's particular conception of justice as fairness. Nor does Rawls expect Shiite Muslims to follow him at home. What Rawls suggests with regard to Muslim societies is defined by his theory of decency. This theory is compatible with religious democracy, which Shiite Islam prescribes for its followers at home. Furthermore, what Rawls proposes with regard to Shiite Muslim citizens of Western liberal societies is defined by his concept of "the reasonable citizen." This concept is compatible with the concept of "the self-restrained Muslim" that Shiite Islam prescribes for its followers abroad.

Practical Reconcilability Proposition

As has been shown, my major concern has been theoretical where Rawls's achievement in softening the secularity of liberalism is considerable. Hence, this book calls Mill's liberalism "deeply secular," whereas Rawls's liberalism is labeled "mildly secular." This distinction concerns the assessment of their liberalism at the theoretical level. However, at the practical level, there is no important difference between the Millian secularist state and the Rawlsian neutral state. Nor is there any ground for conflict between liberal societies and Shiite Muslim citizens.

Chapter 7 of this book examined the Practical Reconcilability Proposition regarding the toleration of Shiite Muslim citizens by the liberal state. Rawls seems to offer to religious citizens what Mill has already offered. Hence, both the Millian and the Rawlsian liberal states accommodate Shiite Muslim citizens. This toleration includes providing necessary and sufficient protections, freedoms, and opportunities in order for Shiite Muslim citizens, among others, to maintain and promote their religion. Freedom of conscience, thought, and religion; freedom of expression; freedom of association; and freedom of action are sufficiently, though unequally, distributed between religious and nonreligious citizens in the Millian and Rawlsian liberal states.

The major possible difference between a Millian society and a Rawlsian society is that in the former, public funds are only available for secular education, whereas religious schools, as complementary educational institutions, are deprived of public funding. By contrast, Rawls seems to have to approve of public funding for religious schools, in which children whose parents have submitted to any reasonable religion are educated. This is the unique major advantage of the Rawlsian ideal liberal state in comparison with the Millian. Yet, Rawls is not explicit about this major privilege that is the logical result of his argument. However, what is important is that almost all Western liberal societies, except the United States, agree with religious schools for minorities with public funding. Therefore, Shiite Muslim citizens of Western liberal societies enjoy both negative freedom and sufficient opportunities for maintaining and promoting their religion safely.

The mentioned toleration by liberal societies of Shiite Muslim citizens is the contribution of liberalism to the practical reconciliation with religious people, including Shiite Muslim citizens. As for the contribution of Shiite Muslim citizens to this practical reconciliation, chapter 8 of this book discussed some ideas and concepts that characterize Shiite Islamic thought. One important idea is the distinction made by Shiite Islamic thought between political theory and ethical theory. Since the former restricts its application to Shiite Islamic societies, Shiite Muslims abroad have no political demand, which might contradict the features of liberal states and societies. This restricted application accounts for toleration of non-Muslims and their principles and values. In addition, what Shiite ethical theory demands of its followers abroad is confined to the concept of "the self-restrained Muslim," which is compatible with Mill's idea of "the harmless person," as well as Rawls's concept of "the reasonable citizen." The duty of Shiite Muslim citizens abroad to be self-restrained Muslims can be fulfilled in the Millian and Rawlsian liberal societies by freedom to practice daily prayers, to wear a headscarf in public places, and the like. In addition, they can choose jobs that are religiously permissible. What is more, according to the ethical code of constructive reciprocity, Shiite Muslim citizens are obliged to respect the basic structure of liberal societies in return for the protections, freedoms, and opportunities that they receive in those societies.

Practical Recommendations of This Research

My investigation has two practical and highly significant recommendations. First, Shiite Muslim majorities at home have to refrain from constructing the basic structure of their societies in accordance with liberal theory. Yet, it does not follow that Shiite Islamic political theory might be illiberal. Rather, it proposes "religious democracy," which guarantees human rights, for an Islamic society with a majority of Shiite Muslims. The second recommendation confirms that the situation of Millian and Rawlsian societies are religiously appropriate for Shiite Muslims to settle in. Since liberal societies tolerate Shiite Muslim citizens, the latter should reciprocally accept the basic structure of the former. However, it should be emphasized that my discussion has focused on the Millian ideal liberal state with no reference to any specific country. Likewise, Rawls's ideal liberal state has been the focus of my examination, rather than any specific country.

Notes

Introduction

1. John Gray, *Liberalisms, Essays in Political Philosophy* (London: Routledge, 1989), p. 217.
2. J. B. Schneewind, "Introduction," in *Mill: A Collection of Critical Essays,* ed. J. B. Schneewind (New York: Anchor Books Edition, 1968), p. ix; and Bertrand Russell, "John Stuart Mill," in Schneewind, *Mill,* p. 21.
3. Acknowledging the significance of Rawls's influence on political philosophy in twentieth century, Raphael suggests that no knowledgeable scholar has accepted his theory as a sound theory of justice. See David. D. Raphael, *Concepts of Justice,* (Oxford: Oxford University Press, 2001), p. 196.
4. Peter Jones, "Two Conceptions of Liberalism, Two Conceptions of Justice," *British Journal of Political Science* 25, no. 4 (October 1995): 515.
5. Cecile Laborde, "The Reception of John Rawls in Europe," *European Journal of Political Theory* 1, no. 2 (October 2002): 133–5.
6. Victoria Davion and Clark Wolf, "Introduction: From Comprehensive Justice to Political Liberalism," in *The Idea of a Political Liberalism, Essays on Rawls,* ed. Victoria Davion and Clark Wolf (Lanham: Rowman and Littlefield, 2000), p. 1.
7. Brooke Ackerly, "John Rawls: An Introduction," *Perspectives on Politics* 4, no. 1 (March 2006): 76.
8. Robert E. Goodin and Philip Pettit (eds.), *A Companion to Contemporary Political Philosophy* (Oxford: Blackwell, 1993), p. 15.
9. Robert Nozick, *Anarchy, State, and Utopia,* (New York: Basic Books, 1974), p. 183.
10. John Rawls, *The Law of Peoples,* (Cambridge, Mass: Harvard University Press, 1999), p. 175. Dombrowski rejects the assumption that Rawls is reluctant about the relationship between religion and politics, and argues that the focal point, which Rawls's political liberalism addresses, suggests a strategy of silence in managing this relationship. See Daniel A. Dombrowski, *Rawls and Religion, The Case for Political Liberalism,* (Albany: State University of New York Press, 2001), p. vii.
11. Manus I. Midlarsky, "Democracy and Islam: Implications for Civilizational Conflict and the Democratic Peace," *International Studies Quarterly* 42, no. 3 (September 1998): 485.

12. Valerie Bunce, "Comparative Democratization, Big and Bounded Generalization," *Comparative Political Studies* 33, no. 6/7 (AugustSeptember 2000): 703–4.
13. Steven Ryan Hofmann, "Islam and Democracy: Micro-Level Indications of Compatibility," *Comparative Political Studies* 37, no. 6 (August 2004): 652.
14. Richard Rose, "How Muslims View Democracy: Evidence from Central Asia," *Journal of Democracy* 13, no. 4 (October 2002): 102.
15. Ibn Al-Manzur, *Lisan Al-Arab*, ed. Ali Shiri, vol. 4 (Beirut: Dar al-Ihya al-Turath al-Arabi, 1988), p. 460.
16. Islmail Ibn Hammad al-Jouhari, *Al-Sihah Taj al-Lughah wa Sihah al-Arabiyyah*, 4th ed., vol. 3 (Beirut: Dar al-Ilm Lilmalayin, 1985), p. 1236.
17. Ibn Al-Manzur, *Lisan Al-Arab*, vol. 6, p. 345.
18. The Qur'an, chapter "The House of Imran," verse 19.
19. Muhammad Hussein Tabatabai, *Qur'an dar Islam*, 2nd ed. (Tehran: Dar al-Kutub al-Islamiyyah, 1974), p. 12.
20. Muhammad Hussein Tabatabai, *Al-Mizan fi Tafsir al-Qur'an*, vol. 18, 2nd ed. (Beirut: Muassasah al-Aalami lil-Matbuaat, 1982), pp. 29–30.
21. The Qur'an, chapter "The Consultation," verse 13.
22. Muhammad Taqi Misbah, *Amuzishi Aqaid*, vols. 1–2, 7th ed. (Qum: Markazi Chap wa Nashri Sazmani Tablighati Islami, 1991), pp. 29–31.
23. Ibn Al-Manzur, *Lisan Al-Arab*, vol. 7, p. 257.
24. Nasir Makarim Shirazi, *Iatiqadi Ma*, 2nd ed. (Qum: Intisharati Nasli Jawan, 1997), pp. 115–16.
25. Muhammad Hussein Tabatabai, *Shia dar Islam*, 2nd edition, (Qum: Markazi Matbouaati-yi Dar al-Tablighi Islami, 1969), p. 39.
26. Makarim Shirazi, *Iatiqadi Ma*, pp. 116–19.
27. Tabatabai, *Shia dar Islam*, pp. 31–2.
28. The Largest Shiite Communities, http://www.adherents.com/largecom/com_shiite.html.
29. Makarim Shirazi, *Iatiqadi Ma*, p. 119; also see: Tabatabai, *Shia dar Islam*, p. 32.
30. Nasir Makarim Shirazi, *Panjah Darsi Usouli Aqaid barayi Jawanan*, 9th ed. (Qum: Madrasah Imam Ali, 1997), pp. 223–4.
31. Muhammad Rida Muzaffar, *Aqaid al-Imamiyyah*, 8th ed. (Beirut: Dar Al-Zahra, 2000), pp. 102–17.
32. Tabatabai, *Shia dar Islam*, p. 149.
33. Muhammad Taqi Misbah, *Amuzishi Aqaid: Imamshinasi* (Qum: Markazi Mudiriyyati Hawzi-yi Ilmiyyi-yi Qum, 1988), pp. 17–27, 121–34, and 439–41.
34. Muzaffar, *Aqaid al-Imamiyyah*, p. 89.
35. Imam Khomeini, *Chihil Hadith*, 13th ed. (Tehran: Institute of Compilation and Publication of Imam Khomeini's Works, 1997), pp. 456–7, 462–3.
36. Misbah, *Amuzishi Aqaid*, pp. 207–13.
37. Muzaffar, *Aqaid al-Imamiyyah*, p. 87.
38. Muzaffar, *Aqaid al-Imamiyyah*, p. 111.

39. Al-Fazil Al-Miqdad, *Sharhi Babi al-Hadi Ashar* (Qum: Matbaah al-Islam, 1974), p. 75.

40. Murtaza Mutahhari, *Wahy wa Nubuwwah,* (Qum: Intisharati Hikmah, 1979), pp. 36–8.

41. For a list of these traits and practices see Muhammad Mahdi Naraqi, *Jami al-Saadat* (The Collector of Felicities), http://www.al-islam.org/al-tawhid/felicities.

42. Imam Khomeini, *Wilayati Faqih: Hokoumati Islami,* 7th ed. (Tehran: Institute of Compilation and Publication of Imam Khomeini's Works, 1998), pp. 17, 22–5, 28, 31.

43. Muhammad Hussein Tabatabai is a prominent philosopher and interpreter of the Qur'an, usually called *allama,* meaning highly knowledgeable, and *mufassiri kabir,* meaning the great interpreter of the Qur'an. His masterpiece is his interpretation of the Qur'an, *Al-Mizan fi Tafsir al-Qur'an,* in 20 volumes, that has been repeatedly published in Beirut, Tehran, and Qum in the second half of the twentieth century. A well-known Iranian philosopher, Murtaza Mutahhari, describes Tabatabai's interpretation of the Qur'an as the greatest interpretation that has been ever written in Islamic history. See Abul Qasim Razzaqi, "Ba Allama-yi Tabatabai dar al-Mizan," in *Yadnami-yi Mufassiri Kabir Ustad Allama-yi Tabatabai* (Qum: Intisharati Shafaq, 1982), p. 212. Misbah, an influential thinker in contemporary Iran, describes Tabatabai as the greatest interpreter and philosopher in the contemporary Shiite world. See Muhammad Taqi Misbah, "Sukhani Piramouni Shakhsiyyati Ustad Allama-yi Tabatabai," in *Yadnami-yi Mufassiri Kabir Ustad Allama-yi Tabatabai* (Qum: Intisharati Shafaq, 1982), p. 41. Sobhani, a distinguished philosopher and jurist, argues that Tabatabai has delivered an original style of the interpretation of the Qur'an. See Jaafar Sobhani, "Nazari wa Gozari bar Zindigani-yi Ustad Allama-yi Tabatabai," in *Yadnami-yi Mufassiri Kabir Ustad Allama-yi Tabatabai* (Qum: Intisharati Shafaq, 1982), pp. 70–2. Jawadi Amoli, a prominent Shiite philosopher and interpreter of the Qur'an, argue that in addition to his innovation in the interpretation of the Qur'an, Tabatabai has promoted Islamic philosophy and made a strong attempt to reconcile between the teachings of the Qur'an and Islamic philosophy and mysticism. See Muhammad Taqi Misbah, "Naqshi Ustad Allama-yi Tabatabai dar Nihzati Fikri-yi Hawzi-yi Ilmiyyi-yi Qum', in *Yadnami-yi Mufassiri Kabir Ustad Allama-yi Tabatabai* (Qum: Intisharati Shafaq, 1982), pp. 141–3; and Abdullah Jawadi-yi Amoli, "Siri-yi Falsafi-yi Ustad Allama-yi Tabatabai," in *Yadnami-yi Mufassiri Kabir Ustad Allama-yi Tabatabai,* (Qum: Intisharati Shafaq, 1982), pp. 167–8.

44. Among their students are the following: Murtaza Mutahhari, a unique Islamic thinker in the contemporary Shiite world whose books have been broadly studied in the last three decades; Muhammad Hussein Beheshti and Abdulkarim Mousavi Ardabili, the first and the second head of the judiciary of the Islamic Republic of Iran; Ibrahim Amini, the deputy director of the Assembly of Experts for the appointment of the supreme leader in Iran; Hassan Hassanzadi

Amoli and Abdullah Jawadi Amoli, the most distinguished philosophers of present Iran; Muhammad Taqi Misbah, the most influential religious scholar in present Iranian politics; Nasir Makarim Shirazi, and Hussein Nouri Hamidani, two top jurists of present Iran; and finally Jaafar Sobhani, the most prominent theologian in the contemporary Shiite world. See Sobhani, "Nazari wa Gozari bar Zindigani-yi Ustad Allama-yi Tabatabai," p. 73.

45. J. A. Simpson and E. S. C. Weiner (eds.), *The Oxford English Dictionary,* 2nd ed., Vol. 8, (Oxford: Oxford University Press, 1989), p. 881.
46. Seymour Martin Lipset, *The Encyclopedia of Democracy* (London: Routledge, 1995), p. 756; Patrick Neal and David Paris, "Liberalism and the Communitarian Critique: A Guide for the Perplexed," *Canadian Journal of Political Science* 23, no. 3 (September 1990): 431.
47. John Kekes, *Against Liberalism* (Ithaca: Cornell University, 1997), p. 2.
48. Richard Bellamy, *Rethinking Liberalism* (London: Pinter, 2000), p. 43.
49. John Gray, *Liberalism,* 2nd ed. (Berkshire: Open University Press, 1995), pp. xi, 46.
50. Anthony Arblaster, *The Rise and Decline of Western Liberalism* (Oxford: Basil Blackwell, 1984), p. 56.
51. Richard Bellamy, *Liberalism and Modern Society: An Historical Argument* (Cambridge: Polity Press, 1992), p. 2.
52. Benjamin Constant, "Liberty Ancient and Modern," in *The History of European Liberalism,* ed. G. de Ruggiero(Oxford: Oxford University Press, 1927), pp. 167–8.
53. Isaiah Berlin, *Four Essays on Liberty* (London: Oxford University Press, 1969), p. lvi.
54. Ibid., pp. lvii, 132, 144.
55. Andrew Mason, "Imposing Liberal Principles," in *Pluralism and Liberal Neutrality,* ed. Richard Bellamy and Martin Hollis (London: Frank Cass, 1999), p. 99.
56. Chandran Kukathas. "Are There Any Cultural Rights?" *Political Theory* 20, no. 1 (February 1992): 116, 128.
57. A. H. Robertson and J. G. Merrills, *Human Rights in the World,* 4th ed. (Manchester: Manchester University Press, 1996), pp. 2–7.
58. Eric Heinze, *The Logic of Liberal Rights: A Study in the Formal Analysis of Legal Discourse* (London: Routledge, 2003), p. 13.
59. Bellamy, *Rethinking Liberalism,* pp. 146, 176–7.
60. Gray, *Liberalism,* pp. xii, xiii.
61. Richard Bellamy, "Liberalism," in *Contemporary Political Ideologies,* ed. Roger Eatwell and Anthony Wright (London: Pinter, 1993), p. 24.
62. John Gray, *Post-Liberalism, Studies in Political Thought,* 2nd ed. (London: Routledge, 1996), p. 287.
63. Bellamy, *Liberalism and Modern Society,* p. 24.
64. Look for instance at Charles Larmore, *The Morals of Modernity,* (Cambridge: Cambridge University Press, 1996), p. 127; Bellamy, *Liberalism and Modern*

Society, p. 7; William A. Galston, *Liberal Purposes, Goods, Virtues, and Diversity in the Liberal State* (Cambridge: Cambridge University Press, 1991), pp. 80–1; John Rawls, *Political Liberalism* (New York: Columbia University Press, 1996), p. 196.

65. Kekes, *Against Liberalism,* p. 2.
66. Galston, *Liberal Purposes, Goods, Virtues, and Diversity,* p. 80.
67. Charles Larmore, *Patterns of Moral Complexity* (Cambridge: Cambridge University Press, 1987), p. 46.
68. William A. Galston, "Two Concepts of Liberalism," *Ethics* 105, no. 3 (April 1995): 525.
69. Rawls, *Political Liberalism,* pp. xx, xxvi.
70. Ibid., pp. xxviii, xxix.
71. Ibid., pp. xxix, 37, 199–200.
72. Since the concept of toleration implies disagreement and disapproval of what is tolerated, liberal citizens, who are self-restrained towards their disagreeing people, should be appreciated. See Steven Kautz, "Liberalism and the Idea of Toleration," *American Journal of Political Science* 37, no. 2 (May 1993): 610. Of course, as this book will demonstrate, peaceable religious people are, also, tolerant of those whom they believe to follow false conceptions of the good.
73. Nick Fotion and Gerard Elfstrom, *Toleration* (London and Tuscaloosa: University of Alabama Press, 1992), pp. 13, 117, 4.
74. Mary Warnock, "The Limits of Toleration," in *On Toleration,* ed. Susan Mendus and David Edwards (New York: Oxford University Press, 1987), pp. 126–7.
75. Preston King, *Toleration,* 2nd ed. (London: Frank Cass, 1998), pp. xiii, xiv, 21–29.
76. Richard C. Sinopoli, "Liberalism and Contested Conceptions of the Good: The Limits of Neutrality," *The Journal of Politics* 55, no. 3 (August 1993): 644.
77. Ibid., p. 4.
78. Ibid., pp. xxix, 4.
79. Galston, "Two Concepts of Liberalism," p. 525.
80. *The Oxford English Dictionary,* vol. 14, p. 848.
81. Iain McLean (ed.), *The Concise Oxford Dictionary of Politics* (Oxford: Oxford University Press, 1996), p. 445.
82. Bernard Eugene Meland, *The Secularisation of Modern Cultures* (New York: Oxford University Press, 1966), pp. 4, 15.
83. Rajeev Bhargava, "Introduction," in *Secularism and Its Critics,* ed. Rajeev Bhargava (Delhi: Oxford University Press, 1998), pp. 3, 7–8.
84. Veit Bader, "Religious Diversity and Democratic Institutional Pluralism," *Political Theory* 31, no. 2 (April 2003): 269–71.
85. Karel Dobbelaere, "Secularization: A Multi-Dimensional Concept," *Current Sociology* 29, no. 2 (Summer 1981): 8–9.
86. Steve Bruce, "Introduction," in *Religion and Modernisation, Sociologists and Historians Debate the Secularisation Book,* ed. Steve Bruce (Oxford: Oxford University Press, 1992), p. 6.

87. George Jacob Holyoake, *English Secularism, A Confession of Belief* (Chicago: Open Court, 1896), pp. 1, 35.

88. Meland, *The Secularisation of Modern Cultures,* p. 3.

89. Heiner Bielefeldt, "Western versus Islamic Human Rights Conceptions? A Critique of Cultural Essentialism in the Discussion on Human Rights," *Political Theory* 28, no. 1 (February 2000): 112.

90. D. L. Munby, *The Idea of a Secular Society, and Its Significance for Christians* (London: Oxford University Press, 1963), p. 12.

91. Richard Vernon, "J. S. Mill and the Religion of Humanity," in *Religion, Secularisation and Political Thought, Thomas Hobbes to J. S. Mill,* ed. James E. Crimmins (London: Routledge, 1990), p. 169.

92. Ibid., pp. 169–70.

93. Munby, *The Idea of a Secular Society,* pp. 14–32.

94. Meland, *The Secularisation of Modern Cultures,* pp. 37–8.

95. Robert Audi and Nicholas Woltersorff, *Religion in the Public Square, the Place of Religious Convictions in Political Debate* (Lanham: Rowman and Littlefield, 1997), pp. 2–14, 38–42, 73.

96. This book defines religion as a doctrine, which suggests that there are supernatural or revelational principles that have come down from God as the original source of existence. In addition, religion suggests that there is a perpetual life man experiences after death. This definition fully applies to Abrahamian religions, including Judaism, Christendom, Islam, as well as Zoroastrianism.

97. Rawls, *Political Liberalism,* pp. 191–2.

98. King, *Toleration,* p. 73.

99. Ibid., pp. 77, 126.

100. Ibid., p. 114.

101. Following political theorists such as Joseph Raz and William Galston, this book rejects even the feasibility of constructing a neutral state. See Joseph Raz, *The Morality of Freedom* (New York: Oxford University Press, 1986), pp. 110–33; and Galston, *Liberal Purposes, Goods, Virtues, and Diversity,* pp. 79–97.

102. William Safran, "Introduction," in *The Secular and the Sacred: Nation, Religion and Politics,* ed. William Safran (London: Frank Cass, 2003), pp. 1–2.

103. George Joffe, "Democracy, Islam and the Culture of Modernism," *Democratization* 4, no. 3 (Autumn 1997): 135–8.

104. P. L. Berger, *Modernisation and Religion* (Dublin: Brunswick Press, 1981), p. 9.

105. Jurgen Moltmann, *God for a Secular Society, the Public Relevance of Theology* trans. Margaret Kohl (London: SCM Press, 1999), p. 211.

106. As Charles Taylor argues, the solution suggested by Hobbes and Grotius to the problem of religious conflicts rests on the supposition that there is "an independent political ethics." Whether or not God exists, all human beings understand some ethical codes, which should reign supreme in politics, such as keeping one's promise. Not only do Hobbes and Grotius propose the availability of a

collection of independent political ethics, but to distinguish them from religious ethics they also argue that religion is a private issue. The public sphere, thus, should be exclusively entrusted to independent political ethics. As Taylor expounds, Locke and Pufendrof's alternative solution to overcome religious conflicts suggests "the common ground strategy." To establish peace among the followers of all sects of Christianity, they searched for some religious, even Christian, principles in which all sects of this religion share. . This solution rests on the idea of Natural Law, which can be discovered by the same reason that brings us to submit to God. See Charles Taylor, "Modes of Secularism," in Rajeev Bhargava (ed.), *Secularism and Its Critics* (Delhi: Oxford University Press, 1998), pp. 33–5.

107. Meland, *The Secularisation of Modern Cultures,* pp. 15–7, 25, 43.
108. Hugh McLeod, "Secular Cities? Berlin, London, and New York in the Later Nineteenth and Early Twentieth Centuries," in *Religion and Modernisation, Sociologists and Historians Debate the Secularisation Book,* ed. Steve Bruce (New York: Oxford University Press, 1992), p. 59.
109. Pippa Norris and Ronald Inglehart, *Sacred and Secular, Religion and Politics Worldwide* (Cambridge: Cambridge University Press, 2004), p. 3.
110. Anthony Gill, "Religion and Comparative Politics," *Annual Review of Political Science* 4 (2001): 117.
111. Leonard Binder, *Islamic Liberalism, a Critique of Development of Ideologies,* (Chicago: University of Chicago Press, 1988), pp. 131–5.
112. Veit Bader, "Religious Pluralism: Secularism or Priority for Democracy?" *Political Theory* 27, no. 5 (October 1999): 597–8.
113. Eldon J. Eisenach, *Two Worlds of Liberalism: Religion and Politics in Hobbes, Locke, and Mill* (Chicago: University of Chicago, 1981), pp. 3–5.

Chapter 1

1. J. B. Schneewind, "Introduction," in *Mill: A Collection of Critical Essays,* ed. J. B. Schneewind (New York: Anchor Books Edition, 1968), pp. x, xi.
2. Jan Wolenski, "The History of Epistemology," in *Handbook of Epistemology,* ed. Ilkka Niiniluoto, Matti Sintonen, and Jan Wolenski (Dordrecht: Kluwer Academic Publishers, 2004), pp. 38–9.
3. Alan Ryan, *John Stuart Mill* (New York: Pantheon Books, 1970), pp. 90, 94.
4. John Stuart Mill, *An Examination of Sir William Hamilton's Philosophy and of the Principal Philosophical Questions Discussed in His Writings,* ed. J. M. Robson, (Toronto: University of Toronto Press, 1979), p. 221.
5. Ryan, *John Stuart Mill,* pp. 91–4.
6. Mill, *Hamilton's Philosophy,* p. 229.
7. R. P. Anschutz, "The Logic of J. S. Mill," in *Mill: A Collection of Critical Essays,* ed. J. B. Schneewind (New York: Anchor Books Edition, 1968), pp. 60–3.
8. Christopher Turk, *Coleridge and Mill: A Study of Influence* (Aldershot: Avebury, 1988), pp. 118–9.

9. Mill, *Hamilton's Philosophy,* p. 143.

10. John Stuart Mill, *A System of Logic, Ratiocinative and Induction, Collected Works of J. S. Mill,* vol. 7, ed. J. M. Robson (1843; repr. Toronto: University of Toronto Press, 1973), II, vii, 1.

11. Turk, *Coleridge and Mill,* p. 117.

12. Gerd Buchdahl, "Inductivist vs. Deductivist Approaches in the Philosophy of Science as Illustrated by Some Controversies between Whewell and Mill," in *The General Philosophy of John Stuart Mill,* ed. Victor Sanchez Valencia (Aldershot, Hants, Burlington, VT: Ashgate, 2002), p. 124.

13. William Whewell, *The Philosophy of Inductive Science,* 2nd ed., vol. 1 (London, 1847), pp. 19, 55.

14. Mill, *A System of Logic,* II, vii, 1.

15. Mill, *Hamilton's Philosophy,* pp. 139–40, 143.

16. Buchdahl, "Inductivist vs. Deductivist Approaches," pp. 113–14.

17. Mill, *A System of Logic,* II, vii, 1.

18. Karl R. Popper, *Logic of Scientific Discovery* (New York: Basic Books, 1963), pp. 59, 75.

19. Ryan, *John Stuart Mill,* p. 9.

20. Anschutz, "The Logic of J. S. Mill," pp. 48–9.

21. John Stuart Mill, "Archbishop Whately's Elements of Logic," *Westminster Review* 9 (1828): 147, 150.

22. Ibid., p. 150.

23. Oskar Alfred Kubitz, *Development of John Stuart Mill's System of Logic* (Urbana: University of Illinois, 1932), p. 203.

24. Henry M. Magid, "John Stuart Mill," in *History of Political Philosophy,* 3rd ed., ed. Leo Strauss and Joseph Cropsey, (Chicago: University of Chicago Press, 1987), pp. 784–5.

25. Anschutz, "The Logic of J.S. Mill," pp. 51–2.

26. Mill, *A System of Logic,* II, vii, 1.

27. Mill, *Hamilton's Philosophy,* p. 139.

28. Kubitz, *Development of John Stuart Mill's System of Logic,* p. 204.

29. Ryan, *John Stuart Mill,* p. 18.

30. Mill, "Introduction," *A System of Logic,* 4.

31. Ryan, *John Stuart Mill,* p. 18.

32. Mill, *Hamilton's Philosophy,* pp. 457, 462.

33. Victor Sanchez Valencia, "Introduction," in *The General Philosophy of John Stuart Mill,* ed. Victor Sanchez Valencia (Aldershot, Hants, Burlington, VT: Ashgate, 2002), p. xxvi.

34. Mill, *A System of Logic,* II, iii, 4.

35. In a further explanation about induction, following Whately, Mill distinguishes between induction as "investigation," and induction as "inference" (Kubitz, *Development of John Stuart Mill's System of Logic,* p. 140). In the process of investigation, we are concerned with collecting evidence about a fact through experience, correcting "a narrower generalisation by a wider" generalization

achieved by experiences. The leading principle in our investigation is the law of universal causation. Since Mill sees experiment as the only valid method, he suggests that even the knowledge of human beings about the law of universal causation as the most general knowledge is due to the historical experience of humankind. According to this law, "To certain facts, certain facts always do, and, as we believe, always will, succeed. The invariable antecedent is termed the cause; the invariable consequent, the effect." Or, "every fact which has a beginning has a cause." The validity of any induction is subject to further experiments that verify some induction and not another, and human experience throughout history has demonstrated that with regard to the phenomena of coexistence there is one certain law that is universal in numbers and spaces, that is, the law of universal causation (Mill, *A System of Logic*, III, v, 1–2; III, iv, 2). In the process of induction as inference or reasoning, we generalize what we have found by experience about facts. This inference is from particulars to generalities on the basis of the law of "uniformity of nature" expressing that "what is true of certain individuals of a class is true of the whole class, or that what is true at certain times will be true in similar circumstances at all time." Induction as inference that generalizes from experience concludes "from some individual instances in which a phenomenon is observed to occur, that it occurs in all instances of a certain class; namely, in all which resemble the former." This assumption is present in all inductions. For, as Mill argues, "The universe, so far as known to us, is so constituted, that whatever is true in any one case, is true in all cases of a certain description; the only difficulty is, to find what description" (Mill, *A System of Logic*, II, ii, 1; III, iii, 1). However, as is recognizable from the distinction between induction as investigation and induction as inference, one can notice the element of deduction in the inductive method in the inference stage. It is for this element of deduction in Mill's inference that John Skorupski maintains that Mill "is . . . an inductivist. But that does not blind him to the deductive structure of scientific theory." See John Skorupski, *John Stuart Mill* (London: Routledge, 1991), pp. 255–6.

36. Mill, *A System of Logic*, III, i, 2; II, iii, 7.
37. Ibid., II, iii, 2.
38. It is worth noting that the petitio principii problem with syllogism was recognized by Sextus Empiricus 16 centuries before Mill dealt with it. See Geoffrey Scarre, "Proof and Implication in Mill's Philosophy of Logic," in *The General Philosophy of John Stuart Mill*, ed. Victor Sanchez Valencia (Aldershot, Hants, Burlington, VT: Ashgate, 2002), p. 293.
39. Mill, *A System of Logic*, II, iii, 2.
40. Ibid., II, iii, 4.
41. Ryan, *John Stuart Mill*, pp. 25–6.
42. Mill, *A System of Logic*, II, iii, 3.
43. Ryan, *John Stuart Mill*, p. 26.
44. Mill, *A System of Logic*, II, iii, 3.
45. Ryan, *John Stuart Mill*, pp. 26–7.

46. Mill, *A System of Logic,* II, iii, 3–5.

47. Mill, *Hamilton's Philosophy,* pp. 372–3, 379, 381.

48. Muhammad Baqir Al-Sadr, *Falsafatuna* (Beirut: Dar al-Kutub al-Islami, 1958), p. 63.

49. Ibid., p. 69.

50. Ibid., p. 68.

51. The intellectual demonstration, which is invoked to prove the truth of the Qur'an as a divine revelation, consists of the following premises:

    1. The person who broughtthis book was illiterate.
    2. His homeland was not civilized, except in the field of poetry.
    3. The Qur'an brought a collection of human values that were significantly higher than the level of its time, especially in the Saudi Arabian peninsula.
    4. The Qur'an broughtsome reports about the history of other nations that were unknown to the Prophet's compatriots.
    5. "The linguistic level and style of the Qur'an was unique and innovative enough to be acknowledged by experienced poets of the Prophet's time.

    We can conclude, therefore, that Muhammad was not in a position to be able to create this book. Hence, it should have been revealed from a supernatural entity. See Muhammad Baqir Al-Sadr, *Al-Fatawa al-Wazihah Wafqan li-Madhhab Ahlulbeit,* 8th ed., vol. 1 (Beirut: Dar al-Taaruf lil-Matbuaat, 1992), pp. 61–74.

52. Murtaza Mutahhari, *Kulliyyati Uloumi Islami,* vol. 3, *Usouli Fiqh and Fiqh,* 24th ed. (Qum: Intisharati Sadra, 2001), pp. 16–23, 34–6.

53. Muhammad Hussein Tabatabai, *Shia dar Islam,* 2nd ed. (Qum: Markazi Matbouaati-yi dar al-Tablighi Islami, 1969), pp. 42–4.

54. However, even if we submit to the Millian scientific method, there is still a possibility to support the basic doctrines of Islam, such as the existence of God, the Messengerhood of Muhammad, and the validity of the Qur'an. For instance, as a Shiite Muslim philosopher argues, in the first place we can collect by experience many facts about the required conditions for human life on earth. Then, we consider that the hypothesis that "there is a wise creator who has deliberately provided all these conditions for man to live on earth" can explain all these facts. By contrast, the rejection of this hypothesis requires that several different facts coincide by accident, the probability of which is almost equal to zero. Then, he concludes that the affirmative hypothesis should be true. See Al-Sadr, *Al-Fatawa al-Wazihah Wafqan li-Madhhab Ahlulbeit,* pp. 19–39, and 61–74. Also for a similar discussion see Nasir Makarim Shirazi, *Payami Qur'an,* vol. 2, 5th ed. (Tehran: Dar al-Kutub al-Islamiyyah, 1997), pp. 54–9.

55. John Stuart Mill, "Utilitarianism," in *Utilitarianism, on Liberty, Considerations of Representative Government, Remarks on Bentham's Philosophy,* ed. Geraint Williams, 3rd ed (London: Every Man's Library, 1993), pp. 2–3.

56. Ryan, *John Stuart Mill,* p. 188.

57. Mill, "Utilitarianism," pp. 4–5.
58. Speaking about the ultimate moral standard, Mill says: "The subject is within the cognisance of the rational faculty; and neither does that faculty deal with it solely in the way of intuitionism. Considerations may be presented capable of determining the intellect either to give or withhold its assent to the doctrine; and this is equivalent to proof. Mill, "Utilitarianism," p. 5.
59. Mill, *A System of Logic,* VI, xii, 6.
60. John Stuart Mill, *Dissertations and Discussions: Political, Philosophical, and Historical,* vol. 1 (London: W. Parker, 1859), p. 148.
61. John Stuart Mill, "On Liberty," *Utilitarianism, on Liberty, Considerations of Representative Government, Remarks on Bentham's Philosophy,* ed. Geraint Williams, 3rd ed. (London: Every Man's Library, 1993), pp. 74, 77.
62. Wolenski, "The History of Epistemology," p. 39.
63. Wikipedia, "Ethical Naturalism," http://en.wikipedia.org/wiki/Ethical_naturalism.
64. Ryan, *John Stuart Mill,* p. 190.
65. Mill, *A System of Logic,* I, v, 1.
66. Ryan, *John Stuart Mill,* p. 191.
67. Mill, *A System of Logic,* VI, xi, 2.
68. Ryan, *John Stuart Mill,* p. 193.
69. Mill, "Utilitarianism," p. 36.
70. Not only is the utility principle the criterion for assessment of ethical conduct as right, but it is also the criterion for assessing the prudence or policy as expedient, and for assessing as beauty or noble that together comprise the whole "Art of Life," as Mill calls it. See Mill, *A System of Logic,* VI, xii, 6.
71. Ryan, *John Stuart Mill,* p. 195.
72. Mill, "Utilitarianism," p. 5.
73. Muhammad Hussein Tabatabai, *Usouli Falsafa wa Rawishi Rialism,* 3 vols., ed. Murtaza Mutahhari (Qum: Dafteri Intisharati Islami), pp. 270–9, 314–32.
74. Imam Khomeini, *Chihil Hadith,* 13th ed. (Tehran: Institute of Compilation and Publication of Imam Khomeini's Works, 1997), pp. 180–4.
75. Alasdair MacIntyre, *After Virtue,* 2nd ed. (London: Duckworth, 2002), p. 56.

Chapter 2

1. R. P. Anschutz, *The Philosophy of J. S. Mill,* 3rd ed. (Oxford: Oxford University Press, 1969), p. 12.
2. Geraint Williams, "Notes," in John Stuart Mill, *Utilitarianism, On Liberty, Considerations of Representative Government, Remarks on Bentham's Philosophy,* ed. by Geraint Williams, 3rd ed. (London: Every Man's Library, 1993), p. 448n3.
3. William Whewell, *Elements of Morality, Including Polity,* 4th ed. (Cambridge: Cambridge University Press, 1864), pp. 26, 40–1, 48–9.
4. Ibid., pp. 49, 53–5.
5. Ibid., pp. 49–53, 58.

6. W. D. Ross, *The Right and the Good* (Oxford: Oxford University Press, 1930), pp. 19–21, 23.
7. John Stuart Mill, "Utilitarianism," in *Utilitarianism, on Liberty, Considerations of Representative Government, Remarks on Bentham's Philosophy,* ed. Geraint Williams, 3rd ed (London: Every Man's Library, 1993), p. 4.
8. Immanuel Kant, *Political Writings,* ed. H. S. Reiss, 2nd ed. (Cambridge: Cambridge University Press, 1991), p. 69.
9. J. B. Schneewind, "Autonomy, Obligation, and Virtue: An Overview of Kant's Moral Philosophy," in *The Cambridge Companion to Kant,* ed. Paul Guyer (Cambridge: Cambridge University Press, 1992), pp. 318–20.
10. Ibid., pp. 316–7.
11. Ronald Dworkin, "The Original Position," in *Reading Rawls, Critical Studies on Rawls's A Theory of Justice,* ed. Norman Daniels (California: Stanford University Press, 1975), pp. 40–1.
12. Geoffrey Scarre, *Utilitarianism* (London: Routledge, 1996), p. 82.
13. Wendy Donner, *The Liberal Self: John Stuart Mill's' Moral and Political Philosophy* (London: Cornell University Press, 1991), p. 2.
14. Schneewind, "Autonomy, Obligation, and Virtue," p. 326.
15. Andrew Levine, *Engaging Political Philosophy, from Hobbes to Rawls* (Oxford: Blackwell, 2002), p. 133.
16. John Stuart Mill, *A System of Logic Ratiocinative and Inductive, Being a Connected View of the Principles of Evidence and the Methods of Scientific Investigation,* Book IV–VI and Appendices, ed. J. M. Robson (1843, repr. Toronto: University of Toronto Press, 1974), p. 951.
17. Ibid., p. 951.
18. Utilitarianism more or less can be characterized as being "consequentialist," "welfarist," "aggregative," "maximising," and "universalist." All consequentialists prioritize the concept of good over the right, because the very meaning of right is dependent on a specific notion of the good. Utilitarians agree that the good is utility, although they differ over the meaning of utility. As for the interpretation of the type of welfare or utility the achievement of which is the goal of the utility principle, to Aristotle it is happiness in the sense of those worthwhile activities that promote human talents and bring about excellence, whereas Bentham, in sharp contrast, considers it as pleasure. Utilitarian morality assumes that utility is something measurable, which is distributed among individuals so as to be summed up in total. Commensurability of the utility of all individuals, along with the possibility of calculating the total or the aggregate utility, is another component of utilitarianism. Utilitarianism, furthermore, is maximizing in the sense that it receives its force from a rational principle of practical reason, which indicates that if a good is achievable at a higher degree it is irrational to behave in such a way as to produce it at a lower degree. A further assumption of utilitarians suggests that the increase in everyone's utility necessarily leads to the increase of social utility. Yet, when taking into consideration the conflicts of interests with regard to scarce natural resources, as well as conflicting values

indispensable in culturally diverse societies, the possibility of connecting the increase of individual utility with the increase of society's utility seems problematic. A further feature of utilitarianism concerns the subject of maximization; hence, while traditional utilitarians generally affirm that the "total utility" is the subject of the maximising element of this theory, Harsanyi suggests that it is "the average per capita utility" that should be maximized. Finally, what utilitarian moralists propose, the greatest happiness, should be distributed as widely among relevant individuals as possible. To the question "Who is my neighbour?" utilitarians will answer "Everyone." This feature of utilitarianism is partly accounted for by the idea that every citizen's interests should be counted equally and not inferior to some others (Scarre, *Utilitarianism,* pp. 4–24).

19. Benthamite utilitarianism, according to Anschutz, consists of three principles— individualism, greatest happiness principle, and hedonism. Individualism requires the reduction of all social and private matters to a simple question of individual utility. According to the greatest happiness principle, those questions may be reduced to questions concerning individual happiness. And finally, the principle of hedonism reduces all those questions to the question about individual measurable pleasures and pains. Hence, what Bentham suggests amounts to the view that every public and private action can be judged as being right or wrong on the basis of its productivity of measurable pleasure or pain (Anschutz, *The Philosophy of J. S. Mill,* pp. 9, 11, 14). As Postema argues, Bentham suggested that utility "is not only the ultimate evaluative principle, it is the sole sovereign *decision principle*" (Gerald J. Postema, *Bentham and the Common Law Tradition* [New York: Oxford University Press, 1986], pp. 157–9). Admitting that the generally accepted interpretation of Benthamite system of morality has characterized him as a "crude act-utilitarian," Paul Kelly rejects this common interpretation, and suggests that "Bentham did not employ a direct act-utilitarian theory of moral obligation" (Paul Kelly, *Utilitarianism and Distributive Justice: Jeremy Bentham and the Civil Law* [Oxford: Clarendon, 1990], pp. 39–40, 43).

20. Jeremy Bentham, *The Principles of Morals and Legislation* (New York: Prometheus Books, 1988), p. 1.

21. Geraint Williams, "Introduction," in John Stuart Mill, *Utilitarianism, on Liberty, Considerations of Representative Government, Remarks on Bentham's Philosophy,* ed. Geraint Williams, 3rd ed. (London: Every Man's Library, 1993), p. xxiv.

22. John Plamenatz, *The English Utilitarians,* 2nd ed (Oxford: Basil Blackwell, 1958), p. 134; Williams, "Introduction," p. xxiv.

23. Mill, "Utilitarianism," pp. 55–6.

24. Ibid., p. 66.

25. Ibid., pp. 57, 60.

26. Ibid., p. 7.

27. Ibid., p. 12.

28. Ibid., pp. 13, 36.
29. Ibid., pp. 36, 40.
30. Ibid., p. 8.
31. Wendy Donner, "Mill's Utilitarianism," in *The Cambridge Companion to Mill,* ed. John Skorupski (Cambridge: Cambridge University Press, 1998), p. 257.
32. Ibid., p. 263.
33. Fredrick Rosen, *Classical Utilitarianism from Hume to Mill,* (London: Routledge, 2003), pp. 172, 173.
34. Mill, "Utilitarianism," pp. 9–10, 37–8.
35. Fred Berger, *Happiness, Justice, and Freedom: The Moral and Political Philosophy of John Stuart Mill* (Berkeley: University of California Press, 1984), pp. 12–17.
36. Mill, *A System of Logic,* pp. 842–3, 952.
37. Karl Britton, *John Stuart Mill* (London: Penguin, 1953), p. 53.
38. Mill, "Utilitarianism," p. 40.
39. Ibid., pp. 8, 9.
40. Donner, *The Liberal Self,* p. 5.
41. Britton, *John Stuart Mill,* p. 52.
42. Mill, "Utilitarianism," pp. 10–11.
43. Ibid., pp. 16–17, 38–9.
44. Richard B. Brandt, "A Utilitarian Theory of Excuses," *The Philosophical Review* 78, no. 3 (July 1969): 343.
45. J. D. Mabbott, "Interpretation of Mill's Utilitarianism," in *Mill: A Collection of Critical Essays,* ed. J. B. Schneewind (New York: Anchor Books, 1968), pp. 190, 192.
46. R. G. Frey, "Introduction: Utilitarianism and Persons," in *Utility and Rights,* ed. R. G. Frey (Oxford: Basil Blackwell, 1985), p. 5.
47. J. O. Urmson, "The Interpretation of the Moral Philosophy of J. S. Mill," in *Mill: A Collection of Critical Essays,* ed. J. B. Schneewind (New York: Anchor Books, 1968), pp. 182–3.
48. Mill, "Utilitarianism," p. 25.
49. Frey, "Introduction: Utilitarianism and Persons," p. 3.
50. Mill, "Utilitarianism," p. 25.
51. Urmson, "The Interpretation of the Moral Philosophy of J. S. Mill," p. 186.
52. Mabbott, "Interpretation of Mill's Utilitarianism," p. 191.
53. Mill, "Utilitarianism," p. 20. The emphasis is added.
54. Ibid., p. 36.
55. John Skorupski, *John Stuart Mill* (London: Routledge, 1991), p. 286.
56. Maurice Mandelbaum, "Two Moot Issues in Mill's Utilitarianism," in *Mill: A Collection of Critical Essays,* ed. J. B. Schneewind (New York: Anchor Books, 1968), pp. 231–2.
57. Mill, "Utilitarianism," p. 17.
58. Britton, *John Stuart Mill,* p. 53.
59. Mill, "Utilitarianism," p. 11.
60. Ibid., pp. 17–18.

61. Alan Ryan, *John Stuart Mill* (New York, Pantheon Books, 1970), pp. 196–205.
62. Mill, "Utilitarianism," p. 33.
63. Ryan, *John Stuart Mill,* p. 197.
64. Mill, "Utilitarianism," p. 18.
65. As Kymlicka argues, Mill and other utilitarian moralists advanced the most powerful alternative to religious morality. See Will Kymlicka, *Contemporary Political Philosophy, An Introduction* (New York: Oxford University Press, 1990), p. 10.
66. Muhammad Hussein Tabatabai, *Usouli Falsafa wa Rawishi Rialism,* 5 vols.,ed. Murtaza Mutahhari (Qum: Dafteri Intisharati Islami), p. 314.
67. Muhammad Hussein Tabatabai, *Shia dar Islam,* 2nd ed. (Qum: Markazi Matbouaati-yi dar al-Tablighi Islami, 1969), pp. 1–3.
68. *The Qur'an,* chapter "The Spider," verse 64.
69. *The Qur'an,* chapter "Golden Ornaments," verses 70–1.
70. Mill, "Utilitarianism," pp. 23, 25.
71. *The Qur'an,* chapter "The Sun," verses 7–8, trans. 'Ali Qulī Qarā'ī (London: Islamic College for Advanced Studies Press, 2004), p. 851.
72. Muhammad Hussein Tabatabai, *Al-Mizan fi Tafsir al-Qur'an,* vol. 16, 2nd ed. (Beirut: Muassasah al-Aalami lil-Matbuaat, 1982), pp. 119–20.
73. *The Qur'an,* chapter "The Heavenly Food," verse 8.
74. *The Qur'an,* chapter "The Women," verse 135.
75. Robert Carr, "The Religious Thought of John Stuart Mill: A Study in Reluctant Scepticism," in *The General Philosophy of John Stuart Mill,* ed. Victor Sanchez Valencia (Aldershot, Hants, Burlington, VT: Ashgate, 2002), p. 413.
76. Richard Vernon, "J. S. Mill and the Religion of Humanity," in *Religion, Secularisation and Political Thought, Thomas Hobbes to J. S. Mill,* ed. James E. Crimmins (London: Routledge, 1990), p. 169.
77. Carr, "The Religious Thought of John Stuart Mill," pp. 423–4, 428.
78. J. S. Mill, "Utility of Religion," in *Essays on Ethics, Religion and Society, Collected Works of John Stuart Mill,* vol. 10, ed. J. M. Robson (Toronto: University of Toronto Press, 1969), pp. 418–19.
79. Ibid., pp. 417–22.
80. Allan D. Megill, "J. S. Mill's Religion of Humanity and the Second Justification for the Writing of *On Liberty,*" *The Journal of Politics* 34, no. 2 (May 1972): 616–17.
81. Mill, "Utility of Religion," pp. 426–7.
82. David Lyons, "Mill's Theory of Justice," in *Values and Morals: Essays in Honour of William Frankena, Charles Stevenson, and Richard Brandt,* ed. Alvin I. Goldman and Jaegwon Kim (Dordrecht, Holland: D. Reidel, 1978), pp. 1, 4–5.
83. Kelly, *Utilitarianism and Distributive Justice,* p. 43.
84. Lyons, "Mill's Theory of Justice," pp. 6–7, 12.
85. John Gray, *Mill on Liberty, a Defence* (London: Routledge and Kegan Paul, 1983), pp. 36, 38–9, 46–7.

86. Mill, "Utilitarianism," p. 7.
87. Ibid., p. 49.
88. Lyons, "Mill's Theory of Justice," pp. 1, 5.
89. Mill, "Utilitarianism," pp. 49, 53–4.
90. Ibid., p. 51–5.
91. Ibid., p. 51.
92. David. D. Raphael, *Concepts of Justice* (Oxford: Oxford University Press, 2001), p. 133.
93. Donner, "Mill's Utilitarianism," p. 285.
94. Mill, "Utilitarianism," pp. 62–3.
95. Donner, "Mill's Utilitarianism," p. 282.
96. Mill, "Utilitarianism," pp. 45–7.
97. Donner, "Mill's Utilitarianism," p. 285.
98. Mill, "Utilitarianism," p. 66.
99. John Stuart Mill, *Dissertations and Discussions: Political, Philosophical, and Historical,* vol. 1 (London: W. Parker, 1859), p. 495.
100. Mill, "Utilitarianism," pp. 55–6.
101. The conviction in rule-utilitarianism along with derivation of the principle of justice from the general good, along with the supremacy of justice over all other happiness, dismiss some objections addressed to Mill on the assumption that since Mill is an act-utilitarian, he cannot account for individual rights. Therefore, Frey is right to assume that Mill attempts to accommodate vital rights by grounding them in a utilitarian basis. Yet, he misrepresents Mill by supposing that this accommodation is impossible because the view that any act is right or wrong owing to its real consequences is incompatible with the view that a right is independent of any consequence of a given act (R. G. Frey, "Act-Utilitarianism, Consequentialism, and Moral Rights," in *Utility and Rights,* ed. R. G. Frey [Oxford: Basil Blackwell, 1985], pp. 62, 65). Also, Donner who suggests that Mill proposes two *independent* criteria for appraisal of a given action as right or wrong (Donner, "Mill's Utilitarianism," p. 283), in Berger's terms: the "proportionality criterion" and the "punishability criterion" (Berger, *Happiness, Justice, and Freedom,* pp. 66, 105), seems to misrepresent Mill's moral theory. Equally irrelevant is Sumner's objection that "what distinguishes consequentialist theories from their rivals is that they are goal-based—that is, at bottom they counsel the pursuit of some global synoptic goal. By contrast, rights appear to function normatively as constraints on the pursuit of such goals." Then, he shows the dilemma in this way: "If right is to be grounded in a goal then the goal must justify constraints on its own pursuit. But surely if we once adopt a goal then we are committed to doing on every occasion whatever will best achieve it, in which case we are committed to ignoring or overriding any such constraints" (L. W. Sumner, *The Moral Foundation of Rights* (Oxford: Clarendon, 1987), pp. vii, 177). All these objections seem not to address to Mill's particular theory of utilitarianism.

Chapter 3

1. John Skorupski, *John Stuart Mill* (London: Routledge, 1991), pp. 248–50.
2. John Stuart Mill, *A System of Logic, Ratiocinative and Induction, Being a Connected View of the Principles of Evidence and the Methods of Scientific Investigation, Collected Works of J. S. Mill*, book 8<, 1843, ed. J. M. Robson (Toronto: University of Toronto Press, 1974), VI, i. 2.
3. Ibid., VI, ii, 2, 3.
4. Skorupski, *John Stuart Mill*, p. 251.
5. Mill, *A System of Logic*, VI, ii, 3.
6. Skorupski, *John Stuart Mill*, pp. 253, 254.
7. Ibid., p. 254.
8. Mill, *A System of Logic*, ii, 3.
9. At the beginning of his essay *On Liberty*, Mill says: "The subject of this Essay is not the so-called Liberty of the Will, . . . but Civil, or Social Liberty: the nature and limits of the power which can be legitimately exercised by society over the individual." See John Stuart Mill, "On Liberty," in *Utilitarianism, on Liberty, Considerations of Representative Government, Remarks on Bentham's Philosophy*, ed. Geraint Williams, 3rd ed. (London: Every Man's Library, 1993), p. 69.
10. Isaiah Berlin, *Four Essays on Liberty* (London: Oxford University Press, 1969), pp. lvi–lvii, 122–3, 127, 131–2, 144.
11. Don A. Habibi, *John Stuart Mill and the Ethic of Human Growth* (Dordrecht: Kluwer Academic Publishers, 2001), pp. 121–2.
12. Berlin, *Four Essays on Liberty*, pp. 132–4.
13. Habibi, *John Stuart Mill and the Ethic of Human Growth*, p. 122.
14. Richard Bellamy, *Rethinking Liberalism* (London: Pinter, 2000), pp. 22–5.
15. Habibi, *John Stuart Mill and the Ethic of Human Growth*, p. 123; lists are in pages 145–8n33 and 148n35.
16. Habibi, *John Stuart Mill and the Ethic of Human Growth*, pp. 123, 125; and Richard Vernon, "J. S. Mill and the Religion of Humanity," in *Religion, Secularisation and Political Thought, Thomas Hobbes to J. S. Mill*, ed. James E. Crimmins (London: Routledge, 1989), p. 176.
17. Habibi, *John Stuart Mill and the Ethic of Human Growth*, pp. 127–8, 142.
18. Skorupski, *John Stuart Mill*, p. 343.
19. Mill, "On Liberty," pp. 69, 81.
20. As will be demonstrated in chapter 6, Rawls suggests that the concept of liberty has one meaning. Hence, Mill should be interpreted as implicitly proposing what Rawls explicitly affirms.
21. Mill, "On Liberty," p. 78.
22. Ibid., p. 71–3.
23. Ibid., p. 81.
24. Ibid., pp. 78, 163.
25. Skorupski, *John Stuart Mill*, p. 342.

26. Joel Feinberg, *The Moral Limits of the Criminal Law*, vol. 2, *Offense to Others* (New York: Oxford University Press, 1985), pp. ix, xiii.
27. Mill, "On Liberty," pp. 166–72.
28. Ryan, *John Stuart Mill*, p. 245.
29. J. C. Rees, "A Re-Reading of Mill on Liberty," *Political Studies* 8, no. 2 (1960): 115–17, 123–4; the emphasis is added.
30. Mill, "On Liberty," pp. 149–50.
31. Ibid., p. 79.
32. Bhikhu Parekh argues that Mill among all nineteenth-century liberal thinkers justified the necessity of not only promoting individuality in European countries, but also imposing individuality on citizens of Eastern countries through colonization. As Parekh expounds, Mill's idea of individuality suggested that since citizens of uncivilized societies were in their premature age "they had no *political* claims to independence and self-determination," though as human beings they "had equal *moral* claims to the pursuit and protection of their interests with the members of civilzed societies." See Bhikhu Parekh, "Decolonizing Liberalism," in *The End of "Isms"? Reflections on the Fate of Ideological Politics after Communism's Collapse*, ed. Aleksandras Shtromas (Oxford: Blackwell Publishers, 1994), pp. 86–91.
33. Mill, "On Liberty," pp. 70, 78, 162.
34. John Gray, *Two Faces of Liberalism* (Cambridge: Polity Press, 2000), p. 85.
35. Mill, "On Liberty," p. 85.
36. Ibid., pp. 80–1, 123.
37. Of course, the concept of harm can be widely or narrowly interpreted. As was mentioned above, Mill himself accepts that harm to the decency of society is prohibited. Equally possible is the prohibition of serious harm to the feelings of individuals.
38. Henry M. Magid, "John Stuart Mill," in *History of Political Philosophy*, 3rd ed., ed. Leo Strauss and Joseph Cropsey (Chicago: University of Chicago Press, 1987), p. 799.
39. Gray, *Two Faces of Liberalism*, p. 85.
40. Mill, "On Liberty," p. 85.
41. Michael J. Sandel, "Morality and the Liberal Ideal," *The New Republic*, no. 7 (May 1984): 15.
42. Mill, "On Liberty," p. 85.
43. Ibid., p. 79.
44. Ibid., pp. 85, 88.
45. Ibid., pp. 111, 113–14, 116.
46. Ibid., pp. 85, 102–4.
47. A major problem with Mill's utility argument is that, according to Gray, our moral heritage should be only refashioned and should receive only piecemeal amendment, rather than become corrected by experiment. What is more, the absolute liberty of discussion Mill emphatically advocates requires us to allow the presence of doctrines, which have proved experimentally to be disastrous, a

view which is quite unjustifiable. Furthermore, it seems quite unreasonable to provide absolute freedom of discussion for disastrous opinions merely for the freshness of the true opinion. According to Gray, the equation of human well-being with the promotion of scientific knowledge has been questioned by contemporary moralists. For instance, they note that the weapons of mass destruction that have resulted from the promotion of scientific knowledge in modern times threaten the whole life of humanity and hence are definitely implausible. Moreover, the growth of knowledge within other cultures may decrease the self-confidence among people from a given culture when they learn the new knowledge, and this consequence is implausible. More significantly, the self-critical reflexivity of modern life has replaced inappropriately most of our moral knowledge with doubt and hesitation. Furthermore, Mill's assumption that the intrinsic value of scientific knowledge can only be achieved in free societies of the West can be countered by the erstwhile Soviet Union situation that what is required for the growth of scientific knowledge is the freedom of scientific community that can be achieved even when the freedom for society at large is denied. See John Gray, *Liberalisms, Essays in Political Philosophy*, (London: Routledge, 1989), pp. 241–4.

48. Some argue that blasphemy should be legally banned or morally condemned for violating the minimum right to "respectful discussion." An alternative view suggests that since blasphemy might cause social disorder, freedom of expression should give way to the value of "social order." Another view suggests that the prohibition of blasphemy is based upon the immorality of "group defamation." See John Horton, "Liberalism, Multiculturalism and Toleration," in *Liberalism, Multiculturalism and Toleration*, ed. John Horton (London: Macmillan Press, 1993), pp. 9–11. By contrast, Brian Barry supports full freedom of expression, including "the right to mock, ridicule and lampoon" religious beliefs. He grounds the legitimacy of blasphemy on the inseparability of criticism of religious beliefs from ridiculing them. Furthermore, he argues that since respectful discussion is not the common way for conversion from, or to, a religion, the only way to counteract the effects of religious fanaticism is "making people ashamed of it." See Brian Barry, *Culture and Equality, an Egalitarian Critique of Multiculturalism* (Cambridge: Polity Press, 2001), pp. 31–2. The argument of this chapter is based on Mill's concept of harm and his particular methodology. The gist of the argument is that the concept of harm should be determined by an inductive experimental investigation that considers the feeling of all citizens, including religious people.

49. Bellamy, *Rethinking Liberalism*, p. 32.

50. Skorupski, *John Stuart Mill*, pp. 366–7.

51. Feinberg, *The Moral Limits of the Criminal Law*, p. 49. The term "harm" is defined as (1) evil (physical or otherwise); hurt, injury, damage, mischief, and a loss; (2) grief, sorrow, pain, trouble, distress, affliction; and (3) pity. The term "offence" is defined as (1) stumbling; (2) a cause of spiritual or moral stumbling; (3) attack, assault, obstruction, opposition; (4) hurt, harm, injury, damage, pain,

as well as a feeling of being hurt, a painful or unpleasant sensation; (5) the condition of being regarded with displeasure, disfavor, disgrace; (6) something that causes annoyance or disgust, a nuisance; and (7) a fault, wrong, sin, and misdeed. See J. A. Simpson and E. S. C. Weiner (eds.), *The Oxford English Dictionary*, 2nd ed. (Oxford: Oxford University Press, 1989), vol. 6, p. 1121; and vol. 10, p. 724.

52. A Millian method of inductive experimentalism is expected to suggest a type of "democratic liberalism," as Bellamy calls it, in which basic concepts and principles should be determined through actual reference to participating citizens who aim to advance their plural interests through social life with submitting to the central principle of equal respect and its resulting principles. See Richard Bellamy, *Liberalism and Pluralism, towards a Politics of Compromise* (London: Routledge, 1999), pp. 38–40.

53. Jaafar Sobhani, *Azadi wa Din Salary* (Qum: Muassasah Imam Sadiq, 2005), pp. 94–101.

54. Mill, "On Liberty," pp. 62–3, 123–4.

55. Ibid., p. 124.

56. Ryan, *John Stuart Mill*, p. 255.

57. Mill, "On Liberty," pp. 79, 124.

58. Ibid., pp. 127–8.

59. Ibid., pp. 126, 140.

60. Skorupski, *John Stuart Mill*, p. 348.

61. Mill, "On Liberty," p. 127.

62. Ibid., pp. 81, 126, 133–4, 138.

63. Skorupski, *John Stuart Mill*, pp. 354–5.

64. Mill, "On Liberty," p. 126.

65. Fred Berger, *Happiness, Justice, and Freedom: The Moral and Political Philosophy of John Stuart Mill* (Berkeley: University of California Press, 1984), p. 233.

66. Mill, "On Liberty," pp. 136, 142.

67. Ibid., pp. 9, 10.

68. Ibid., p. 78.

69. Karl Britton, *John Stuart Mill* (London: Penguin, 1953), pp. 103–4.

70. Andrew Levine, *Engaging Political Philosophy from Hobbes to Rawls* (Oxford: Blackwell, 2002), p. 145.

71. Maurice Cowling, "Mill and Liberalism," in *Mill: A Collection of Critical Essays*, ed. J. B. Schneewind (New York: Anchor Books, 1968), pp. 332–5.

72. Wendy Donner, *The Liberal Self: John Stuart Mill's Moral and Political Philosophy* (London: Cornell University Press, 1991), pp. 3–4.

73. Gray, *Liberalisms, Essays in Political Philosophy*, pp. 133–4, 136.

74. Fredrick Rosen, *Classical Utilitarianism from Hume to Mill*, (London: Routledge, 2003), pp. 193–4, 197.

75. Richard Wollheim, "John Stuart Mill and Isaiah Berlin, the Ends of Life and the Preliminaries of Morality," in *The Idea of Freedom, Essays in Honour of Isaiah Berlin*, ed. Alan Ryan (Oxford: Oxford University Press, 1979), p. 254.

76. Gray, *Two Faces of Liberalism,* pp. 86–8.
77. Muhammad Hussein Tabatabai, *Qur'an dar Islam,* 2nd ed. (Tehran: Dar al-Kutub al-Islamiyyah, 1974), p. 12.
78. Sobhani, *Azadi wa Din Salary,* pp. 53–5, 74.
79. Imam Khomeini, *Chihil Hadith,* 13th ed. (Tehran: Institute of Compilation and Publication of Imam Khomeini's Works, 1997), pp. 180–4.

Chapter 4

1. A revised version of this chapter has already been published as an independent article. See Hamid Hadji Haidar, "Rawls and Religion: Between the Decency and Justice of Reasonable Religious Regimes," *Politics and Ethics Review* 2, no. 1 (Spring 2006): 62–78.
2. John Rawls, "Justice as Fairness: Political not Metaphysical," in *Collected Papers,* ed. Samuel Freeman (Cambridge, MA: Harvard University Press, 1999), pp. 390–1.
3. John Rawls, "The Idea of an Overlapping Consensus," in *Collected Papers,* ed. Samuel Freeman (Cambridge, MA: Harvard University Press, 1999), p. 421.
4. Rawls, "Justice as Fairness," p. 395.
5. Rawls, "The Idea of an Overlapping Consensus," pp. 445–6.
6. Rawls, "Justice as Fairness," pp. 391, 395.
7. On the whole, the purpose of modern political philosophy for Rawls is to articulate a ground for "stable agreement" among adherents of divergent doctrines about the good life in modern pluralistic societies. To assess Rawls's view about the task of modern political philosophy, one should distinguish between "political philosophy" entrusted to philosophers and "political activity" assignable to politicians. Then, Rawls's theory of justice can be placed in the latter category with the aim to search for an agreeable ground for social cooperation, as opposed to his contention that it is *a form* of political philosophy. Essentially required by every branch of philosophy is the aim of "exploration" of some principles as true, valid, reliable, agreeable, and the like, irrespective of the action of acceptance by others. Political philosophy in the first place is a branch of general philosophy with its domain being restricted to government, state, and the public realm. While the subject of this branch of philosophy is specific and distinctive from other branches, its methodology as well as its aim should remain the same as that of other branches. Hence, a philosopher might be reasonably motivated by the crucial importance of peace and stability to argue for the necessity and justifiability of finding a ground for "agreement" or "compromise" among citizens in deeply pluralistic societies. Yet, the act of suggesting some principles as the ground for such a crucial compromise or agreement is the job of politicians of every given society at a given time. The "making" of the components of the package for agreement or compromise should be entrusted to real politicians at any given time and vary across liberal societies.

The idea of "compromise" developed by Bellamy as "democratic liberalism," which intends to overcome the tension between liberalism and democracy by attaching supreme importance to the value of compromise, should be considered as a political philosophy. See Richard Bellamy, *Liberalism and Pluralism, towards a Politics of Compromise* (London: Routledge, 1999), p. 93. Addressing the problem of inevitable plurality of ideas and cultures in modern industrial societies, this political philosophy is aimed to suggest fair conditions for construction of the common good through a procedure of negotiation by which all those who are committed to the value of compromise are accommodated with equal and mutual respect empowered with reciprocity. See Richard Bellamy and Martin Hollis, "Consensus, Neutrality and Compromise," in *Pluralism and Liberal Neutrality,* ed. Richard Bellamy and Martin Hollis (London: Frank Cass, 1999), pp. 62–3, 69. Therefore, Rawls's contention that his philosophy is political in that its *scope* is restricted to political and public realm, which he labels the "basic structure" of society, rather than encompassing all aspects of human life, seems sound. Yet, his characterization of its *content* as being built upon an articulated set of implicit shared fundamental ideas found in the public political culture of a democratic society (John Rawls, *Political Liberalism* [New York: Columbia University Press, 1996], pp. 11, 13; my emphasis), along with setting its aim—the attainment of agreement on his specific package—bring his theory into the category of political activity. Rawls himself tends to accept the objection that his political liberalism is closer to politics than philosophy (Rawls, "The Idea of an Overlapping Consensus," p. 447).

What logically follows from the distinction between the aim and methodology of political philosophy and political activity lies in their different force. The force of political activity assigned to politicians of a given society at a given time is restricted to those citizens who freely accept its presuppositions in the process of socialization in that society as valid. By contrast, political philosophy is capable of providing a convincing argument with regard to those who have been socialized differently. Political activity, hence, is an attempt to bring individuals with some shared convictions to acknowledge the requirements of those shared principles that are controversial or unclear to them. In distinguishing between proof and justification, Rawls acknowledges this feature of his theory. He writes: "Justification proceeds from what all parties to the discussion hold in common. Ideally, to justify a conception of justice to someone is to give him a proof of its principles from premises that we both accept." See John Rawls, *A Theory of Justice,* 2nd ed. (Oxford: Oxford University Press, 1999), p. 508.

8. Jean Hampton, "Should Political Philosophy be Done Without Metaphysics?" *Ethics* 99, no. 4 (July 1989): 795–6.
9. Ibid., pp. 794, 801.
10. Rawls, "Justice as Fairness," p. 394.
11. Ibid., pp. 394–5.
12. Rawls, *Political Liberalism,* pp. 191–2.

13. David C. Paris, "The Theoretical Mystique: Neutrality, Plurality, and the Defence of Liberalism," *American Journal of Political Science* 31, no. 4 (November 1987): 913.
14. Ibid., p. 915.
15. Rawls, *Political Liberalism,* pp. 191–2.
16. Ibid., pp. 9–11, 192.
17. Ibid., pp. 168–70.
18. John Rawls, *The Law of Peoples* (Cambridge, MA: Harvard University Press, 1999), p. 143.
19. Ibid.
20. Rawls, *Political Liberalism,* pp. 9–11.
21. Ibid., p. 169.
22. Rawls, *The Law of Peoples,* p. 132.
23. Ibid., 143.
24. Rawls, *Political Liberalism,* p. 168–9.
25. Rawls, *The Law of Peoples,* pp. 132, 172–3.
26. Rawls, *Political Liberalism,* pp. 134, 169–71, 139–40, 243.
27. Ibid., p. xl.
28. Rawls, *The Law of Peoples,* pp. 175–6.
29. Rawls, *Political Liberalism,* pp. 89, 91.
30. Ibid., p. 91.
31. Ibid., pp. 91–2.
32. Ibid., p. 92.
33. Ibid.
34. Ibid., pp. 99–100.
35. John Rawls, "Themes in Kant's Moral Philosophy," in *Collected Papers,* ed. Samuel Freeman (Cambridge, MA: Harvard University Press, 1999), p. 512.
36. Stephen Mulhall and Adam Swift, *Liberals and Communitarians,* 2nd ed. (Oxford: Blackwell, 2001), pp. 180–1.
37. Rawls, *Political Liberalism,* p. 93.
38. Ibid.
39. Ibid., pp. 94, 96n8, 119–20.
40. Ibid., p. 93.
41. Rawls, *A Theory of Justice,* p. 506.
42. Wikipedia. "Ethical Naturalism." http://en.wikipedia.org/wiki/Ethical_naturalism.
43. Rawls, *A Theory of Justice,* p. 506.
44. Philosophy.lander.edu. "Ethics." http://philosophy.lander.edu/ethics/naturalism.html.
45. Scanlon recognizes three methods of justification in Rawls's view, that is, reflective equilibrium, the original position, and public reason. See T. M. Scanlon, "Rawls and Justification," in *The Cambridge Companion to Rawls,* ed. Samuel Freeman (Cambridge: Cambridge University Press, 2003), p. 139. It seems that the original position, far from being an independent method in Rawls's methodology, is

a complementary device facilitating the technique of reflective equilibrium. In addition, Rawls's idea of public reason far from being a method of justification for his political theory is another consequence along with his two principles of justice as fairness conceived of as being a procedure to legitimize public decision making. Put another way, Rawls's liberal political theory encompasses two main values: the first concerns the "principles of justice" and the second concerns the idea of public reason as the "guidelines of inquiry." See Rawls, *Political Liberalism,* pp. 223–4. Hence, what Rawls offers as valid justification is his technique of reflective equilibrium.

46. Muhammad Hussein Tabatabai, *Al-Mizan fi Tafsir al-Qur'an,* vol. 15, 2nd ed. (Beirut: Muassasah al-Aalami lil-Matbuaat, 1982), p. 65.
47. David Lyons, "Nature and Soundness of the Contract and Coherence Arguments," in *Reading Rawls, Critical Studies on Rawls' A Theory of Justice,* ed. Norman Daniels (Palo Alto, CA: Stanford University Press, 1975), p. 145.
48. James van Cleve, "Why Coherence Is Not Enough: A Defense of Moderate Foundationalism," in *Contemporary Debates in Epistemology,* ed. Matthias Steup and Ernest Sosa (Oxford: Blackwell Publishing, 2005), p. 169.
49. Ronald Dworkin, "The Original Position," in *Reading Rawls, Critical Studies on Rawls' A Theory of Justice,* ed. Norman Daniels (Palo Alto, CA: Stanford University Press, 1975), pp. 22, 27.
50. Richard Rorty, "Idealizations, Foundations, and Social Practices," in *Democracy and Difference, Contesting the Boundaries of the Political,* ed. Seyla Benhabib (Princeton, NJ: Princeton University Press, 1996), p. 333.
51. Scanlon, "Rawls and Justification," p. 140.
52. Rawls, *Political Liberalism,* p. 124.
53. Rawls, *A Theory of Justice,* p. 42.
54. John Rawls, "Outline of a Decision Procedure for Ethics," in *Collected Papers,* ed. Samuel Freeman (Cambridge, MA: Harvard University Press, 1999), p. 6.
55. Scanlon, "Rawls and Justification," p. 143.
56. Rawls, *A Theory of Justice,* p. 42.
57. Scanlon, "Rawls and Justification," p. 145.
58. Ibid., p. 140.
59. Rawls, *A Theory of Justice,* p. 18.
60. Scanlon, "Rawls and Justification," p. 141.
61. Rawls, *A Theory of Justice,* p. 43.
62. Scanlon, "Rawls and Justification," p. 142.
63. Rawls, *A Theory of Justice,* p. 46.
64. Ibid., p. 43.
65. John Rawls, *Justice as Fairness: A Restatement,* ed. Erin Kelly (Cambridge, MA: Harvard University Press, 2001), p. 30.
66. Rawls, "'Justice as Fairness," pp. 401–2; the emphasis is mine.
67. Rawls, *A Theory of Justice,* p. 11.
68. Ibid., p. 118.
69. Ibid., p. 11.

70. Rawls, *Justice as Fairness,* p. 16.
71. Dworkin, "The Original Position," pp. 17–18, 19–20.
72. Rawls, "Justice as Fairness," p. 401.
73. Rawls is dissatisfied with Dworkin's interpretation of the idea of the original position. The interpretation this chapter adopts is based on Rawls's comments in that essay, which suggests that his "account of use of the original position resembles in some respects an account that Dworkin rejects." See Rawls, "Justice as Fairness," p. 401n19.
74. Chandran Kukathas and Philip Pettit, *Rawls: A Theory of Justice and Its Critics* (Cambridge: Polity Press, 1990), p. 27.
75. Rawls, *Justice as Fairness,* p. 32.
76. Richard B. Brandt, *A Theory of the Good and the Right* (Oxford: Clarendon, 1979), p. 20.
77. Scanlon, "Rawls and Justification," p. 152.
78. The dependence of any justification upon "truths about human nature, human rights, rationality, or politics that are self-evident, rationally incontestable, or axiomatic" is what Amy Gutmann calls "foundationalism" in political philosophy. See Amy Gutmann, "Democracy, Philosophy, and Justification," in *Democracy and Difference, Contesting the Boundaries of the Political,* ed. Seyla Benhabib (Princeton, NJ: Princeton University Press, 1996), p. 340.
79. As Richard Rorty has put it, "antifoundationalism" or idealizationalism in political philosophy attempts to make a coherent picture of the present practices, or to show how to make them more coherent. He suggests that Rawls wants to remind Americans merely of what they do in courts of law. See Rorty, "Idealizations, Foundations, and Social Practices," p. 333.
80. Rawls, *The Law of Peoples,* pp. 78, 85–6.

Chapter 5

1. Categorizing moral theories into "goal-based," "duty-based," and "right-based" theories, Dworkin suggests that Rawls's theory of justice is a right-based theory. See Ronald Dworkin, "The Original Position," in *Reading Rawls, Critical Studies on Rawls' A Theory of Justice,* ed. Norman Daniels (Palo Alto, CA: Stanford University Press, 1975), pp. 40, 42. Yet, not only does Rawls dismiss the characterization of his theory of justice as a right-based theory, but also he is not satisfied with Dworkin's tripartite categorization of moral theories. He prefers to call his theory a "conception-based" or an "ideal-based" view, as there are some other important possibilities. See John Rawls, "Justice as Fairness: Political Not Metaphysical," in *Collected Papers,* ed. Samuel Freeman (Cambridge, MA: Harvard University Press, 1999), p. 400n19.
2. W. K. Frankena, *Ethics* (Englewood Cliffs, NJ: Prentice Hall, 1963), p. 13.
3. John Rawls, *A Theory of Justice,* 2nd ed. (Oxford: Oxford University Press, 1999), pp. 21–2, 26.
4. Ibid., pp. 26–8.

5. Ronald Dworkin, "Liberalism," in *Public and Private Morality,* ed. Stuart Hampshire (New York: Cambridge University Press, 1978), pp. 127–9.

6. As for the conflict between utility and justice, Mackie proposes that the utilitarian stipulation that each person should count for one and nobody for more than one is less than a guaranteed fair go for each individual that justice requires. See J. L. Mackie, "Rights, Utility, and Universalisation," in *Utility and Rights,* ed. R. G. Frey (Oxford: Basil Blackwell, 1985), p. 87. By contrast, Hare assumes that these two verdicts are the same, since utilitarianism in line with justice requires the pursuit of the interest of each person equally. See R. M. Hare, "Rights, Utility, and Universalisation, Reply to J. L. Mackie," in *Utility and Rights,* ed. R. G. Frey (Oxford: Basil Blackwell, 1985), pp. 106–7.

7. David Lyons, "Nature and Soundness of the Contract and Coherence Arguments," in *Reading Rawls, Critical Studies on Rawls' A Theory of Justice,* ed. Norman Daniels (Palo Alto, CA: Stanford University Press, 1975), p. 142–4.

8. Rawls, *A Theory of Justice,* pp. 22–4, 27, 181, 183, 187.

9. H. L. A. Hart, "Between Utility and Rights," in *Ronald Dworkin and Contemporary Jurisprudence,* ed. Marshall Cohen (London: Duckworth, 1983), pp. 215–16.

10. Andrew Levine, *Engaging Political Philosophy, from Hobbes to Rawls* (Oxford: Blackwell, 2002), p. 179.

11. Rawls, *A Theory of Justice,* pp. 73–7.

12. Ibid., pp. 74–5.

13. Robert Paul Wolff, *Understanding Rawls, a Reconstruction and Critique of A Theory of Justice* (Princeton, NJ: Princeton University Press, 1977), p. 5.

14. Peter Jones, "Two Conceptions of Liberalism, Two Conceptions of Justice," *British Journal of Political Science* 25, no. 4 (October 1995): 515.

15. Iris Marion Young, "Political Theory: An Overview," in *A New Handbook of Political Science,* ed. Robert E. Goodin and Hans-Dieter Klingemann (Oxford: Oxford University Press, 1996), p. 497.

16. John Rawls, *The Law of Peoples* (Cambridge, MA: Harvard University Press, 1999), pp. 179–80.

17. John Rawls, *Political Liberalism* (New York: Columbia University Press, 1996), p. 175.

18. Rawls, *A Theory of Justice,* pp. 7–9.

19. Since "the structure and content of *Theory,*" as Rawls admits, "remain substantially the same," it is quite strange that he expects that utilitarianism be an alternative to the principles of justice as fairness presented in *TJ,* and utilitarians should accept the same principles when presented in *PL.* Therefore, rivalry seems to persist among Rawls's theory of justice and all the others, no matter how far he develops the *presentation* of his principles of justice. See Rawls, *Political Liberalism,* pp. xviii, 168–70.

20. Ibid., pp. 168–70.

21. Rawls, *A Theory of Justice,* p. 3.

22. Rawls, *Political Liberalism,* pp. xxi, xxii, 192.

23. Rawls, *A Theory of Justice*, pp. 3, 8–9, 41–4.
24. Rawls, *Political Liberalism*, p. 4.
25. John Rawls, *Justice as Fairness: A Restatement*, ed. Erin Kelly (Cambridge, MA: Harvard University Press, 2001), p. 9.
26. Levine, *Engaging Political Philosophy, from Hobbes to Rawls*, p. 184.
27. Rawls, *The Law of Peoples*, pp. 64–6.
28. Rawls, *Political Liberalism*, pp. xvii, xviii.
29. Rawls, *The Law of Peoples*, pp. 179–80.
30. Rawls, *Political Liberalism*, p. xliiin7, xliiin8.
31. Rawls, *A Theory of Justice*, pp. 3–4. Michael Sandel criticizes Rawls's proposition that justice is the first virtue of social institutions. He maintains that not only is justice not the prime social virtue, but also that since justice has a remedial value, in some cases it is a "vice." According to Sandel, justice is a social virtue only where the following conditions hold together: a high degree of scarcity of resources, conflict of demands, and the absence of benevolence. It is only in this situation that justice is a pressing social priority. See Michael J. Sandel, *Liberalism and the Limits of Justice* (Cambridge: Cambridge University Press, 1982), p. 34. Baker contends that Sandel misunderstands Rawls's view of the primacy of justice. The primacy of justice means that in case of conflict between justice and other social values, justice takes precedence over other social values. According to Baker, Rawls is articulating the just institutions, which do not prevent people from acting on the motives of fraternity and benevolence in their community. Moreover, just institutions do not require each person to claim and pursue his due; rather they enable individuals to claim their due if they choose to do so. Hence, the primacy of justice is consistent with the domination of the spirit of fraternity and benevolence. See C. Edwin Baker, "Sandel on Rawls: Justice as a Vice," *University of Pennsylvania Law Review* 133, no. 4 (April 1985): 917–18.
32. *The Qur'an*, chapter "The Heavenly Food," verse 8.
33. *The Qur'an*, chapter "The Women," verse 135.
34. Rawls, *A Theory of Justice*, p. 5.
35. John Rawls, "Justice as Reciprocity," in *Collected Papers*, ed. Samuel Freeman (Cambridge, MA: Harvard University Press, 1999), p. 191.
36. Rawls, *A Theory of Justice*, p. 54.
37. Ibid., p. 12.
38. Rawls, *Political Liberalism*, pp. 5–6.
39. Rawls, *A Theory of Justice*, pp. 53–4, 72.
40. However, in the case of extreme poverty, inequality, and anarchy in a society, it may be justifiable to establish a developmental dictatorial government that seeks to construct the basic structure of a just and liberal society. Put another way, the provision of the minimum subsistence is the first duty of public duty of the government. See Rawls, *A Theory of Justice*, pp. 252–3; and Isaiah Berlin, "Introduction," *Four Essays on Liberty* (New York: Oxford University Press, 1969).

41. Rawls, *A Theory of Justice,* pp. 6–7, 53–4.
42. Rawls, *Political Liberalism,* pp. 5–7.
43. Thomas Nagel, "Rawls and Liberalism," in *The Cambridge Companion to Rawls,* ed. Samuel Freeman (Cambridge: Cambridge University Press, 2003), p. 63.
44. Rawls, *The Law of Peoples,* p. 78.
45. Ibid., pp. 59, 62.
46. Ibid., p. 65.
47. Ibid., pp. 64–6.
48. Rawls, *Justice as Fairness,* p. 37.
49. Ibid., pp. 25, 41.
50. Grounding his argument in some empirical researches conducted by political scientists in the second half of twentieth century, Goerge Klasko sheds doubt on Rawls's claim that public political culture of liberal democratic societies embodies his asserted elements. See George Klosko, "Rawls's 'Political' Philosophy and American Democracy," *The American Political Science Review* 87, no. 2 (June 1993): 352–4.
51. Rawls, *Justice as Fairness,* pp. 25, 33–6.
52. As Kymlicka puts it, Western liberal democracies, including the United States, with which Rawls is chiefly concerned, are multicultural. See Will Kymlicka, *Multicultural Citizenship* (New York: Oxford University Press, 1995), pp. 10–11. Hence, Rawls ignores an important philosophical issue of "the rights of minority cultures." See Will Kymlicka, *Liberalism, Community, and Culture* (New York: Oxford University Press, 1989), p. 3. The consequence of this omission, as Parekh puts it, is that Rawls's argument might be unconvincing to those citizens who belong to other cultures. See Bhikhu Parekh, *Rethinking Multiculturalism, Cultural Diversity and Political Theory* (New York: Palgrave, 2000), p. 10. Therefore, dismissing implicitly the value of multiculturalism in liberal democratic societies, Rawls seems to be constructing his argument on the assumption that the ideas implicit in the mainstream culture in liberal democratic societies should be imposed on all alternative cultures to which minority groups in these societies have subscribed. See Andrew Mason, "Imposing Liberal Principles," in *Pluralism and Liberal Neutrality,* ed. Richard Bellamy and Martin Hollis (London: Frank Cass, 1999), p. 102. Yet, it should be conceded that Rawls's political liberalism, by narrowing down its application to liberal democratic societies, has succeeded to be fairer to cultural diversity than other comprehensive theories of liberalism that assert universality. See John Kane, "Democracy and Group Rights," in *Democratic Theory Today,* ed. April Carter and Geoffrey Stokes (Cambridge: Polity Press, 2002), p. 101.
53. Will Kymlicka, *Multicultural Citizenship* (New York: Oxford University Press, 1995), p. 18. See also: Chandran Kukathas, "Are There Any Cultural Rights?" *Political Theory* 20, no. 1 (February 1992): 115, 120.
54. According to Rawls's idea of "public reason," "citizens are to conduct their fundamental discussions within the framework of what each regards as a political conception of justice based on values that others can reasonably be

expected to endorse." See Rawls, *Political Liberalism,* p. 226. Critics of Rawls's idea of public reason have suggested that such a shared and public reason is not actually available. Therefore, any argument, religious or nonreligious, would be drawn on various particular comprehensive conceptions of the good. See James P. Sterba, "Rawls and Religion," in *The Idea of a Political Liberalism, Essays on Rawls,* ed. Victoria Davion and Clark Wolf (Lanham: Rowman and Littlefield, 2000), p. 36. This section intends to show that Rawls's argument is based on several premises that are specifically secular, and hence cannot be justifiable to committed religious citizens.

55. Richard A. Posner, "Review of Jeremy Waldron, 'Law and Disagreement,'" *Columbia Law Review* 100, no. 2 (March 2000): 586.

56. Jeremy Waldron, *Law and Disagreement* (Oxford: Oxford University Press, 1999), pp. 158–9.

57. Rawls, *Justice as Fairness,* p. 33.

58. John Gray, *Liberalism,* 2nd ed. (Berkshire: Open University Press, 1995), p. 85.

59. Rawls, *Political Liberalism,* pp. xviii, 4, 36.

60. In his post-Rawlsian liberal theory, Waldron argues that not only do we disagree about the basic issues of life, such as the existence of God and the meaning of life, but we also disagree about the meaning of justice. The fair terms of cooperation among disagreeing people are also controversial. He concludes that in the situation of deep disagreement about a good life, as well as about the principles of justice, it is the public who should select from the list of varying views, rather than have a philosopher impose his view about justice on people. See Waldron, *Law and Disagreement,* pp. 1–2. In his review of Waldron's *Law and Disagreement* and *The Dignity of Legislation,* Whittington argues that Waldron's "post-Rawlsian" liberalism can be characterized by his democratic emphasis on legislatures. According to Whittington, Waldron dismisses Rawls's emphasis on the supremacy of judiciary, which is entrusted with guaranteeing liberal basic rights determined by philosophers. See Keith E. Whittington, "In Defense of Legislatures," *Political Theory* 28, no. 5 (October 2000): 692.

61. Daniel A. Dombrowski, *Rawls and Religion, the Case for Political Liberalism* (Albany: State University of New York Press, 2001), p. 9.

62. Rawls, *Political Liberalism,* pp. xix, 56–9.

63. In a similar way, Sandel criticizes Rawls's idea of "the circumstances of justice" as formulated in *TJ.* He argues that justice is the prime virtue of industrial, individualistic, divided societies, which lack a sense of community and shared identity. See Sandel, *Liberalism and the Limits of Justice,* pp. 30–1.

64. Rawls, *The Law of Peoples,* p. 78.

65. Rawls, *Justice as Fairness,* p. 5.

66. Rawls, *A Theory of Justice,* pp. 126–8.

67. Ibid., p. 4.

68. Carnes Lord, "Aristotle," in *History of Political Philosophy,* 3rd ed., ed. Leo Strauss and Joseph Cropsey (Chicago: University of Chicago Press, 1987), pp. 135, 136.

69. Rawls, *Justice as Fairness,* pp. 3–4.
70. Rawls, *Political Liberalism,* p. 15.
71. Rawls, *Justice as Fairness,* p. 6.
72. Rawls, *Political Liberalism,* p. 16.
73. Brian Barry, *Theories of Justice* (London: Harvest-Wheatsheaf 1989), p. 373.
74. In the chapter "The Iron," verse 25, the Qur'an says: "Indeed, We sent Our Messengers with the clear signs, and We sent the Balance so that men might uphold justice."
75. *The Qur'an,* chapter "The All-Merciful," verse 60, trans. Arthur J. Arberry (Qum: Ansariyan Publication, 1995), p. 559.
76. Rawls, *Justice as Fairness,* p. 5.
77. Rawls, *The Law of Peoples,* p. 172.
78. Rawls, *Political Liberalism,* p. lxii.
79. Jones, "Two Conceptions of Liberalism, Two Conceptions of Justice," p. 521. Gray argues that "recent controversy in sociobiology suggests that competition among theories of human nature is not merely a competition among rival empirical conjectures, but also among incompatible metaphysical and episte-mological views." Hence, "adopting the conception of the person," Gray continues, "will entail adopting or endorsing substantive positions in philo-sophical inquiry." See John Gray, *Liberalisms, Essays in Political Philosophy* (London: Routledge, 1989), p. 168.
80. Rawls, *Political Liberalism,* pp. 18–9, 30.
81. Ibid., pp. 19, 370.
82. Rawls, *The Law of Peoples,* p. 128.
83. Rawls, *A Theory of Justice,* p. 41.
84. Rawls, *Political Liberalism,* p. 142.
85. Ibid., pp. 19–20, 30–1. Communitarians have questioned the Rawlsian notion of the "self" as detachable from his ends. See Robert E. Goodin and Philip Pettit (eds.), *A Companion to Contemporary Political Philosophy* (Oxford: Blackwell, 1993), p. 19. As Sandel argues, Rawls's assumption about the detachability of man from his ends is not a neutral premise that all who live in liberal democratic societies affirm. Rather, Sandel contends that in many cases—such as our membership "of this family or community or nation or people, as bearers of this history, as sons and daughters of that revolution, as citizens of this republic"—we connect to our ends and goals not through acts of choice and decision, rather through acts of cognition. See Sandel, *Liberalism and the Limits of Justice,* p. 179.
86. Rawls, *Political Liberalism,* pp. 32–3.
87. Ibid., p. 79.
88. Veit Bader, "Religious Pluralism: Secularism or Priority for Democracy?" *Political Theory* 27, no. 5 (October 1999): 599, 600.
89. Jean Hampton, "Should Political Philosophy be Done Without Metaphysics?" *Ethics* 99, no. 4 (July 1989): 813.
90. Rawls, *A Theory of Justice,* pp. 123–4.

91. In *TJ*, Rawls argues that in the original position parties that are delegated the task of determining the principles of social justice are supposed not to be envious or altruist, as rationality requires. In his transformed theory, these characters should be discussed here.
92. Rawls, *A Theory of Justice,* pp. 123–5.
93. Jones, "Two Conceptions of Liberalism, Two Conceptions of Justice," p. 522.
94. Rawls, *Political Liberalism,* pp. 49, 54.
95. Ibid., pp. 52–4.
96. While for Rawls, the difference between the rationality of behaving justly and the reasonableness and virtue of impartiality is motivational, for Brian Barry it is definitional. Brian Barry categorizes all theories of justice into two groups. In the first group, the central concepts are advantage, bargaining power, self-interestedness, and prudence. Since each individual seeks his own benefits by entering social life and he finds cooperation more effective than a thorough conflict with others, he submits to the principles of justice by which he can get what he wants more safely. In this sense, justice is the minimum price that the self-interested rational person has to pay in order to obtain others' cooperation. In this sense, justice recognizes different bargaining powers of individuals in setting some principles of social cooperation. Hence, if a more powerful participant finds that his share is disproportionate to his power, he has no rational reason to accept the agreement. He calls this notion of justice "justice as mutual advantage." The key development in this line of argument, as Barry argues, is "the invention of game theory." Barry argues that this notion of justice is mooted in Plato's *Republic,* and Hobbes is the most famous commentator of this notion of justice. The second sense of justice detaches the bargaining power from the principles of justice and tries to prevent translation of bargaining power into advantage. In this sense, "a just state of affairs is one that people can accept not merely in the sense that they cannot reasonably *expect* to get more but in the strongest sense that they cannot reasonably *claim* more." He calls this notion "justice as impartiality." In this sense, people are expected to find another motivation to follow the just state of affairs, other than their self-interest. One way to determine the demands of justice as impartiality is to assume "an impartial observer." Hence, "justice is seen as what someone with no stake in the outcome would approve of as a distribution of benefits and burdens." An alternative way is to ask one to put himself in other's shoes, for instance, by asking him to ignore his specific position in society and his real bargaining power. The motive to follow the requirements of justice in the second sense is "the desire to act justly." He further assumes that the desire to act justly is "an original principle in human nature and one that develops under the normal conditions of human life." However, Barry argues that a system of sanctions against non-compliance is required as a complementary source of motivation in addition to the sense of justice. The main development in this line of argument, as Barry suggests, is the invention of the notion of the "original position" put forward by Rawls as "an ethically privileged choice situation." Barry argues that this view

of justice is due to the Enlightenment and all who follow it are in debt to Kant. See Barry, *Theories of Justice,* pp. 8, 362–6, 375.

97. Richard Bellamy and Martin Hollis, "Liberal Justice: Political and Metaphysical," *The Philosophical Quarterly* 45, no. 178 (January 1995): 4–6.

98. *The Qur'an,* chapter "The Women," verse 135.

99. *The Qur'an,* chapter "Muhammad," verse 24, and chapter "Aali Imran," verses 190–1.

100. *The Qur'an,* chapter "The Sun," verses 7–8; trans. 'Ali Qulī Qarā'ī (London: Islamic College for Advanced Studies Press, 2004), p. 851.

101. *The Qur'an,* chapter "Marry," verse 95.

102. *The Qur'an,* chapter "The Livestock," verse 164.

103. Muhammad Hussein Tabatabai, *Al-Mizan fi Tafsir al-Qur'an,* vol. 16, 2nd ed., (Beirut: Muassasah al-Aalami lil-Matbuaat, 1982), pp. 119–20.

104. Rawls, *Political Liberalism,* pp. 37–8, 217.

105. Jeremy Waldron, *Liberal Rights: Collected Papers 1981–1991* (Cambridge: Cambridge University Press, 1993), pp. 36–7; the emphasis is added.

106. Thomas Nagel, *Equality and Partiality* (New York: Oxford University Press, 1991), pp. 8, 33; the emphasis is added.

107. Marilyn Friedman, "John Rawls and the Political Coercion of Unreasonable People," in *The Idea of a Political Liberalism, Essays on Rawls,* Victoria Davion and Clark Wolf (eds.), (Lanham: Rowman and Littlefield, 2000), p. 30. This idea poses another problem, namely political obligation. Pateman claims that "political obligation in the liberal democratic state constitutes an insoluble problem." The liberal idea that individuals are born free and equal to one another gives rise to the insoluble question of political obligation, that is, "why and how can some individuals rule legitimately some others who are also free and equal to the ruler?" Liberal thinkers assume that it is the free and equal individuals themselves who voluntarily restrict their freedom by making social contracts and entering into a social and political life based upon political obligation, which individuals voluntarily undertake. According to Pateman, voluntarist justifications *"far from providing a solution, they define the problem"* because "a free and equal individual can always question political authority and political obligation in general terms." He continues to argue that "consent theory has long been embarrassed by the fact it always runs into difficulties when confronted by the demand to show who has, and when, and how, actually and explicitly consented in the liberal democratic state." See Carole Pateman, *The Problem of Political Obligation: A Critique of Liberal Theory* (Cambridge: Polity Press, 1985), pp. 1, 12–15.

108. *The Qur'an,* chapter "The Bee," verse 125, trans. Qarā'ī, p. 387.

109. *The Qur'an:* chapter "The Cow," verse 256, trans. Qarā'ī, p. 59.

110. Tabatabai, *Al-Mizan fi Tafsir al-Qur'an,* vol. 2, p. 343.

111. Nasir Makarim Shirazi, *Al-Amthal fi Tafsir Kitabi Allah al-Munzal,* vol. 2 (Qum: Madrasah Imam Ali, 2000), p. 261.

112. Rawls, *Political Liberalism,* p. 14.

113. Rawls, *Justice as Fairness,* pp. 8–9.
114. Rawls, *Political Liberalism,* p. 35.
115. Rawls, *Justice as Fairness,* p. 9.
116. This is, of course, a substantive idea supported by liberal societies. See Dombrowski, *Rawls and Religion, the Case for Political Liberalism,* p. 28.
117. Rawls, *Political Liberalism,* p. 24.
118. Ibid., p. 26.
119. Rawls, *A Theory of Justice,* pp. 16–7.
120. Ibid., p. 118.
121. As Dombrowski suggests, Rawls's idea of the original position can be used by religious believers in sorting out disagreement about divine commands. See Dombrowski, *Rawls and Religion, the Case for Political Liberalism,* pp. 17–19.
122. Abu Mohammed Al-Harrani (ed.), *Tuhaf Al-Uqoul,* trans. Badr Shahin (Qum: Ansariyan Publications, 2001), p. 26.
123. Rawls, *A Theory of Justice,* pp. 130–1.
124. Lyons, "Nature and Soundness of the Contract and Coherence Arguments," p. 161.
125. Dombrowski, *Rawls and Religion, the Case for Political Liberalism,* p. 33.
126. Brian Barry, *The Liberal Theory of Justice:* A Critical Examination of the Principal Doctrines in *A Theory of Justice* by John Rawls (Oxford: Clarendon Press, 1973), p. 88.
127. Lyons, "Nature and Soundness of the Contract and Coherence Arguments," pp. 161–2.
128. Barry, *The Liberal Theory of Justice,* p. 103.
129. Rawls, *A Theory of Justice,* p. 135.
130. This picture of the derivation of the two principles of justice matches coherently in the reconstruction of Rawls's argument as I have drawn. However, Simone Chambers contends that there are two more arguments in Rawls's discussion in support of the difference principle. First, Rawls objects to utilitarian ignorance of the worth of each person by legitimizing the sacrifice of the gains of some persons if this sacrifice leads to the overall gains of society. For Rawls, this ignorance of the distinction between persons opposes the Kantian idea of the categorical imperative, which states no one should be used as means for others. Hence, if we are to consider each person as an end in himself, we should care more about the worst-off members of society. Otherwise, the market economy would result in less life chances for those who are naturally worst-off. The second argument concerns the arbitrariness of natural endowments, such as race, gender, talents, and abilities. Those with better endowments do not deserve their talents more than other members of society do, which is a joint venture for all to benefit from. Hence, the members with better talents and abilities are justified to benefit from their native talents only in so far as they benefit the worst-off members of society. Hence, the economic system should provide all members of society with a reasonable and dignified life, rather than

rewarding those with better native talents. See Simone Chambers, "The Politics of Equality: Rawls on the Barricades," *Perspectives on Politics* 4, no. 1 (March 2006): 84–5. It seems that what Chambers considers as Rawls's two additional arguments for the difference principle should not be counted as independent arguments. Rather, they are some intuitive ideas that motivate Rawls to construct the original position in such a way as to lead to the difference principle and hence satisfy those intuitive judgments in reflective equilibrium.

131. Chambers, "The Politics of Equality," p. 81.

Chapter 6

1. John Rawls, *A Theory of Justice,* 2nd ed. (Oxford: Oxford University Press, 1999), pp. 176–7.
2. Ibid., pp. 177–8.
3. Jeffrey Paul, "Rawls on Liberty," in *Conceptions of Liberty in Political Philosophy,* ed. Zbignew Pelczynski and John Gray (London: Athlone, 1984), p. 387.
4. Rawls, *A Theory of Justice,* p. 176.
5. Brian Barry, *Culture and Equality, an Egalitarian Critique of Multiculturalism* (Cambridge: Polity Press, 2001), p. 7.
6. Andrew Levine, *Engaging Political Philosophy, from Hobbes to Rawls* (Oxford: Blackwell, 2002), p. 187.
7. John Rawls, "Justice as Fairness: Political Not Metaphysical," in *Collected Papers,* ed. Samuel Freeman (Cambridge, MA: Harvard University Press, 1999), pp. 48–9.
8. Rawls, *A Theory of Justice,* p. 220.
9. Onora O'Neill, "The Most Extensive Liberty," *Proceedings of Aristotelian Society* 80 (1979): 50.
10. Ibid., p. 51. See also John Gray, *Two Faces of Liberalism* (Cambridge: Polity Press, 2000), p. 79.
11. O'Neill, "The Most Extensive Liberty," pp. 51–2.
12. John Rawls, *Political Liberalism* (New York: Columbia University Press, 1996), pp. 331–5.
13. Rawls, *A Theory of Justice,* pp. 53–4, 175, 220.
14. Harry Brighouse, "Egalitarian Liberalism and Justice in Education," *Political Quarterly* 73, no. 2 (April–June 2002): 182.
15. Rawls, *Political Liberalism,* p. 295.
16. Rawls, *A Theory of Justice,* p. 186.
17. Rawls, *Political Liberalism,* pp. 297, 346, 348.
18. H. L. A. Hart, "Rawls on Liberty and Its Priority," in *Reading Rawls, CriticalSstudies on Rawls' A Theory of Justice,* ed. Norman Daniels (Palo Alto, CA: Stanford University Press, 1975), p. 245.
19. Rawls, "Justice as Fairness," p. 48.

20. Rawls, *A Theory of Justice*, p. 220.
21. Thomas W. Pogge, *Realizing Rawls* (New York: Cornell University Press, 1989), p. 128.
22. Rawls, *A Theory of Justice*, p. 179.
23. Rawls, *Political Liberalism*, p. 5.
24. Norman Daniels, "Equal Liberty and Unequal Worth of Liberty," in *Reading Rawls, Critical Studies on Rawls' A Theory of Justice*, ed. Norman Daniels (Palo Alto, CA: Stanford University Press, 1975), p. 253.
25. Ibid., pp. 254–7.
26. Ibid., pp. 257–8.
27. Rawls, *A Theory of Justice*, pp. 198–9, 212.
28. Daniels, "Equal Liberty and Unequal Worth of Liberty," p. 263. The force of this objection will be more demonstrably severe if one considers the historical discrimination made against the members of some minority groups. As Galeotti argues, "Treating people equally does not always coincide with treating them as equals, which is precisely the aim of liberal equality." She suggests that in the situation of historical discrimination, the mere indifference is insufficient in providing equal opportunity. For "in evolving societies, where privileges and costs have already been linked to moral and cultural differences and have been rooted in a history of discrimination and oppression, the adoption of a neutral attitude towards those differences, far from neutralising the effects of previous discrimination, reproduces them." See Anna Elisabetta Galeotti, "Neutrality and Recognition," in *Pluralism and Liberal Neutrality*, ed. Richard Bellamy and Martin Hollis (London: Frank Cass, 1999), pp. 40, 49. What results from Galeotti's objection is "preferential policies" or "reverse discrimination," according to which there should be some privileges for those groups that are historically discriminated against in order to rectify past injustice, rather than equalizing the situation for all.
29. Rawls, *A Theory of Justice*, p. 182.
30. Rawls, *Political Liberalism*, pp. 193–4.
31. Stephen Macedo, "Liberal Civic Education and Religious Fundamentalism: The Case of God v. John Rawls," *Ethics* 105 (April 1995): 485.
32. Hart contends that the shift in the formulation of the principle of liberty from the general principle of the greatest equal liberty in "Justice as Fairness" to a certain collection of basic liberties in *TJ* is not complete, because Rawls still commits himself to the value of the most extensive liberty. See Hart, "Rawls on Liberty and Its Priority," pp. 236–7. By dismissing the idea of maximum liberties in *PL*, Rawls seems to meet both objections raised by Hart.
33. Rawls, *A Theory of Justice*, p. 53.
34. Ibid.; John Rawls, *The Law of Peoples* (Cambridge, MA: Harvard University Press, 1999), p. 134.
35. Rawls, *A Theory of Justice*, p. 53.

36. Some other liberal theorists support the compatibility of a just constitution with either socialism or capitalism. Among these liberal theorists are the following: Allan Bloom, "Justice: John Rawls vs. the Tradition of Political Philosophy," *American Political Science Review* 69, no. 2 (June 1975): 649; Benjamin R. Barber "Justifying Justice: The Problems of Psychology, Politics, and Measurement in Rawls," in *Reading Rawls, Critical Studies on Rawls' A Theory of Justice* ed. Norman Daniels (Palo Alto, CA: Stanford University Press, 1975), pp. 312–3; and Brian Barry, *The Liberal Theory of Justice,* A Critical Examination of the Principal Doctrines in *A Theory of Justice* by John Rawls, (Oxford: Clarendon, 1973), p. 166. See David Lewis Schaefer, *Justice or Tyranny? A Critique of John Rawls's A Theory of Justice* (Washington, London: Kennikat Press, 1979), p. 45.

37. Rawls, *Political Liberalism,* pp. 298–9.

38. Rex Martin, *Rawls and Rights* (Kansas: University Press of Kansas, 1985), p. 47.

39. Amy Gutmann, "Rawls on the Relationship between Liberalism and Democracy," in *The Cambridge Companion to Rawls,* ed. Samuel Freeman (Cambridge: Cambridge University Press, 2003), pp. 170–8.

40. Ibid., pp. 182–3; See Rawls, *Political Liberalism,* pp. 360–1.

41. Rawls, *Political Liberalism,* p. 299.

42. Rawls, *A Theory of Justice,* pp. 195, 197, 201; the emphasis is added.

43. This inappropriateness is also recognized by Martin. See Martin, *Rawls and Rights,* p. 47.

44. Rawls, *A Theory of Justice,* pp. 53, 177–8.

45. Richard Bellamy, *Rethinking Liberalism* (London: Pinter, 2000), pp. 176–7.

46. All these seven premises are discussed in detail in the previous chapter.

47. Rawls, *A Theory of Justice,* p. 181.

48. The derivation of the first principle of justice from the original position is discussed at the end of the previous chapter.

49. Rawls, *A Theory of Justice,* pp. 181–2.

50. Hart, "'Rawls on Liberty and Its Priority," pp. 230–52.

51. Rawls, *Political Liberalism,* pp. 289–90, 292–3.

52. Ibid., pp. 293–4, 299.

53. Ibid., p. 304.

54. Ibid., p. 307.

55. Ibid., pp. 308–9.

56. Ibid., pp. 316, 318–21.

57. Ibid., pp. 334–5.

58. Ibid., p. 335.

59. Ibid., pp. 310, 313–4.

60. Ibid., p. 335.

61. Rawls, *A Theory of Justice,* p. 210.

62. Gray, *Two Faces of Liberalism,* pp. 70–2.

63. Rawls, *Political Liberalism,* pp. 295, 334–5.

64. Gray, *Two Faces of Liberalism,* pp. 73–9.
65. Ibid., pp. 80–2.

Chapter 7

1. John Stuart Mill, "On Liberty," *Utilitarianism, on Liberty, Considerations of Representative Government,* ed. Geraint Williams, 3rd ed. (London: Every Man's Library, 1993), p. 85.
2. Ibid., p. 85.
3. Ibid., p. 78.
4. Ibid., pp. 80–81, 174.
5. F. W. Garforth, *Educative Democracy, John Stuart Mill on Education in Society* (New York: Oxford University Press, 1980), p. 160.
6. John Stuart Mill, "Utilitarianism," *Utilitarianism, on Liberty, Considerations of Representative Government,* ed. Geraint Williams, 3rd ed. (London: Every Man's Library, 1993), p. 18.
7. Liberal educational systems in general, as Levinson argues, require the intrusion of the liberal state into children's life in the form of compulsory public education. This compulsory education should be separate from the environment of children's home, that is, through public schools. See Meira Levinson, *The Demands of Liberal Education,* (Oxford: Oxford University Press, 1999), p. 58. Hence, public schooling is the major assurance that citizens will support national values. See Thomas J. La Belle and Christopher R. Ward, *Multiculturalism and Education, Diversity and Its Impact on Schools and Society* (Albany: State University of New York, 1994), p. 69. These shared values, as Zhidas Daskalovski suggests, are necessary grounds for nation building, which "is a phenomenon of the modern liberal democratic state." See Zhidas Daskalovski, "Neutrality, Liberal Nation Building and Minority Cultural Rights," *Critical Review of International and Political Philosophy* 5, no. 3 (Autumn 2002): 31. For the survival of the liberal state in a diverse society depends on maintaining some "common substantive purposes" that should be transmitted to the next generation through civic education. See Larry Becker and Will Kymlicka, "Introduction," *Ethics* 105, no. 3 (April 1995): 466.
8. Garforth, *Educative Democracy,* pp. 100, 113, 149–50.
9. Mill, "On Liberty," p. 176.
10. Garforth, *Educative Democracy,* p. 116.
11. Mill, "Utilitarianism," p. 18.
12. John Stuart Mill, "Utility of Religion," *Essays on Ethics, Religion and Society, Collected Works of John Stuart Mill,* vol. 10, ed. J. M. Robson (Toronto: University of Toronto Press, 1969), p. 422.
13. Levinson, *The Demands of Liberal Education,* p. 57.
14. It is argued that the Millian educational system would be, more or less, similar to what prevails in contemporary public schools in Western societies. Parekh argues that this kind of educational system is deeply secular or has a monocultural

orientation with regard to "curriculum, the organisation, personnel, the structure of authority, the pedagogical techniques, the competitive ethos," and the like. See Bhikhu Parekh, "The Concept of Multi-Cultural Education," in *Multi-Cultural Education, the Interminable Debate,* ed. Sohan Modgil et al. (Sussex: Falmer Press, 1986), pp. 20–1.

15. Brian Barry, *Culture and Equality, an Egalitarian Critique of Multiculturalism* (Cambridge: Polity Press, 2001), p. 29.

16. Christine R. Barker, "Church and State: Lessons from Germany?" *Political Quarterly* 75, no. 2 (April–June 2004): 171–5.

17. An alternative possibility is that a secular political philosophy justifies in some circumstances a religionist state on usefulness grounds. Rawls, indisputably, is not an advocate of a religionist state.

18. John Rawls, *A Theory of Justice,* 2nd ed. (Oxford: Oxford University Press, 1999), p. 53.

19. John Rawls, *The Law of Peoples* (Cambridge, MA: Harvard University Press, 1999), p. 134.

20. Amy Gutmann, "Civic Education and Social Diversity," *Ethics* 105, no. 3 (April 1995): 559–60.

21. Stephen Macedo, "Liberal Civic Education and Religious Fundamentalism: The Case of God v. John Rawls," *Ethics* 105 (April 1995): 479.

22. Gutmann, "Civic Education and Social Diversity," p. 577.

23. Rawls, *The Law of Peoples,* p. 161.

24. Ibid., pp. 133–4, 144, 148, 167.

25. Will Kymlicka calls Rawls's idea of neutrality of aim "justificatory neutrality" and his idea of neutrality of effects "consequential neutrality." See: Will Kymlicka, "Liberal Individualism and Liberal Neutrality," *Ethics* 99, no. 4 (July 1989): 884.

26. John Rawls, *Political Liberalism* (New York: Columbia University Press, 1996), pp. 193–4.

27. Macedo, "Liberal Civic Education and Religious Fundamentalism," p. 485.

28. Rawls, *Political Liberalism,* pp. 192–4.

29. Daskalovski, "Neutrality, Liberal Nation Building and Minority Cultural Rights," p. 29.

30. Rawls, *Political Liberalism,* p. 197.

31. Ibid., p. 199.

32. Gutmann, "Civic Education and Social Diversity," p. 559.

33. Rawls, *Political Liberalism,* p. 199.

34. Gutmann, "Civic Education and Social Diversity," p. 567.

35. Rawls, *Political Liberalism,* pp. 194, 196–7.

36. Gutmann, "Civic Education and Social Diversity," p. 559.

37. Macedo, "Liberal Civic Education and Religious Fundamentalism," p. 486.

38. John Horton, "Liberalism, Multiculturalism and Toleration," in *Liberalism, Multiculturalism and Toleration,* ed. John Horton (London: Macmillan Press, 1993), p. 3.

39. William A. Galston, "Two Concepts of Liberalism," *Ethics* 105, no. 3 (April 1995): 528.

40. Chandran Kukathas, "Are There Any Cultural Rights?" *Political Theory* 20, no. 1 (February 1992): 116, 128.

Chapter 8

1. Imam Khomeini, *Wilayati Faqih: Hokoumati Islami,* 7th ed. (Tehran: Institute of Compilation and Publication of Imam Khomeini's Works, 1998), pp. 15, 26.

2. Mutahhari has written many books explaining Islamic thought in various aspects that have been widely read over the last three decades in Iran as well as in other parts of the Shia Islamic world.

3. Murtaza Mutahhari, *Wahy wa Nubuwwah* (Qum: Intisharati Hikmah, 1979), pp. 36–8.

4. *The Qur'an,* chapter "The Iron," verse 25, trans. Arthur J. Arberry (Qum: Ansariyan Publication, 1995), p. 567.

5. Muhammad Hussein Tabatabai, *Al-Mizan fi Tafsir al-Qur'an,* vol. 19, 2nd ed. (Beirut: Muassasah al-Aalami lil-Matbuaat, 1982), p. 171.

6. Imam Khomeini, *Kitab al-Bei,* vol. 2 (Najaf: Nashri Adab, 1975), p. 462.

7. *The Qur'an,* chapter "The Congregation," verse 2, trans. Arthur J. Arberry (Qum: Ansariyan Publication), p. 583.

8. Tabatabai, *Al-Mizan fi Tafsir al-Qur'an,* vol. 19, p. 265.

9. Nasir Makarim Shirazi, *Nafahat al-Qur'an,* vol. 10 (Qum: Muassasah abi-Salih lil-Nashri wa al-Thiqafah, 1995), pp. 24–6.

10. Imam Khomeini, *Sahifi-yi Nour,* ed. T.C.O.C.D.O.I.R., vol. 20 (Tehran: Intisharati Shirkati Sahami-yi Chapkhani-yi Wizarati Irshad, 1990), p. 102.

11. Muhammad Hussein Tabatabai, *Maqalat Tasisiyyah fil-Fikr al-Islami,* trans. Jawad Ali Kassar, 2nd ed. (Beirut: Muassasah Umm al-Qura Littahqiq wa al-Nashr, 1997), p. 42.

12. Ahmad Vaezi, *Hokoumati Dini,* 4th ed. (Qum: Intisharati Mirsad, 2000), chapters 1–2.

13. Mahdi Haeri, *Hikmah wa Hokoumah* (London: Intisharati Shadi, 1995), pp. 141, 143, 152.

14. Abdullah Jawadi-yi Amoli, *Wilayati Faqih: Rahbari dar Islam* (Tehran: Markazi Nashri Farhangi-yi Raja, 1988), p. 189.

15. Brian Rosebury argues that apart from appreciating the "good government" in the sense of a democratic government with fair and frequent elections, majority vote, separation of powers, and the like, there is a rational and moral ground for approving the idea of "government for good purposes," which equals suggesting the necessity of ideology. See Brian Rosebury, "Why Good Government Is Not Enough," *Political Quarterly* 72, no. 3 (July–September 2001): 345–6. The argument for the necessity of the Shia state for the purposes appreciated by Shia society is grounded on similar idea as Rosebury develops in the mentioned article.

16. Imam Khomeini, *Wilayati Faqih,* pp. 3, 17.
17. Makarim Shirazi, *Nafahat al-Qur'an,* vol. 10, p. 23–4.
18. Imam Khomeini, *Wilayati Faqih,* p. 17.
19. Imam Khomeini, *Kitab al-Bei,* vol. 2, p. 462.
20. Imam Khomeini, *Sahifi-yi Nour,* vol. 18, p. 33.
21. Imam Khomeini, *Wilayati Faqih,* pp. 17, 22–5, 28, 31.
22. Imam Khomeini, *Sahifi-yi Nour,* vol. 12, p. 217.
23. Imam Khomeini, *Chihil Hadith,* 13th ed. (Tehran: Institute of Compilation and Publication of Imam Khomeini's Works, 1997), p. 182.
24. *The Qur'an,* chapter "Joseph," verse 103, trans. 'Ali Quli Qarā'i (London: Islamic College for Advanced Studies Press, 2004), p. 338.
25. *The Qur'an,* chapter 'The Cattle', verse 35, trans. Qarā'i, p. 177.
26. *The Qur'an,* chapter "Hood," verse 118, trans. Qarā'i, p. 320.
27. Muhammad Hassan Tabarsi, *Majma al-Bayan,* vol. 5 (Beirut: Dar al-Hikmah, 1986), p. 311.
28. Tabatabai, *Al-Mizan fi Tafsir al-Qur'an,* vol. 10, p. 126.
29. Jaafar Sobhani, *Mafahim al-Qur'an,* vol. 7 (Beirut: Dar al-Anwar, 1992), p. 457.
30. *The Qur'an:* chapter "The Cow," verse 256, trans. Qarā'i, p. 59.
31. Tabatabai, *Al-Mizan fi Tafsir al-Qur'an,* vol. 2, p. 343.
32. Nasir Makarim Shirazi, *Al-Amthal fi Tafsir Kitabi Allah al-Munzal,* vol. 2 (Qum: Madrasah Imam Ali, 2000), p. 261.
33. Imam Khomeini, *Tahdhib al-Usoul,* ed. Jaafar Sobhani, 3rd ed., vol. 1 (Qum: Matbaah Dar al-Fikr, 1988), pp. 241–5.
34. This issue is a subject of controversy among Muslim jurisprudents. One alternative idea assumes that all Islamic values are universally applicable to all human beings. On the opposite side is the other view affirming that even in the establishment stage, Islamic values are restricted only to Muslims. As is seen, Imam Khomeini's view lies in between these two alternatives.
35. Rom Harre and Michael Krausz, *Varieties of Relativism* (Oxford: Blackwell, 1996), p. 3.
36. Imam Khomeini, *Wilayati Faqih,* p. 21.
37. Jean Hampton, "Should Political Philosophy Be Done Without Metaphysics?" *Ethics* 99, no. 4 (July 1989): 810–11.
38. A. James Reichley, "Democracy and Religion," *Political Science and Politics* 19, no. 4 (Autumn 1986): 801.
39. I am inspired by the initiation of the term "peaceable religions" by Timothy S. Shah's characterization of Grotius's liberalism as affirming in "peaceable Christianity." See Timothy Samuel Shah, "Making the Christian World Safe for Liberalism: From Grotius to Rawls," in *Religion and Democracy,* ed. David Marquand and Ronald L. Nettler (Oxford: Blackwell, 2000), p. 128. Veit Bader calls these religions as "modern," "liberalised," and "anti-fundamentalist" religions. See Veit Bader, "Religious Pluralism: Secularism or Priority for Democracy?" *Political Theory* 27, no. 5 (October 1999): 602.

40. Susan Mendus and David Edwards, "Introduction," in *On Toleration,* ed. Susan Mendus and David Edwards (New York: Oxford University Press, 1987), pp. 4–5.
41. John Gray, *Liberalisms, Essays in Political Philosophy* (London: Routledge, 1989), p. 12.
42. Mendus and Edwards, "Introduction," pp. 6–7.
43. John Horton and Susan Mendus, "Locke and Toleration," in *John Locke: A Letter Concerning Toleration in Focus,* ed. John Horton and Susan Mendus (London: Rutledge, 1991), p. 2.
44. Jeremy Waldron, "Locke: Toleration and the Rationality of Persecution," in *John Locke: A Letter Concerning Toleration in Focus,* ed. John Horton and Susan Mendus (London: Rutledge, 1991), pp. 103–4.
45. Susan Mendus, "Locke: Toleration, Morality and Rationality," in *John Locke: A Letter Concerning Toleration in focus,* John Horton and Susan Mendus (ed.), (London: Rutledge, 1991), p. 150–1.
46. Imam Khomeini in one of his discussion employs the concept of "the first rank successor of Prophet" and "the second rank successor of Prophet" to point to two levels of Imamate. Hence I used the notion of the first rank Imam and the second rank Imam in the text. See Imam Khomeini, *Wilayati Faqih,* p. 65.
47. Muhammad Taqi Misbah, *Amuzishi Aqaid: Imamshinasi,* (Qum: Markazi Mudiriyyati Hawzi-yi Ilmiyya-yi Qum, 1988), pp. 17–27, 121–34, 439–41.
48. Imam Khomeini, *Chihil Hadith,* pp. 456–7, 462–3.
49. Misbah, *Amuzishi Aqaid,* pp. 207–13.
50. Muhammad Riza Muzaffar, *Aqaid al-Imamiyyah,* 8th ed. (Beirut: Dar Al-Zahra, 2000), p. 87.
51. Ibid., p. 103.
52. Al-Fazil Al-Miqdad, *Sharhi Babi al-Hadi Ashar* (Qum: Matbaah al-Islam, 1974), p. 75.
53. Shia Muslims believe that after the demise of the Prophet Muhammad there have been 12 infallible Imams succeeding him one by one until the twelfth, Al-Mahdi, went into occultation in the second half of ninth century.
54. Imam Khomeini, *Al-Rasail,* vol. 2 (Qum: Muassisi-yi Matbuaati-yi Ismailian, 1963), p. 100.
55. Imam Khomeini, *Sahifi-yi Nour,* vol. 7, p. 122.
56. Ibid., vol. 10, p. 155.
57. Ibid., vol. 5, p. 105.
58. Ibid., vol. 17, p. 160.
59. Ibid., vol. 18, pp. 203, 245–6.
60. Hussein Al-Nuri Al-Tabarsi, *Mustadrak Al-Wasa'il,* vol. 12 (Qum: Muassasah Ahlulbeit li-Ihya al-Turath, 1986), p. 89.
61. *The Qur'an,* chapter "The Apartments," verse 13, trans. Qarā'ī, p. 730.
62. Tabatabai, *Al-Mizan fi Tafsir al-Qur'an,* vol. 18, pp. 354–6.
63. Nasir Makarim Shirazi, *Tafsiri Nimounih,* 16th ed., vol. 22 (Tehran: Dar al-Kutub al-Islamiyyah, 1999), p. 201.

64. In a similar theorization, John Locke derives the idea of "basic human equality" from the religious view about equality of each member of the species of man in their godly endowment, including their personal faculties and abilities, as well as natural recourses. According to Jeremy Waldron, Locke suggests that since God has given the world to the species of man, no one can dominate others. Thus, the world belongs to all human beings and each is equal to all others in his entitlement to rule over himself. Moreover, the fact that all human beings resemble each other in possessing "the complex property of corporeal rationality" rejects any ground for subordination and subjection. The legitimacy of authority, therefore, lies in the consent of each man. See Jeremy Waldron, *God, Locke, and Equality, Christian Foundations of John Locke's Political Thought* (Cambridge: Cambridge University Press, 2002), pp. 25, 32, 66–8.

65. For a discussion of Shia Islamic account of religious democracy see Hamid Hadji Haidar, *A Theory of Religious Democracy: A Proceduralist Account of Shia Islamic Democracy for Modern Shia Society* (London: ICAS Press, 2006), ch. 5.

66. For a discussion of freedom in religious democracy see Hamid Hadji Haidar, "Azadi dar Andishi-yi Siyasi-yi Hazrati Imam Khomeini," *Matin* 1, no. 2 (Spring 1999): 117–52.

67. Charles Taylor criticizes liberalism as subscribing to the false idea of emptiness of the "self" empowered only with the capacity for choosing and revising our ends. See Charles Taylor, *Hegel and Modern Society* (Cambridge: Cambridge University Press, 1979), p. 157.

68. *The Qur'an,* chapter "Byzantium," verse 30, trans. Qarā'ī, pp. 568–9.

69. Tabatabai, *Al-Mizan fi Tafsir al-Qur'an,* vol. 16, pp. 178–9.

70. *The Qur'an,* chapter "The Sun," verses 7–8, trans. Qarā'ī, p. 851.

71. Tabatabai, *Al-Mizan fi Tafsir al-Qur'an,* vol. 20, pp. 297–8.

72. Imam Khomeini, *Chihil Hadith,* pp. 180–4.

73. Alasdair MacIntyre, *After Virtue,* 2nd ed. (London: Duckworth, 2002), p. 56.

74. Shafer-Landau distinguishes between realism and constructivism in ethics, locating both in the category of objectivism, as opposed to noncognitivist systems of morality. See Russ Shafer-Landau, "Ethical Disagreement, Ethical Objectivism and Moral Indeterminacy," *Philosophy and Phenomenological Research* 54, no. 2 (June 1994): 6.

75. In his *Law and Disagreement,* Waldron goes further and rejects moral objectivity. He argues that the obvious disagreement about justice and the fact that moral realists (unlike natural scientists) have failed to provide any method that can settle fundamental moral disputes, indicate the invalidity of moral objectivism. See Waldron, *Law and Disagreement,* pp. 176–80.

76. Tabatabai, *Al-Mizan fi Tafsir al-Qur'an,* vol. 2, pp. 118, 130–3.

77. Ibid., vol. 16, pp. 119–20.

78. *The Qur'an,* chapter "Ta Ha," verses 2–3.

79. Tabatabai, *Al-Mizan fi Tafsir al-Qur'an,* vol. 12, p. 371.

80. *The Qur'an,* chapter "The Bee," verse 125, trans. Qarā'ī, p. 387.

81. Al-Feiz Al-Kashani *Kitab al-Safi fi Tafsir al-Qur'an,* vol. 4 (Tehran: Dar al-Kutub al-Islamiyyah, 1998), pp. 365–6.
82. Tabatabai, *Al-Mizan fi Tafsir al-Qur'an,* vol. 12, pp. 371–2.
83. Here are two key verses of the *Qur'an* about migration: (1) "Indeed, those whom the angels take away while they are wronging themselves, they ask, 'What state were you in?' They reply, 'We were abased in the land.' They say, 'Was not Allah's earth vast enough so that you might migrate in it?' The refuge of such shall be hell, and it is an evil destination. Except the abased among men, women and children, who have neither access to any means nor are guided to any way." See *The Qur'an,* chapter "The Women," verses 97–8, trans. Qarā'ī, p. 128. (2) "Those who migrate for the sake of Allah after they have been wronged, We will surely settle them in a good place in the world, and the reward of the Hereafter is surely greater, had they known." See *The Qur'an,* chapter "The Bee," verse 41, trans. Qarā'ī, p. 374. These two verses connect the prohibition of residence in nonreligious societies with deprivation of maintaining one's religion that requires the permissibility of residence when Muslims can maintain their commitment to religious basic convictions and exercise their practical duties.
84. Muhammad Hassan Najafi, *Jawahir al-Kalam,* 4th ed., vol. 21 (Tehran: Dar al-Kutub al-Islamiyyah, 1990), pp. 34–8.
85. Tabatabai, *Al-Mizan fi Tafsir al-Qur'an,* vol. 5, p. 49.
86. Najafi, *Jawahir al-Kalam,* pp. 34–8.
87. For a discussion of Shia Islamic view about peace and war in comparison with international law, see the following Farsi book, Hamid Hadji Haidar, *Tawassul bi Zour dar Rawabiti Bein al-Milal, az Didgahi Huqouqi bein al-Milali Umoumi wa Fiqhi Shia* (Tehran: Intisharati Ittilaat, 1997), ch. 3. A short discussion of the main Shia argument for peace is also available in the following English chapter: Hamid Hadji Haidar, "Islamic Jihad and Terrorism," in *Terrorism: Definition, Roots and Solution,* ed. Hassan Bashir (London: Institute of Islamic Studies, 2003).
88. *The Qur'an,* chapter "The All-Merciful," verse 60, trans. Arberry, p. 559.
89. Tabarsi, *Majma al-Bayan,* vol. 9, pp. 315–16.
90. John Horton, *Political Obligation* (London: Macmillan, 1992), pp. 100–1.
91. *The Qur'an,* chapter "The Believers," verse 96, trans. Qarā'ī, p. 484.
92. Tabatabai, *Al-Mizan fi Tafsir al-Qur'an,* vol. 15, p. 65.

Conclusion

1. There is a fourth question concerning peaceability of Islamic regimes that sometimes worries Western liberals. I have shown elsewhere that not only is peace in the settlement of conflicts of interests and disagreement on the conception of the good valuable from a Shiite Islamic perspective, but that it is also the purpose of religion. In fact, the restoration of the initial situation of peace in human society was the reason for appointing Messengers and sending down the scriptures to

people. Peace and justice are two supreme divine values by which Muslims are instructed to manage their relationships with non-Muslims. The Qur'an moral system does not allow Muslims to violate the principles of justice, even where they are justified to resort to defensive war against their enemies who are not committed to the principles of justice and just conduct of war. This moral verdict is important owing to the misconception in the West today about Islamic ideas on *jihad*, war, and peace. Far from leading its believers to initially fight against nonbelievers, the Qur'an teaches them to uphold peace to the most possible degree. See Hamid Hadji Haidar, "'The Qur'anic Idea of Peace," *PSA Contemporary Political Studies: Conference Proceedings 2006,* www.psa.ac.uk/journals/pdf/5/2006/Haidar.pdf.

Bibliography

Ackerly, Brooke (2006) "John Rawls: An Introduction." *Perspectives on Politics* 4, no. 1 (March).

Al-Harrani, Abu Mohammed (ed.) (2001) *Tuhaf Al-Uqoul.* Translated by Badr Shahin. Qum: Ansariyan Publications.

Al-Jouhari, Ismail Ibn Hammad (1985) *Al-Sihah Taj al-Lughah wa Sihah al-Arabiyyah.* 4th ed. Vol. 3. Beirut: Dar al-Ilm Lilmalayin.

Al-Kashani, Al-Feiz (1998) *Kitab al-Safi fi Tafsir al-Qur'an.* Vols. 1, 4. Tehran: Dar al-Kutub al-Islamiyyah.

Al-Miqdad, Al-Fazil (1974) *Sharhi Babi al-Hadi Ashar.* Qum: Matbaah al-Islam.

Al-Nuri Al-Tabarsi, Hussein (1986) *Mustadrak Al-Wasail.* Vol. 12. Qum: Muassasah Ahlulbeit li-Ihya al-Turath.

Al-Sadr, Muhammad Baqir (1958) *Falsafatuna.* Beirut: Dar al-Kutub al-Islami.

——— (1992) *Al-Fatawa al-Wazihah Wafqan Li-Madhhab Ahlulbeit,* 8th ed. Vol. 1. Beirut: Dar al-Taaruf lil-Matbuaat.

Al-Toosi, Muhammad Hassan (n.d.) *Al-Tibyan fi Tafsir al-Qur'an.* Vol. 1. Beirut: Dar al-Ihya al-Turath al-Arabi.

Anschutz, R. P. (1968) "The Logic of J. S. Mill." In *Mill: A Collection of Critical Essays,* edited by J. B. Schneewind. New York: Anchor Books Edition.

——— (1969) *The Philosophy of J. S. Mill,* 3rd ed. Oxford: Oxford University Press.

Arblaster, Anthony (1984) *The Rise and Decline of Western Liberalism.* Oxford: Basil Blackwell.

Audi, Robert, and Nicholas Woltersorff (1997) *Religion in the Public Square, the Place of Religious Convictions in Political Debate.* Lanham: Rowman and Littlefield.

Bader, Veit (1999) "Religious Pluralism: Secularism or Priority for Democracy." *Political Theory* 27, no. 5 (October).

——— (2003) "Religious Diversity and Democratic Institutional Pluralism." *Political Theory* 31, no. 2 (April).

Baker, C. Edwin (1985) "Sandel on Rawls: Justice as a Vice." *University of Pennsylvania Law Review* 133, no. 4 (April).

Barber, Benjamin R. (1975) "Justifying Justice: The Problems of Psychology, Politics, and Measurement in Rawls." In *Reading Rawls, Critical Studies on Rawls' A Theory of Justice,* edited by Norman Daniels. Palo Alto, CA: Stanford University Press.

Barker, Christine R. (2004) "Church and State: Lessons from Germany?" *Political Quarterly* 75, no. 2 (April–June).

Barry, Brian (1973) *The Liberal Theory of Justice:* A Critical Examination of the Principal Doctrines in *A Theory of Justice* by John Rawls. Oxford: Clarendon Press.

———— (1989) *Theories of Justice.* London: Harvest-Wheatsheaf.

———— (2001) *Culture and Equality, an Egalitarian Critique of Multiculturalism.* Cambridge: Polity Press.

Becker, Larry, and Will Kymlicka (1995) "Introduction." *Ethics* 105, no. 3 (April).

Bellamy, Richard (1992) *Liberalism and Modern Society: An Historical Argument.* Cambridge: Polity Press.

———— (1993) "Liberalism." In *Contemporary Political Ideologies,* edited by Roger Eatwell, and Anthony Wright. London: Pinter.

———— (1999) *Liberalism and Pluralism, towards a Politics of Compromise.* London: Routledge.

———— (2000) *Rethinking Liberalism.* London: Pinter.

Bellamy, Richard, and Martin Hollis (1995) "Liberal Justice: Political and Metaphysical." *The Philosophical Quarterly* 45, no. 178 (January).

———— (1999) "Consensus, Neutrality and Compromise." In *Pluralism and Liberal Neutrality,* edited by Richard Bellamy and Martin Hollis. London: Frank Cass.

Bentham, Jeremy (1988) *The Principles of Morals and Legislation.* New York: Prometheus Books.

Berger, Fred (1984) *Happiness, Justice, and Freedom: The Moral and Political Philosophy of John Stuart Mill.* Berkeley: University of California Press.

Berger, P. L. (1981) *Modernisation and Religion.* Dublin: Brunswick Press.

Berlin, Isaiah (1969) *Four Essays on Liberty.* London: Oxford University Press.

Bhargava, Rajeev (1998) "Introduction." In *Secularism and Its Critics,* edited by Rajeev Bhargava. Delhi: Oxford University Press.

Bielefeldt, Heiner (2000) "Western versus Islamic Human Rights Conceptions? A Critique of Cultural Essentialism in the Discussion on Human Rights." *Political Theory* 28, no. 1 (February).

Binder, Leonard (1988) *Islamic Liberalism, a Critique of Development of Ideologies.* Chicago: University of Chicago Press.

Bloom, Allan (1975) "Justice: John Rawls vs. the Tradition of Political Philosophy." *American Political Science Review* 69, no. 2 (June): 649.

Brandt, Richard B. (1969) "A Utilitarian Theory of Excuses." *The Philosophical Review* 78, no. 3 (July).

———— (1979) *A Theory of the Good and the Right.* Oxford: Clarendon Press.

Brighouse, Harry (2002) "Egalitarian Liberalism and Justice in Education." *Political Quarterly* 73, no. 2 (April–June).

Britton, Karl (1953) *John Stuart Mill.* London: Penguin.

Bruce, Steve (1992) "Introduction." In *Religion and Modernisation, Sociologists and Historians Debate the Secularisation Book,* edited by Steve Bruce. Oxford: Oxford University Press.

Bunce, Valerie (2000) "Comparative Democratization, Big and Bounded Generalization." *Comparative Political Studies* 33, no. 6/7 (August–September).

Buchdahl, Gerd (2002) "Inductivist vs. Deductivist Approaches in the Philosophy of Science as Illustrated by Some Controversies between Whewell and Mill." In *The General Philosophy of John Stuart Mill,* edited by Victor Sanchez Valencia. Aldershot, Hants, Burlington, VT: Ashgate.

Carr, Robert (2002) "The Religious Thought of John Stuart Mill: A Study in Reluctant Scepticism." In *The General Philosophy of John Stuart Mill,* edited by Victor Sanchez Valencia. Aldershot, Hants, Burlington, VT: Ashgate.

Chambers, Simone (2006) "The Politics of Equality: Rawls on the Barricades." *Perspectives on Politics* 4, no. 1 (March).

Cleve, James van (2005) "Why Coherence Is Not Enough: A Defense of Moderate Foundationalism." In *Contemporary Debates in Epistemology,* edited by Matthias Steup and Ernest Sosa. Oxford: Blackwell.

Constant, Benjamin (1927) "Liberty Ancient and Modern." In *The History of European Liberalism,* edited by G. de Ruggiero. Oxford: Oxford University Press.

Cowling, Maurice (1968) "Mill and Liberalism." In *Mill: A Collection of Critical Essays.* edited by J. B. Schneewind. New York: Anchor Books.

Daniels, Norman (1975) "Equal Liberty and Unequal Worth of Liberty." In *Reading Rawls, Critical Studies on Rawls' A Theory of Justice,* edited by Norman Daniels. Palo Alto, CA: Stanford University Press.

Daskalovski, Zhidas (2002) "Neutrality, Liberal Nation Building and Minority Cultural Rights." *Critical Review of International and Political Philosophy* 5, no. 3 (Autumn).

Davion, Victoria, and Clark Wolf (2000) "Introduction: From Comprehensive Justice to Political Liberalism." In *The Idea of a Political Liberalism, Essays on Rawls,* edited by Victoria Davion and Clark Wolf Lanham: Rowman and Littlefield.

Dobbelaere, Karel (1981) "Secularization: A Multi-Dimensional Concept." *Current Sociology* 29, no. 2 (Summer).

Dombrowski, Daniel A. (2001) *Rawls and Religion, the Case for Political Liberalism.* Albany: State University of New York Press.

Donner, Wendy (1991) *The Liberal Self: John Stuart Mill's Moral and Political Philosophy.* London: Cornell University Press.

———— (1998) "Mill's Utilitarianism." In *The Cambridge Companion to Mill,* edited by John Skorupski. Cambridge: Cambridge University Press.

Dworkin, Ronald (1975) "The Original Position." In *Reading Rawls, Critical Studies on Rawls's A Theory of Justice,* edited by Norman Daniels. Palo Alto, CA: Stanford University Press.

———— (1978) "Liberalism." In *Public and Private Morality,* edited by Stuart Hampshire. New York: Cambridge University Press.

Eisenach, Eldon J. (1981) *Two Worlds of Liberalism: Religion and Politics in Hobbes, Locke, and Mill.* Chicago: University of Chicago.

Feinberg, Joel (1985) *The Moral Limits of the Criminal Law.* Vol. 2. *Offense to Others.* New York: Oxford University Press.

Fotion, Nick, and Gerard Elfstrom (1992) *Toleration.* London and Tuscaloosa: University of Alabama Press.

Frankena, W. K. (1963) *Ethics.* Englewood Cliffs, NJ: Prentice Hall.

Frey, R. G. (1985a) "Act-Utilitarianism, Consequentialism, and Moral Rights." In *Utility and Rights,* edited by R. G. Frey. Oxford: Basil Blackwell.

——— (1985b) "Introduction: Utilitarianism and Persons." In *Utility and Rights,* edited by R. G. Frey. Oxford: Basil Blackwell.

Friedman, Marilyn (2000) "John Rawls and the Political Coercion of Unreasonable People." In *The Idea of a Political Liberalism, Essays on Rawls,* edited by Victoria Davion and Clark Wolf. Lanham: Rowman and Littlefield.

Galeotti, Anna Elisabetta (1999) "Neutrality and Recognition." In *Pluralism and Liberal Neutrality,* edited by Richard Bellamy and Martin Hollis. London: Frank Cass.

Galston, William A. (1991) *Liberal Purposes, Goods, Virtues, and Diversity in the Liberal State.* Cambridge: Cambridge University Press.

——— (1995) "Two Concepts of Liberalism." *Ethics* 105, no. 3 (April).

Garforth, F. W. (1980) *Educative Democracy, John Stuart Mill on Education in Society.* New York: Oxford University Press.

Gill, Anthony (2001) "Religion and Comparative Politics." *Annual Review of Political Science* 4.

Goodin, Robert E., and Philip Pettit (1993) *A Companion to Contemporary Political Philosophy.* Oxford: Blackwell.

Gray, John (1983) *Mill on Liberty, a Defence.* London: Routledge and Kegan Paul.

——— (1989) *Liberalisms, Essays in Political Philosophy.* London: Routledge.

——— (1995) *Liberalism,* 2nd ed. Berkshire: Open University Press.

——— (1996) *Post-Liberalism, Studies in Political Thought,* 2nd ed. London: Routledge.

——— (2000) *Two Faces of Liberalism.* Cambridge: Polity Press.

Gutmann, Amy (1995) "Civic Education and Social Diversity." *Ethics* 105, no. 3 (April).

——— (1996) "Democracy, Philosophy, and Justification." In *Democracy and Difference, Contesting the Boundaries of the Political,* edited by Seyla Benhabib New Jersey: Princeton University Press.

——— (2003) "Rawls on the Relationship between Liberalism and Democracy." In Samuel Freeman. *The Cambridge Companion to Rawls.* Cambridge: Cambridge University Press.

Habibi, Don A. (2001) *John Stuart Mill and the Ethic of Human Growth.* Dordrecht: Kluwer Academic Publishers.

Haeri, Mahdi (1995) *Hikmah wa Hokoumah.* London: Intisharati Shadi.

Hadji Haidar, Hamid (1997) *Tawassul bi Zour dar Rawabiti bein al-Milal, az Didgahi Huqouqi bein al-Milali Umoumi wa Fiqhi Shia.* Tehran: Intisharati Ittilaat.

———— (1999) "Azadi dar Andishi-yi Siyasi-yi Hazrati Imam Khomeini." *Matin* 1, no. 2 (Spring).

———— (2003) "Islamic Jihad and Terrorism." In *Terrorism: Definition, Roots and Solution,* edited by Hassan Bashir. London: Institute of Islamic Studies.

———— (2006) "Rawls and Religion: Between the Decency and Justice of Reasonable Religious Regimes." *Politics and Ethics Review* 2, no. 1 (Spring).

———— (2006) *A Theory of Religious Democracy: A Proceduralist Account of Shia Islamic Democracy for Modern Shia Society.* London: ICAS Press.

Hampton, Jean (1989) "Should Political Philosophy be Done Without Metaphysics?" *Ethics* 99, no. 4 (July).

Hare, R. M. (1985) "Rights, Utility, and Universalisation, Reply to J. L. Mackie." In *Utility and Rights,* edited by R. G. Frey. Oxford: Basil Blackwell.

Harre, Rom, and Michael Krausz (1996) *Varieties of Relativism.* Oxford: Blackwell.

Hart, H. L. A. (1975) "Rawls on Liberty and its Priority." In *Reading Rawls, Critical Studies on Rawls' A Theory of Justice,* edited by Norman Daniels. Palo Alto, CA: Stanford University Press.

———— (1983) "Between Utility and Rights." In *Ronald Dworkin and Contemporary Jurisprudence,* edited by Marshall Cohen. London: Duckworth.

Heinze, Eric (2003) *The Logic of Liberal Rights: A Study in the Formal Analysis of Legal Discourse.* London: Routledge.

Hofmann, Steven Ryan (2004) "Islam and Democracy: Micro-Level Indications of Compatibility." *Comparative Political Studies* 37, no. 6 (August).

Holyoake, George Jacob (1896) *English Secularism, a Confession of Belief.* Chicago: Open Court Publishing Company.

Horton, John (1992) *Political Obligation.* London: Macmillan.

———— (1993) "Liberalism, Multiculturalism and Toleration." In *Liberalism, Multiculturalism and Toleration,* edited by John Horton. London: Macmillan.

Horton, John, and Susan Mendus (1991) "Locke and Toleration." In *John Locke: A Letter Concerning Toleration in Focus,* edited by John Horton and Susan Mendus London: Rutledge.

Ibn Al-Manzur (1988) *Lisan Al-Arab.* Edited by Ali Shiri. Vols. 4–7. Beirut: Dar al-Ihya al-Turath al-Arabi.

Imam Khomeini (1963) *Al-Rasail.* 2 vols. Qum: Muassisi-yi Matbuaati-yi Ismailian.

———— (1975) *Kitab al-Bei.* 2 vols. Najaf: Nashri Adab.

———— (1982–1990) *Sahifi-yi Nour.* Edited by T.C.O.C.D.O.I.R. 21 vols. Tehran: Intisharati Shirkati Sahami-yi Chapkhani-yi Wizarati Irshad.

———— (1988) *Tahdhib al-Usoul.* Edited by Sobhani, Jaafar, 3rd ed. 2 vols. Qum: Matbaah Dar al-Fikr.

———— (1997) *Chihil Hadith,* 13th ed. Tehran: Institute of Compilation and Publication of Imam Khomeini's Works.

———— (1998) *Wilayati Faqih: Hokoumati Islami,* 7th ed. Tehran: Institute of Compilation and Publication of Imam Khomeini's Works.

Jawadi-yi Amoli, Abdullah (1982) "Siri-yi Falsafi-yi Ustad Allama-yi Tabatabai." In *Yadnami-yi Mufassiri Kabir Ustad Allama-yi Tabatabai.* Qum; Intisharati Shafaq.

———— (1988) *Wilayati Faqih: Rahbari dar Islam.* Tehran: Markazi Nashri Farhangi-yi Raja.

Joffe, George (1997) "Democracy, Islam and the Culture of Modernism." *Democratization* 4, no. 3 (Autumn).

Jones, Peter (1995) "Two Conceptions of Liberalism, Two Conceptions of Justice." *British Journal of Political Science* 25, no. 4 (October).

Kane, John (2002) "Democracy and Group Rights." In *Democratic Theory Today,* edited by April Carter and Geoffrey Stokes. Cambridge: Polity Press.

Kant, Immanuel (1991) *Political Writings.* Edited by H. S. Reiss. 2nd ed. Cambridge: Cambridge University Press.

Kautz, Steven (1993) "Liberalism and the Idea of Toleration." *American Journal of Political Science* 37, no. 2 (May).

Kekes, John (1997) *Against Liberalism.* Ithaca: Cornell University.

Kelly, Paul (1990) *Utilitarianism and Distributive Justice: Jeremy Bentham and the Civil Law.* Oxford: Clarendon.

King, Preston (1998) *Toleration,* 2nd edition. London: Frank Cass.

Klosko, George (1993) "Rawls's "Political" Philosophy and American Democracy." *The American Political Science Review* 87, no. 2 (June).

Kubitz, Oskar Alfred (1932) *Development of John Stuart Mill's System of Logic.* Urbana: University of Illinois Press.

Kukathas, Chandran (1992) "Are There Any Cultural Rights?" *Political Theory* 20, no. 1 (February).

Kukathas, Chandran, and Philip Pettit (1990) *Rawls: A Theory of Justice and Its Critics.* Cambridge: Polity Press.

Kymlicka, Will (1989) "Liberal Individualism and Liberal Neutrality." *Ethics* 99, no. 4 (July).

———— (1989) *Liberalism, Community, and Culture.* New York: Oxford University Press.

———— (1990) *Contemporary Political Philosophy, an Introduction.* New York: Oxford University Press.

———— (1995) *Multicultural Citizenship.* New York: Oxford University Press.

La Belle, Thomas J., and Christopher R. Ward (1994) *Multiculturalism and Education, Diversity and Its Impact on Schools and Society.* Albany: State University of New York.

Laborde, Cecile (2002) "The Reception of John Rawls in Europe." *European Journal of Political Theory* 1, no. 2 (October).

Larmore, Charles (1987) *Patterns of Moral Complexity.* Cambridge: Cambridge University Press.

———— (1996) *The Morals of Modernity.* Cambridge: Cambridge University Press.

Levine, Andrew (2002) *Engaging Political Philosophy from Hobbes to Rawls.* Oxford: Blackwell.

Levinson, Meira (1999) *The Demands of Liberal Education.* Oxford: Oxford University Press.

Lipset, Seymour Martin (1995) *The Encyclopedia of Democracy.* London: Routledge.

Lord, Carnes (1987) "Aristotle." In *History of Political Philosophy*, edited by Leo Strauss and Joseph Cropsey. 3rd ed. Chicago: University of Chicago Press.

Lyons, David (1975) "Nature and Soundness of the Contract and Coherence Arguments." In *Reading Rawls, Critical Studies on Rawls' A Theory of Justice*, edited by Norman Daniels. Palo Alto, CA: Stanford University Press.

———— (1978) "Mill's Theory of Justice." In *Values and Morals: Essays in Honour of William Frankena, Charles Stevenson, and Richard Brandt*, edited by Alvin I. Goldman and Jaegwon Kim. Dordrecht, Holland: D. Reidel.

Mabbott, J. D. (1968) "Interpretation of Mill's Utilitarianism." In *Mill: A Collection of Critical Essays*, edited by J. B. Schneewind. New York: Anchor Books.

Macedo, Stephen (1995) "Liberal Civic Education and Religious Fundamentalism: The Case of God v. John Rawls." *Ethics* 105 (April).

MacIntyre, Alasdair (2002) *After Virtue*, 2nd ed. London: Duckworth.

Mackie, J. L. (1985) "Rights, Utility, and Universalisation." In *Utility and Rights*, edited by R. G. Frey. Oxford: Basil Blackwell.

Magid, Henry M. (1987) "John Stuart Mill." In *History of Political Philosophy*, edited by Leo Strauss and Joseph Cropsey. 3rd ed. Chicago: University of Chicago Press.

Makarim Shirazi, Nasir (1995) *Nafahat al-Qur'an*. Vol. 10. Qum: Muassasah abi-Salih lin-Nashri wa al-Thiqafah.

———— (1997) *Iatiqadi Ma*, 2nd ed. Qum: Intisharati Nasli Jawan.

———— (1997) *Panjah Darsi Usouli Aqaid barayi Jawanan*, 9th ed. Qum: Madrasah Imam Ali.

———— (1997) *Payami Qur'an*, Vol. 2. 5th ed. Tehran: Dar al-Kutub al-Islamiyyah.

———— (1999) *Tafsiri Nimounih*, 16th ed. Vol. 22. Tehran: Dar al-Kutub al-Islamiyyah.

———— (2000) *Al-Amthal fi Tafsir Kitabi Allah al-Munzal*. 20 vols. Qum: Madrasah Imam Ali.

Mandelbaum, Maurice (1968) "Two Moot Issues in Mill's Utilitarianism." In *Mill: A Collection of Critical Essays*, edited by J. B. Schneewind. New York: Anchor Books.

Martin, Rex (1985) *Rawls and Rights*. Kansas: University Press of Kansas.

Mason, Andrew (1999) "Imposing Liberal Principles." In *Pluralism and Liberal Neutrality*, edited by Richard Bellamy and Martin Hollis. London: Frank Cass.

McLean, Iain (ed.) (1996) *The Concise Oxford Dictionary of Politics*. Oxford: Oxford University Press.

McLeod, Hugh (1992) "Secular Cities? Berlin, London, and New York in the Later Nineteenth and Early Twentieth Centuries." In *Religion and Modernisation, Sociologists and Historians Debate the Secularisation Book*, edited by Steve Bruce. New York: Oxford University Press.

Megill, Allan D. (1972) "J. S. Mill's Religion of Humanity and the Second Justification for the Writing of *On Liberty*." *The Journal of Politics* 34, no. 2 (May).

Meland, Bernard Eugene (1966) *The Secularisation of Modern Cultures*. New York: Oxford University Press.

Mendus, Susan (1991) "Locke: Toleration, Morality and Rationality." In *John Locke: A Letter Concerning Toleration in Focus,* edited by John Horton and Susan Mendus. London: Rutledge.

Mendus, Susan, and David Edwards (1987) "Introduction." In *On Toleration,* edited by Susan Mendus and David Edwards. New York: Oxford University Press.

Midlarsky, Manus I. (1998) "Democracy and Islam: Implications for Civilizational Conflict and the Democratic Peace." *International Studies Quarterly* 42, no. 3 (September).

Mill, John Stuart (1828) "Archbishop Whately's Elements of Logic." *Westminster Review* 9.

——— (1859) *Dissertations and Discussions: Political, Philosophical, and Historical.* Vol. 1. London: W. Parker.

——— (1969) "Utility of Religion", *Essays on Ethics, Religion and Society, Collected works of John Stuart Mill.* Vol. 10. Edited by J. M. Robson. Toronto: University of Toronto Press.

——— (1973–1974) *A System of Logic Ratiocinative and Inductive, Being a Connected View of the Principles of Evidence and the Methods of Scientific Investigation, Collected Works of J. S. Mill.* Books 4–8 and Appendices. Edited by J. M. Robson. 1843. Reprint, Toronto: University of Toronto Press.

——— (1979) *An Examination of Sir William Hamilton's Philosophy and of the Principal Philosophical Questions Discussed in His Writings.* Edited by J. M. Robson. Toronto: University of Toronto Press.

——— (1993) *Utilitarianism, On Liberty, Considerations of Representative Government, Remarks on Bentham's Philosophy.* Edited by Geraint Williams. 3rd ed. London: Every Man's Library.

Misbah, Muhammad Taqi (1982) "Naqshi Ustad Allama-yi Tabatabai dar Nihzati Fikri-yi Hawzi-yi Ilmiyyi-yi Qum." In *Yadnami-yi Mufassiri Kabir Ustad Allama-yi Tabatabai.* Qum: Intisharati Shafaq.

——— (1982) "Sukhani Piramouni Shakhsiyyati Ustad Allama-yi Tabatabai." In *Yadnami-yi Mufassiri Kabir Ustad Allama-yi Tabatabai.* Qum: Intisharati Shafaq.

——— (1988) *Amuzishi Aqaid: Imamshinasi.* Qum: Markazi Mudiriyyati Hawzi-yi Ilmiyya-yi Qum.

——— (1991) *Amuzishi Aqaid.* 2 vols. 7th ed. Qum: Markazi Chap wa Nashri Sazmani Tablighati Islami.

Moltmann, Jurgen (1999) *God for a Secular Society, the Public Relevance of Theology.* Translated by Margaret Kohl. 1927. Reprint, London: SCM Press.

Muhammad Hussein Tabatabai (1969) *Shia dar Islam.* 2nd edition. Qum: Markazi Matbouaati-yi Dar al-Tablighi Islami.

——— (1974) *Qur'an dar Islam.* 2nd ed. Tehran: Dar al-Kutub al-Islamiyyah.

——— (1982) *Al-Mizan fi Tafsir al-Qur'an.* 20 vols. 2nd ed. Beirut: Muassasah al-Aalami lil-Matbuaat.

——— (1997) *Maqalat Tasisiyyah fil-Fikr al-Islami.* Translated by Jawad Ali Kassar. 2nd ed. Beirut: Muassasah Umm al-Qura Littahqiq wa al-Nashr.

——— (n.d.) *Usouli Falsafa wa Rawishi Rialism.* 3 vols. Edited by Murtaza Mutahhari. Qum: Daftari Intisharati Islami.

Mulhall, Stephen, and Adam Swift (2001) *Liberals and Communitarians,* 2nd ed. Oxford: Blackwell.

Munby, D. L. (1963) *The Idea of a Secular Society, and Its Significance for Christians.* London: Oxford University Press.

Mutahhari, Murtaza (1979) *Wahy wa Nubuwwah.* Qum: Intisharati Hikmah.

——— (2001) *Kulliyyati Uloumi Islami.* Vol. 3. *Usouli Fiqh and Fiqh.* 24th ed. Qum: Intisharati Sadra.

Muzaffar, Muhammad Rida (2000) *Aqaid al-Imamiyyah.* 8nd ed. Beirut: Dar Al-Zahra.

Nagel, Thomas (1991) *Equality and Partiality.* New York: Oxford University Press.

——— (2003) "Rawls and Liberalism." In *The Cambridge Companion to Rawls,* edited by Samuel Freeman. Cambridge: Cambridge University Press.

Najafi, Muhammad Hassan (1990) *Jawahir al-Kalam.* 4th ed. Vol. 21. Tehran: Dar al-Kutub al-Islamiyyah.

Neal, Patrick, and David Paris (1990) "Liberalism and the Communitarian Critique: A Guide for the Perplexed." *Canadian Journal of Political Science* 23, no. 3 (September).

Norris, Pippa, and Ronald Inglehart (2004) *Sacred and Secular, Religion and Politics Worldwide.* Cambridge: Cambridge University Press.

Nozick, Robert (1974) *Anarchy, State, and Utopia.* New York: Basic Books.

O'Neill, Onora (1979) "The Most Extensive Liberty." *Proceedings of Aristotelian Society* 80.

Parekh, Bhikhu (1986) "The Concept of Multi-Cultural Education." In *Multi-Cultural Education, The Interminable Debate,* edited by Sohan Modgil et al. Sussex: Falmer Press.

——— (1994) "Decolonizing Liberalism." In *The End of "Isms"? Reflections on the Fate of Ideological Politics after Communism's Collapse,* edited by Aleksandras Shtromas. Oxford: Blackwell.

——— (2000) *Rethinking Multiculturalism, Cultural Diversity and Political Theory.* New York: Palgrave.

Paris, David C. (1987) "The Theoretical Mystique: Neutrality, Plurality, and the Defence of Liberalism." *American Journal of Political science* 31, no. 4.

Pateman, Carole (1985) *The Problem of Political Obligation: A Critique of Liberal Theory.* Cambridge: Polity Press.

Paul, Jeffrey (1984) "Rawls on Liberty." In *Conceptions of Liberty in Political Philosophy,* edited by Zbignew Pelczynski and John Gray. London: Athlone Press.

Plamenatz, John (1958) *The English Utilitarians.* 2nd ed. Oxford: Basil Blackwell.

Pogge, Thomas W. (1989) *Realizing Rawls.* New York: Cornell University Press.

Popper, Karl R. (1963) *Logic of Scientific Discovery.* New York: Basic Books.

Posner, Richard A. (2000) "Review of Jeremy Waldron, 'Law and Disagreement.'" *Columbia Law Review* 100, no. 2 (March).

Postema, Gerald J. (1986) *Bentham and the Common Law Tradition.* New York: Oxford University Press.

The Qur'an (1995) Translated by Arthur J. Arberry. Qum: Ansariyan Publication.

The Qur'an (2004) Translated by 'Alī Qulī Qarā'ī. London: Islamic College for Advanced Studies Press.

Raphael, David D. (2001) *Concepts of Justice.* Oxford: Oxford University Press.

Rawls, John (1996) *Political Liberalism.* New York: Columbia University Press.

―――― (1999) *Collected Papers.* Edited by Samuel Freeman. Cambridge, MA: Harvard University Press.

―――― (1999) *The Law of Peoples.* Cambridge, MA: Harvard University Press.

―――― (1999) *A Theory of Justice.* 2nd ed. Oxford: Oxford University Press.

―――― (2001) *Justice as Fairness: A Restatement.* Edited by Erin Kelly. Cambridge, MA: Harvard University Press.

Raz, Joseph (1986) *The Morality of Freedom.* New York: Oxford University Press.

Razzaqi, Abul Qasim (1982) "Ba Allama-yi Tabatabai dar al-Mizan." In *Yadnami-yi Mufassiri Kabir Ustad Allama-yi Tabatabai.* Qum: Intisharati Shafaq.

Rees, J. C. (1960) "A Re-Reading of Mill on Liberty." *Political Studies* 8, no. 2.

Reichley, A. James (1986) "Democracy and Religion." *Political Science and Politics* 19, no. 4 (Autumn).

Robertson, A. H. and Merrills, J. G. (1996) *Human Rights in the World.* 4th ed. Manchester: Manchester University Press.

Rorty, Richard (1996) "Idealizations, Foundations, and Social Practices." In *Democracy and Difference, Contesting the Boundaries of the Politica,* edited by Seyla Benhabib. Princeton, NJ: Princeton University Press.

Rose, Richard (2002), "How Muslims View Democracy: Evidence from Central Asia." *Journal of Democracy* 13, no. 4 (October).

Rosebury, Brian (2001) "Why Good Government Is Not Enough." *Political Quarterly* 72, no. 3 (July–September).

Rosen, Fredrick (2003) *Classical Utilitarianism from Hume to Mill.* London: Routledge.

Ross, W. D. (1930) *The Right and the Good.* Oxford: Oxford University Press.

Russell, Bertrand (1968) "John Stuart Mill." In *Mill: A Collection of Critical Essays,* edited by J. B. Schneewind. New York: Anchor Books Edition.

Ryan, Alan (1970) *John Stuart Mill.* New York: Pantheon Books.

Safran, William (2003) "Introduction." In *The Secular and the Sacred: Nation, Religion and Politics,* edited by William Safran. London: Frank Cass.

Sandel, Michael J. (1982) *Liberalism and the Limits of Justice.* Cambridge: Cambridge University Press.

―――― (1984) "Morality and the Liberal Ideal." *The New Republic,* no. 7 (May).

Scanlon, T. M. (2003) "Rawls and Justification." In *The Cambridge Companion to Rawls,* edited by Samuel Freeman. Cambridge: Cambridge University Press.

Scarre, Geoffrey (1996) *Utilitarianism.* London: Routledge.

―――― (2002) "Proof and Implication in Mill's Philosophy of Logic." In *The General Philosophy of John Stuart Mill,* edited by Victor Sanchez Valencia. Aldershot, Hants, Burlington, VT: Ashgate.

Schaefer, David Lewis (1979) *Justice or Tyranny? A Critique of John Rawls's A Theory of Justice.* Washington, London: Kennikat Press.

Schneewind, J. B. (1968) "Introduction." In *Mill: A Collection of Critical Essays,* edited by J. B. Schneewind. New York: Anchor Books Edition.

——— (1992) "Autonomy, Obligation, and Virtue: An Overview of Kant's Moral Philosophy." In *The Cambridge Companion to Kant,* edited by Paul Guyer. Cambridge: Cambridge University Press.

Shafer-Landau, Russ (1994) "Ethical Disagreement, Ethical Objectivism and Moral Indeterminacy." *Philosophy and Phenomenological Research* 54, no. 2 (June).

Shah, Timothy Samuel (2000) "Making the Christian World Safe for Liberalism: From Grotius to Rawls." In *Religion and Democracy,* edited by David Marquand and Ronald L. Nettler. Oxford: Blackwell.

Simpson, J. A., and E. S. C. Weiner (eds.) (1989) *The Oxford English Dictionary.* 2nd ed. Vols. 6, 8, 10, 14. Oxford: Oxford University Press.

Sinopoli, Richard C. (1993) "Liberalism and Contested Conceptions of the Good: The Limits of Neutrality." *The Journal of Politics* 55, no. 3 (August).

Skorupski, John (1991) *John Stuart Mill.* London: Routledge.

Sobhani, Jaafar (1982) "Nazari wa Gozari bar Zindigani-yi Ustad Allama-yi Tabatabai." In *Yadnami-yi Mufassiri Kabir Ustad Allama-yi Tabatabai.* Qum: Intisharati Shafaq.

——— (1992) *Mafahim al-Qur'an.* Vol. 7. Beirut: Dar al-Anwar.

——— (2005) *Azadi wa Din Salary.* Qum: Muassasah Imam Sadiq.

Sterba, James P. (2000) "Rawls and Religion." In *The Idea of a Political Liberalism, Essays on Rawls,* edited by Victoria Davion and Clark Wolf. Lanham: Rowman and Littlefield.

Sumner, L. W. (1987) *The Moral Foundation of Rights.* Oxford: Clarendon.

Tabarsi, Muhammad Hassan (1986) *Majma al-Bayan.* 10 vols. Beirut: Dar al-Hikmah.

Taylor, Charles (1979) *Hegel and Modern Society.* Cambridge: Cambridge University Press.

——— (1998) "Modes of Secularism." In *Secularism and Its Critics,* edited by Rajeev Bhargava. Delhi: Oxford University Press.

Turk, Christopher (1988) *Coleridge and Mill: A Study of Influence.* Aldershot: Avebury.

Urmson, J. O. (1968) "The Interpretation of the Moral Philosophy of J. S. Mill." In *Mill: A Collection of Critical Essays,* edited by J. B. Schneewind. New York: Anchor Books.

Vaezi, Ahmad (2000) *Hokoumati Dini.* 4th ed. Qum: Intisharati Mirsad.

Valencia, Victor Sanchez (2002) "Introduction." In *The General Philosophy of John Stuart Mill,* edited by Victor Sanchez Valencia Aldershot, Hants, Burlington, VT: Ashgate.

Vernon, Richard (1989) "J. S. Mill and the Religion of Humanity." In *Religion, Secularisation and Political Thought, Thomas Hobbes to J. S. Mill,* edited by James E. Crimmins London: Routledge.

Waldron, Jeremy (1991) "Locke: Toleration and the Rationality of Persecution." In *John Locke: A Letter Concerning Toleration in Focus,* edited by John Horton and Susan Mendus. London: Rutledge.

———— (1993) *Liberal Rights: Collected Papers 1981–1991*. Cambridge: Cambridge University Press.

———— (1999) *Law and Disagreement*. Oxford: Oxford University Press.

———— (2002) *God, Locke, and Equality, Christian Foundations of John Locke's Political Thought*. Cambridge: Cambridge University Press.

Warnock, Mary (1987) "The Limits of Toleration." In *On Toleration*, edited by Susan Mendus and David Edwards. New York: Oxford University Press.

Whewell, William (1847) *The Philosophy of Inductive Science*. 2nd ed. Vol. 1. London.

———— (1864) *Elements of Morality, Including Polity*. 4th ed. Cambridge: Cambridge University Press.

Whittington, Keith E. (2000) "In Defense of Legislatures." *Political Theory* 28, no. 5 (October).

Williams, Geraint (1993) "Introduction" and "Notes." In John Stuart Mill, *Utilitarianism, On Liberty, Considerations of Representative Government, Remarks on Bentham's Philosophy*, edited by Geraint Williams. 3rd ed. London: Every Man's Library.

Wolenski, Jan (2004) "The History of Epistemology." In *Handbook of Epistemology*, edited by Ilkka Niiniluoto et. al. Dordrecht: Kluwer Academic Publishers.

Wolff, Robert Paul (1977) *Understanding Rawls, A Reconstruction and Critique of A Theory of Justice*. New Jersey, Princeton University Press.

Wollheim, Richard (1979) "John Stuart Mill and Isaiah Berlin, the Ends of Life and the Preliminaries of Morality." In *The Idea of Freedom, Essays in Honour of Isaiah Berlin*, edited by Alan Ryan. Oxford: Oxford University Press.

Young, Iris Marion (1996) "Political Theory: An Overview." In *A New Handbook of Political Science*, edited by Robert E. Goodin and Hans-Dieter Klingemann. Oxford: Oxford University Press.

Internet Resources

Muhammad Mahdi Naraqi. Jami al-Saadat. http://www.al-islam.org/al-tawhid/felicities.

Philosophy.lander.edu. "Ethics." http://philosophy.lander.edu/ethics/naturalism.html.

Political Studies Association. "The Qur'anic Idea of Peace." http://www.psa.ac.uk/journals/pdf/5/2006/Haidar.pdf.

The Largest Shiite Communities. http://www.adherents.com/largecom/com_shiite.html.

Wikipedia. "Ethical Naturalism." http://en.wikipedia.org/wiki/Ethical_naturalism.

Index